KEEPING THE FAITH

KEEPING THE FAITH

Memoirs of a Parliamentarian

SOMNATH CHATTERJEE

HarperCollins *Publishers* India

a joint venture with

New Delhi

First published in India in 2010 by
HarperCollins *Publishers* India
a joint venture with
The India Today Group

ISBN: 978-81-7223-925-1

2 4 6 8 10 9 7 5 3

HarperCollins *Publishers*
A-53, Sector 57, Noida 201301, India
77-85 Fulham Palace Road, London W6 8JB, United Kingdom
Hazelton Lanes, 55 Avenue Road, Suite 2900, Toronto, Ontario M5R 3L2
and 1995 Markham Road, Scarborough, Ontario M1B 5M8, Canada
25 Ryde Road, Pymble, Sydney, NSW 2073, Australia
31 View Road, Glenfield, Auckland 10, New Zealand
10 East 53rd Street, New York NY 10022, USA

Typeset in 12/15 Dante MT Std
InoSoft Systems

Printed and bound at
Thomson Press (India) Ltd.

To my parents, **Nirmal Chandra and Binapani**,
who taught their children the importance of discipline in life
and of being responsible and compassionate human beings

and

to my leader, **Jyoti Basu**,
who persuaded me to join politics and taught me that politics
provided the best opportunity to serve the people,
and from whom I received unbounded affection
and inspiring guidance throughout my political career

CONTENTS

1

THE EARLY YEARS

My grandfather, Bholanath Chatterjee, was a person of humble means but spirited character. An officer in the engineering department of the Calcutta municipality, he resigned without a second thought when he was superseded by a British officer. This was some time in 1912. He had a large family, comprising his wife, five sons and a daughter, and no other means of income. My father, Nirmal Chandra Chatterjee, the eldest son, born in 1895, was in college at the time.

My father used to tell us of the difficult days that the family went through after my grandfather suddenly gave up his job. In fact, as he could not afford the bus or tram fare, he would often walk to his college, Scottish Church College in central Calcutta, a distance of nearly seven or eight miles from the family residence in south Calcutta. But all that did not dampen Bholanath's spirit and he never surrendered to injustice and discrimination. The family gradually settled down when he started a small business, which brought in a regular income.

My father was a good student and did well in all his examinations. He was awarded the prestigious Premchand Roychand Scholarship of Calcutta University. During his student days, he enjoyed the affection of Sir Asutosh Mookerjee, a friend of my grandfather. Known as the Bengal Tiger for his courage of conviction and his strong personality, Sir Asutosh had many achievements to his credit and was one of the greatest judges of the Calcutta High Court. He was also the vice chancellor of Calcutta University, a well-known mathematician and a great Sanskrit scholar.

My father (better known as N.C. Chatterjee) did his MA in history, became a law graduate of Calcutta University and, in 1916, started his career as a vakil, as Indian lawyers were then called at the initial stage of their practice. Only later were they eligible to be enrolled as advocates in the High Court. In those days, only barristers could practise in what was known as the Original Side (being the lucrative side) of the Calcutta High Court. In view of my father's consistently good results in different examinations, Sir Asutosh encouraged him to go to England to become a barrister.

But the family had no resources and, obviously, my father, who had just become a lawyer, could not afford to go to England on his own. As such, he borrowed about Rs 3,000 from one of his uncles, my grandfather's cousin, and left for England in 1922. Those days one could survive in England on such a modest amount for about nine or ten months, though with considerable difficulty, often skipping a meal. One had also to pay the necessary tuition fee. As my father was enrolled in the Calcutta High Court as an advocate and had a law degree, the Inns of Court (the society that conducts the Bar examinations) exempted him from appearing in Part I of the Bar examination and also from attending most of the dinners, which a Bar student had to compulsorily attend, and for which one had to pay from one's own pocket. My father realized he had to complete his course before his money ran out and justify the faith reposed in him by Sir Asutosh and his own family. He completed his Bar examination in ten months, which was a record. He stood first in Class I of the Bar examination, one of the most difficult of the lot. He was the first Indian to do so. He also won the prestigious Langdon Medal for his proficiency in Hindu Law. When he left for England, the power of his reading glass was –2. When he came back after his brilliant results, it was –12, which shows how much time and attention he had devoted to his studies and at what cost!

He returned to India in 1923 after becoming a barrister. As he told us later, one of the great moments in his life was when he got down at Howrah Station, Calcutta, to find Sir Asutosh at the platform to receive him. He was overwhelmed with emotion when Sir Asutosh embraced him and said, 'Nirmal, we are proud of you.'

I have often thought about my father's journey to England, and I realize that with determination, discipline, commitment, sincerity and hard work, one can overcome all hurdles. My father proved it. He has been the greatest inspiration in my life.

As a barrister, my father made rapid progress. But there were obstacles too. As he told me, during his early days as a barrister, when he applied to become a member of the Bar Library Club of the Calcutta High Court, without which a barrister could not function, some vested interests tried to create difficulties. There was also a rumour that he might not be admitted to the Bar Library Club. Not being a member of the club would have made it almost impossible for him to practise as a barrister. Coming to know of it, the then Hon. Chief Justice of the High Court told him, 'NC, if you are not given the membership of Bar Library,

I shall provide a room for you next to my chamber, so that you can carry on with your practice.' When this became known, he was admitted as a member. This seemed to me a great example how honesty of purpose and dedication to one's work and merit are always recognized by well-meaning persons. This incident has always inspired me to try my humble best whenever I have had to discharge my duties.

As my father's practice picked up (and the first thing he did was to repay the loan that he had taken from his uncle), it became necessary for him to have more space for his chamber and growing library. Initially, he rented a building across our ancestral house in Bhowanipur. Soon, even that became quite inadequate and in 1934 my grandfather persuaded my father to move to a larger place. At the instance of his father and brothers, Nirmal Chandra purchased a plot of land at Theatre Road (now known as Shakespeare Sarani), which earlier housed a building where the English performed plays, from which the road acquired its name. The house had wooden floors, which were suitable for dancing. It was demolished and under the supervision of my grandfather and uncles, a beautiful house was constructed on that plot of land, No. 5, Theatre Road. We shifted there in 1936 when I was seven years old. I remember my eldest sister's marriage there, an event of great rejoicing for us.

I was born on 25 July 1929 at Tezpur, Assam, where my maternal grandfather, Rai Bahadur Debendra Kumar Mukherjee, the first Indian director of land records, Assam, was then posted. He was a man committed to high principles and was known for his impeccable integrity.

I was the youngest of three sisters and two brothers. My eldest sister, Amita, was born in 1919 at Gauhati, when my father was a practising vakil in Calcutta High Court. The rest of us – including my other sisters, Namita and Sabita, and elder brother, Debnath

– were born after my father returned to Calcutta as a barrister. Debnath, like Amita, was born in Gauhati. He used to tease Amita that she was a vakil's daughter while he was the son of a barrister!

My earliest childhood memories pertain to my schooldays at Gokhale Memorial Girls' School, near our ancestral house in south Calcutta. As my mother told me, up to the age of five, I was almost a bedridden child, being a patient of nephritis with little hope of survival. My mother believed that it was only due to the treatment of Sir Nilratan Sarkar, one of the greatest physicians of this country, that I eventually recovered. When I had grown up, my mother extracted a promise from me that I would never take a bath at Har Ki Pauri in Hardwar because Sir Nilratan had told her that my illness was due to a serious infection from the very cold water there, in which I might have been immersed on a visit to the holy city. I have not defied her in all these years!

I recollect that I was mostly confined to my room and did not have a normal childhood. When I was about six, I was admitted to Gokhale Memorial Girls' School because my sisters were students there, so that if necessary, Amita would be in a position to look after me. I was later told that I was admitted to the school primarily to find out whether I could bear the strain of remaining out of the house for a few hours. I was in that school for about two years and I believe that I was the only boy student there. I still have some hazy recollection of the kindness and affection I received from the teachers, who knew about my indisposition.

It was only at the age of eleven that my proper education began with my admission to a well-known Bengali-medium school, Mitra Institution, Bhowanipur. Before that, arrangements had been made for lessons from a private tutor, Banku Behari Das, a good teacher and a kind-hearted gentleman. He taught me and many of my cousins, who were about the same age as I was, when we lived in a joint family and also later when we shifted to the house on Theatre Road. I remember vividly his care and devotion. He paid special attention to me as I was unwell, and I used to wait for his arrival eagerly. From him I learnt that one has to observe discipline and that there is no alternative to sincerity and truthfulness.

Mitra Institution, Bhowanipur, was founded in 1905 by Sir Asutosh and several other leading citizens of south Calcutta. My father was part of the school's first batch of students but as the school had not yet received an affiliation for Class X, he had to move to London Missionary School, from which he passed his entrance examination. Mitra Institution subsequently became one of the most renowned schools in Calcutta, where the families of Sir Asutosh, Chittaranjan Das, Sir N.N. Sircar, Sir B.C. Mitter, Sir Chandramadhab Ghosh and many other families, including ours, got their sons admitted. My son, Pratap, studied there, while my two daughters, Anuradha and Anushila, were students of Gokhale Memorial Girls' School.

I took admission in Mitra Institution in 1940 as a student of Class VI. By this time I had recovered sufficiently from my illness and the doctors advised that I start getting used to a normal life. We had by then shifted to Theatre Road, and the school was at least four miles away from our residence. My father was a successful lawyer by now and owned more than one car. But I used public transport to attend school right from the beginning. My mother was committed to simple living and high moral values. She was a great disciplinarian who insisted that I go to school like any other student, either on foot or by public transport. We were not allowed the luxury of going to school in a car.

I recount this only to highlight how my siblings and I were taught the importance of humble living and a sense of responsibility to one's duties from a very young age. My mother, being the wife of the eldest son of the family, used to treat all my cousins (I had four uncles and an aunt) equally and nobody could accuse her of discriminating between her own children and our cousins. In fact, she helped many families with regular financial assistance. All that has been a great lesson to me and our family. Although she could afford it, she never indulged in luxury for the sake of it. Both my parents believed in simple living. There was nothing ostentatious in our house. This has helped me tremendously to adjust to the different situations that I have faced in my life. Whatever strength of character and commitment to principles I have been able to acquire are primarily due to my mother's training and her steadfast adherence to discipline and love and affection for everybody in the family.

I had the great fortune of growing up in an atmosphere of mutual affection, where we were taught to respect elders and our teachers and the importance of doing one's duty. That is how we learnt to live together loving each other, to accommodate each other in an atmosphere of goodwill and affection.

My father had become extremely busy with his legal practice and could hardly afford time to look after the family or its affairs. Being the youngest child and having been ill for a long time, I was very close to my mother and perhaps that helped me imbibe some of her lessons. I am indeed proud to be the son of such exceptional parents.

At the age of fifteen, when I was a student of Class X, I had my upanayan ceremony, along with two of my cousins. This required us to shave our heads. I used to go to school in a white half-sleeved shirt and shorts. When I went to school for the first time after the upanayan ceremony, similarly dressed but with a shaven head, Kabishekhar Kalidas Ray, the great poet and litterateur, who was the Bengali teacher in the school, hailed me as the 'Saheb Bamun', which translates to 'English Brahmin'. I felt extremely embarrassed. After returning home, I told my mother that I would never again go to school in shorts. Since then, I always wore a dhoti and shirt to school. Nobody thought of going to school in trousers those days.

As a student I was extremely lucky to have teachers of a very high calibre. Mitra Institution was known for its high standard of education and discipline. Apart from Kalidas Ray, I had great teachers like Keshab Chandra Nag, whose book on mathematics was recommended by all schools; Janaki Nath Shastri, whose book *Helps to the Study of Sanskrit* was referred to by all students of Sanskrit; Suresh De, who taught English; Mani Chakraborty, Nitindra Narayan Roy, Jatin Babu, Mukunda Babu, Prafulla Babu, our principal Haridas Kar, among others. They inculcated in the students a deep commitment towards academic excellence. In 1945, when I passed the matriculation examination, the students of our school occupied four positions – the first, second, fourth and seventh – among the first ten students and were awarded five first-grade scholarships, which was an all-time record. I had the honour of standing seventh among the first ten students in the scholarship list and tenth in the general list.

After matriculation, I took admission in Presidency College, Calcutta, which was (and still is, I believe) one of the best educational institutions in the country. I studied science in the Intermediate course and then switched to economics for my BA course. I had as my contemporaries some of the best students from all over the state. They were extremely successful later in many spheres of our national life. Among them were Amaresh Bagchi, the great economist; Hariananda Barari, director of IB and the governor of Haryana; Nilmoni Mukherjee, historian; Adinath Chatterjee of the Calcutta Electricity Supply Corporation; Dip Sen and Sugata Basu, both stalwarts of the IPS; Kanak Ranjan Dasgupta, engineer, who stood first in the matriculation examination from our school; Amiya Chakrabarti, professor of chemistry in Jadavpur University; Amitabha Chatterjee, engineer; and many others. Though Bengal has been well known for its political activities and its aggressive 'student politics', the Presidency College Students' Union was not active in politics in my time. I had no interest in active politics either.

In 1945, of course, the freedom movement was fast approaching its climax. Everyone knew that sooner or later India was going to become independent. Whether one was active in politics or not, no Indian during those exciting days could be totally disinterested in political developments as freedom was in the air. With demands for the division of the country on a communal basis, there was a lot of discussion about the possibility of Bengal becoming an independent state. There was hardly any Indian who was not aware of the great importance of the naval mutiny of 1946, which shook the British imperialists. All of us hoped for the success of the Indian National Army, founded by Netaji Subhas Chandra Bose. No leader could generate such tremendous enthusiasm and electrify the whole nation as Netaji did. The youth and students in particular were waiting most eagerly for his return at the head of the conquering army, which would free us from bondage and foreign rule. '*Kadam Kadam Badhaye Ja*', the marching song of the Indian National Army, was on the lips of every Indian.

All of us also realized that the political situation in Bengal (before Partition) was volatile, with the Muslim League government ruling in the province, as the states were then called. The British government's pernicious policy of 'divide and rule' and the introduction of communal electorates – creating a clear divide among the two major communities on the basis of religion – had brought the Muslim League to power in Bengal, with the government actually fomenting trouble by indulging in discriminatory actions. It encouraged its supporters to take law into their own hands through state-sponsored communal riots.

The results were ghastly and dehumanizing. The Muslim League had been advocating the partition of India on communal lines and the creation of Pakistan, which would include the Muslim-majority province of Bengal among others. Other political parties opposed this vehemently and the British government too did not accede to the inclusion of Bengal in the proposed state of Pakistan.

To force the situation and with a view to creating irreconcilable differences between the two major communities, the League government let loose a well-organized mayhem through the Great Calcutta Killings from 16 August 1946, the likes of which, I am sure, no country had seen in any peace time. Thousands of innocent people of both communities lost their lives. I had the most shocking experience of learning of the cold-blooded killing of one Dr Jamal, who lived just across the street from our family house in Bhowanipur. He had always been secular in his outlook and was close to everyone in the locality – a Hindu-dominated one. As a doctor he never charged any fee from his neighbours. He was even one of the important organizers of the annual Durga Puja celebration. Despite this, he was killed in the most brutal manner, dragged out of our family house, where he had taken shelter to save himself, mercilessly beaten and his throat slit by the rampaging mob – comprising those who used to call him dada or kaka. I realized what great tragedy ill-feeling and enmity between people could cause and how human beings could turn into demons. That day I also understood how religion, if misused, could cause havoc and bring untold miseries to people's lives.

The Hindu Mahasabha had been founded in the late 1930s to fight the communal politics of the Muslim League and protect the interests of the Hindus. My father was a leader of the Hindu Mahasabha. In 1940 he was elected a councillor of the corporation of Calcutta from Ballygunge constituency, defeating a well-known

Congress candidate. Fifteen out of ninety-eight councillors were from the party. The Hindu Mahasabha had many eminent leaders, such as Sir Manmatha Nath Mukherjee (former acting Chief Justice of the Calcutta High Court), Dr Syama Prasad Mookerjee, S.N. Banerjee (a leading barrister), Ashutosh Lahiry (the great freedom fighter, who spent a number of years in Cellular Jail) and others. The party was then quite a force in Bengal and some other states.

After the communal riots in Calcutta in August 1946, my father, then president of the Bengal Provincial Hindu Mahasabha, along with his party members, played an important role in trying to bring about peace and harmony between the two communities. The riots in Calcutta were followed by ghastly incidents of communal confrontation in Noakhali in eastern Bengal and Bihar. I remember my father visiting several villages in Noakhali in the aftermath of the riots to protect the rights of the grievously affected minority communities and to restore peace.

In 1946-47, Mahatma Gandhi visited Noakhali and Calcutta to bring about harmony and amity among the people and to extinguish the flames of communal passion. In Noakhali, he stayed in Srirampur village, where my father met him on 5 December 1946 to discuss the prevailing situation. After India achieved independence, the communal situation in Calcutta and many areas continued to be tense. In the months of August and September 1947, Gandhiji stayed at Hydari Manzil at Beliaghata, Calcutta, as part of his efforts to restore peace. During that period, my father often went to Hydari Manzil and on a few occasions I was able to persuade him to take me along with him so that I could have the great privilege of meeting Gandhiji. I was then a student of Presidency College. Gandhiji had gone on a fast to bring about a change of heart among the people of Calcutta. Leaders of different communities and parties, including my father, made earnest requests to Gandhiji to break his fast as his condition was deteriorating rapidly. On 4 September 1947, they were able to persuade him to do so. I was present on the historic occasion. Even now I recall the events of the day, particularly when Gandhiji broke his fast by taking a glass of juice.

As has been recorded by Manu Gandhi:

> This long talk (the discussion with different leaders and representatives of communities) exhausted Bapu. He started uttering 'Rama, Rama'. He was feeling giddy and extremely restless. Abhaben and I had been supporting him. He tried to lie down one moment and got up the next. He kept turning his rosary. All the visitors went to another room to decide what they should do. The leaders among them were Rajaji, Kripalaniji, Prafullababu and Shaheed Saheb. After an hour's discussion Nirmalbabu was the first to come in. All the leaders had given in writing that peace would be preserved in Calcutta, and that they would take the responsibility if anything untoward were to happen. They were prepared to die before anyone else. The papers were signed among others by N.C. Chatterjee, Suhrawardy, Surendra Mohan Ghose, Sarat Chandra Bose, Sardar Niranjan Singh Talib, Debendra Nath Mukherjee and R.K. Jaidka.
>
> 'We, the undersigned, promise to Gandhiji that peace and quiet have been restored in Calcutta once again. We shall never again allow communal strife in the city. And shall strive unto death to prevent it.'
>
> This document was signed by the above-mentioned persons. After this, Bapu directed that we arrange a prayer. There was the usual prayer and the recitation of 'Ramanama'. Shaheed Suhrawardy then offered Bapu a glass containing one ounce of sweet lemon juice exactly at 9.15 and having bowed down to him in the Hindu style, burst into tears.
>
> —*A Frank Friendship*, compiled and edited by Gopalkrishna Gandhi

The opportunity I had of seeing Mahatma Gandhi from very close quarters greatly attracted me towards him. I still recall the most penetrating but affectionate look in his eyes, which could not but draw people. I have no hesitation in admitting that I became one of his ardent admirers. I found his charm irresistible and during those days I started attending his prayer meetings at different places. If I remember correctly, I attended at least five or six of his prayer meetings. I must confess that I could not keep myself away from those meetings whenever they were held in and around Calcutta.

This, however, did not result in my getting involved in active politics in any manner whatsoever and my first priority still remained my studies. But I started reading the autobiography of Mahatma Gandhi, which greatly impressed me.

Around this time my father became president of All India Hindu Mahasabha and presided over the Gwalior session of the party. But after Partition and after the assassination of Gandhiji, it appeared to me that he had become somewhat disenchanted with the party's politics. Towards the end of 1947 and early 1948, he fell ill quite frequently and for months could not attend to his professional work. Doctors advised him that because of the serious attack of epidemic dropsy, he would not be able to lead an active life any more. He was then about fifty-three years old and the prospect of a restricted life obviously upset him very much. At this time, as we came to know later, he got an offer for appointment as a judge of the Calcutta High Court and he agreed to accept the offer. In July 1948, he became an additional judge and soon thereafter a permanent judge of the Calcutta High Court.

At that time both my parents were unwell and they were convalescing in Puri, Orissa, where I had accompanied them. I came to know of my father's appointment as a judge from the newspapers. Only my mother knew of it beforehand. I mention this because nowadays everybody seems to know who is aspiring to be a judge and who is supporting whom. There is lobbying with members of the collegium that selects the judges and there is public speculation about appointments too. I wish that the appointment of judges of our higher courts is treated with great sanctity and does not become a matter of 'tadbir' and market gossip. I find it painful that some of the basic ethical standards have lost their importance and that the judiciary is not immune to such weaknesses.

During my father's tenure as a judge, there was obviously no question of his taking part in political activities. However, he resigned within fourteen months of accepting the judgeship along with a few other judges of different High Courts, because the government had proposed in the draft constitution that no one holding a judicial office would be allowed to do any legal work after retirement. My father thought this would seriously interfere with the right of former judges to carry on legal work as lawyers after their resignation or retirement, which was earlier permitted.

In 1950, my father started practising in the Supreme Court and shifted from Calcutta to Delhi, as he could no longer practise in the Calcutta High Court. Soon, he became the vice-president of the Supreme Court Bar Association and executive chairman of the Indian Law Institute. He thereafter also gradually renewed his association with the Hindu Mahasabha. When I was in England for my studies, he contested in the first general election to the Lok Sabha in 1952 from the Hooghly parliamentary constituency in West Bengal as a Hindu Mahasabha candidate and was elected, defeating Renuka Ray, a well-known Congress leader. I will not dwell on his role as an MP during the first Lok Sabha. It is generally accepted that he was one of its most outstanding parliamentarians.

In 1949, I graduated from Presidency College with honours in economics. While I joined MA (economics) in Calcutta University,

I also enrolled in the Law College for an LLB degree, as I wanted to follow my father's profession. Later in the year, I got admission to Jesus College, Cambridge, in the UK. I was very excited to have got the great opportunity of studying at Cambridge and also to qualify as a barrister from Middle Temple, where my father had also been a student.

Immediately thereafter, I was faced with a situation I had not anticipated. My mother, probably because of her abiding affection for me, wanted me to get married before I left for England. She also persuaded my father to agree to her proposal. In those days no one could question the decision taken by one's parents and I never dreamt of defying them. And so it was that while I was a student, I married Renu, a girl selected by my parents, the youngest daughter of Dhirendra Narayan Roy, who belonged to a family of Lalgola in the district of Murshidabad, which was well known for its acts of benevolence and charity.

I left for England from Bombay on 7 September 1950 on the SS *Strathaird*, leaving my young wife in Calcutta. I reached England on 24 September 1950 and stayed there for three years. I returned once in May 1951, when my son Pratap was born. He is now a very successful barrister practising in Calcutta and other High Courts and also in the Supreme Court.

My three-year stay in England was marked by total focus on academic pursuits to the exclusion of almost everything else. In fact, my English landlady often chided the other Indian students, 'Why don't you become like Somnath Chatterjee?' My spartan lifestyle was also necessitated by the limited financial resources at my disposal. I was fortunate that the family I boarded with gave me the occasional dinner!

Two landmark events unfolded in England during my stay there. One was the general election in October 1951, in which Clement Attlee was defeated and Winston Churchill came back to power. I followed the political scene quite closely. I was a regular visitor to the House of Commons when it was in session and was privileged to hear parliamentary stalwarts like Attlee, Churchill, Aneurin Bevan and Richard Butler deliver stirring speeches. What fascinated me about the election was the total absence of wasteful expenditure during canvassing. There wasn't a single poster defacing walls, no screaming loudspeakers, no political processions. The only means of canvassing seemed to be pamphlets left in mailboxes and private meetings.

The other significant development was the death of King George VI and the coronation of Queen Elizabeth II. I came to know of the death of the monarch as I was getting ready to go to college. I was sure that a holiday would be declared. However, to my surprise there was no holiday and life went on as usual. Only the flag flew at half-mast. My professor arrived a few minutes late, apologized for the delay and began his lecture. In contrast, India was on holiday for three days!

I finally returned to India in August 1953 and joined my wife and we have lived together happily thereafter. She has been a great source of strength to me all my life and has always encouraged me in all my activities. She once told me that I could participate in everything that interested me, but no one should ever be able to allege that I was corrupt. I hope I have been able to live up to her expectations.

I joined the Calcutta High Court as a barrister soon after my return. When my father contested the second Lok Sabha elections in 1957 as a candidate of the Hindu Mahasabha, as a dutiful son I tried to help him by arranging for jeeps (which was the only vehicle that could be used effectively in the rural areas then) and organizing election materials like posters and handbills. However, I had nothing to do with his campaign nor did he ask me to take any part in it. He did not express any desire that I should take part in politics. My eldest sister Amita assisted my father in a big way during this and subsequent election campaigns. She single-handedly ran my father's establishment at Chinsurah and Burdwan and was a tower of strength to my father during the strenuous campaign. My father, however, lost the election. By that time the Mahasabha had become a smaller political outfit and did not have much influence among the people.

After a while, my father dissociated himself from active politics and concerned himself more and more with matters of civil liberties. He was one of the most distinguished office-bearers of the All India Civil Liberties Union and its president too. He organized the constitution of the important Mulla Commission and Sarjoo Prasad Commission of Enquiry, non-official bodies that looked into human rights violations and civil liberty issues. The reports of these commissions were outstanding documents with which everyone interested in civil liberties and human rights is well acquainted. He was one of the most renowned lawyers of the Calcutta High Court but often appeared, without charging any fee, in cases concerning civil liberties and human rights. Some of these cases related to well-known communist leaders like Jyoti Basu, who had been detained under the Defence of India Rules. My father got the orders of their detention quashed.

After I joined the Calcutta High Court as a barrister, Snehangshu Kanta Acharya (Dodo-da, as we called him), well-known barrister and leader of the then undivided Communist Party of India (CPI), introduced me to Jyoti Basu and other leaders of the party. Jyoti Basu, Benoy Choudhury and Harekrishna Konar often visited my father. Of course, S.K. Acharya (who was a great admirer of my father and was extremely affectionate towards me) was the driving force in building up the close relationship between my father and important leaders of the CPI. Acharya and Jyoti Basu were very close friends, and the latter often visited Acharya's house. On many occasions, I had the privilege of being asked by Acharya to be present at his house and thus had the opportunity of coming to know Jyoti Basu well.

In 1962, my father again decided to contest the general elections from the Hooghly parliamentary constituency but this time as an independent candidate. He lost by a narrow margin to Prabhat Kar, the CPI leader. Though he won three of the seven assembly segments of the constituency, it was extremely difficult to win an election as an independent. During that election, too, I tried to help him with logistic support. In 1963, a bye-election to the Lok Sabha was held after the member elected from the Burdwan parliamentary constituency was disqualified by the High Court following an election petition over his having entered into a work contract with the government. My father was approached by CPI leaders like Jyoti Basu, Bhawani Sen, Benoy Choudhury (who belonged to Burdwan) and S.K. Acharya to contest the bye-election as an independent candidate supported by the party. At their request and that of many civil rights activists and leaders like Tridib Chowdhury, the well-known RSP leader who was himself an MP, my father agreed. He was elected from the Burdwan parliamentary constituency in 1963. Though an independent member, on many important issues he supported the views of the Left. I believe that in recognition of that, the Communist Party of India (Marxist) – the CPI(M) (by then the CPI had been divided) – decided to support him in the fourth Lok Sabha election from Burdwan, which he won defeating Narayan Choudhuri, the powerful Congress leader.

At the request of S.K. Acharya, I also started representing workers, trade unions and others who were members or functionaries of the CPI and CPI(M) in the High Court without charging any fee. Such appearances gave me the chance to come close to many leaders and workers of the CPI(M). I became a member of the Democratic Lawyers' Association, which was an organ of the party. I had not thought of joining the CPI(M). However, I attended some of the party programmes, including public meetings, and read some Marxist literature which S.K. Acharya had given me. I must confess I was impressed by Marxist theories and principles (as far as I could understand in my imperfect way), the pro-people policies and programmes of the party, and gradually became one of its supporters and sympathizers.

By the time my father was elected to the fourth Lok Sabha in 1967, I had established greater and closer contact with the party, its leaders and workers. During the election campaign in 1967, I took a more active part than earlier, visiting the constituency with leaders and workers of the party. I did not address meetings but I got grassroots exposure to the party's objectives and policies and also the causes espoused by it. I continued to help the party by appearing for the workers in different courts of law as and when the occasion arose and thus got involved in CITU's (Centre of Indian Trade Unions) movement.

Though my father continued to remain an independent member in the House, he worked closely with the CPI(M) on almost all occasions. I remember he also appeared in a few cases concerning civil liberties and trade unions on behalf of the party and its workers before the Supreme Court.

From 1968 onwards, my father's health deteriorated due to an attack of cerebral thrombosis. He was in coma for nearly four months but his recovery surprised even the doctors treating him in Willingdon Hospital (now Ram Manohar Lohia Hospital). In 1969, in the elections held for the assembly in West Bengal, my father campaigned for candidates of the CPI(M) and addressed election meetings too. However, because of his failing health, he found it difficult to appear in courts or attend Parliament. Towards the latter half of 1970 he decided he would no longer actively pursue either his professional or political career and shifted to Calcutta after spending twenty years in Delhi. The fourth Lok Sabha was dissolved on 27 December 1970.

Before the election to the fifth Lok Sabha was announced, it became clear that my father would not be able to participate in it. Then something interesting happened which completely changed my career path. I believe it was due to the active initiative and prodding of S.K. Acharya, my leader in the Bar, that Jyoti Basu and Benoy Choudhury visited my father at our Ballygunge residence – we had left our Theatre Road residence when my father became a judge, as he said he would not be able to meet the expenses of the big establishment on the meagre salary paid to High Court judges. They suggested that I should contest the Lok Sabha election from Burdwan with the support of the party. Neither Acharya nor my father told me about the purpose of their visit. Apart from S.K. Acharya, Jyoti Basu and Benoy Choudhury, other important leaders of the West Bengal unit of the party – like Pramod Dasgupta, secretary of the West Bengal unit, and Harekrishna Konar – had also met my father in this connection on one or two occasions.

Eventually, my father told me of the request. I was pleasantly surprised that CPI(M) leaders wanted me to contest the election to the Lok Sabha. I was not a member of the party and my only contact with the party and some frontal organizations was in my capacity as a lawyer. But I did not take the proposal seriously and told him that it was for him to decide. Whatever decision he took, I would follow. He said he had turned down the proposal because he felt that I should continue with my professional career, where I had been able to make a mark. I should contest after five years, if at all. By that time I was a fairly busy practitioner in the Calcutta High Court, the Supreme Court and other High Courts and also had a family with my wife, son and two daughters, both born after

I joined the Calcutta Bar. They brought immense happiness to us. My children are highly educated – both my daughters are law graduates – happily married and busy with their own lives.

I was not an activist and had not thought of a political career. But S.K. Acharya, whom I met in court every day and who was my 'guru', constantly persuaded me to speak to my father so that he would give me his permission. I told him that there was no question of my taking the plunge unless my father approved. Whenever I thought of it, I felt extremely nervous at the prospect of being a candidate, which would have required me to address public meetings, of which I had no experience. At the same time, I must honestly confess that at the back of my mind a feeling started growing that should the great opportunity come to me, why should I not accept it? It would indeed be a great honour. My wife also felt that if my father gave his consent, I should not hesitate to contest. The visits of party leaders and the discussions in our house became more and more frequent and this was no doubt having an effect on me. I started wondering how I would be able to combine my professional life and parliamentary life, if at all I became an MP.

One day, I summoned the courage to tell my father that S.K. Acharya was pressurizing me to stand for elections. My father reiterated that 'very few lawyers can pick up a practice that you have done in such a short time and therefore it will not be advisable to give it up for an uncertain political career'. I let the matter rest there. After another visit by top leaders of the CPI(M), my father must have given further thought to it. One morning, when I was about to leave for the court, he conveyed to me that to honour the requests of S.K. Acharya, Jyoti Basu and others, I had his permission to contest the election from Burdwan.

When I reached the High Court, I immediately informed S.K. Acharya about my father's decision and he almost jumped out of his chair in joy. I told him that I was still very hesitant because it would be a totally new experience for me and not being active in politics, I might not make the grade. After the court hours that day, S.K. Acharya met my father to finalize the question of my candidature. The leaders assured him that it would not be difficult for me to win in view of the strength of the party in Burdwan. My father was informed that I need not join the party and would contest as an independent candidate. The leaders encouraged me and said that I need not feel apprehensive as the party would support my candidature. I recall that Pramod Dasgupta, one of the greatest leaders of the party, asked me not to worry about addressing meetings. He told me that he would be present at the inaugural meeting to be held in support of my candidature in the constituency.

That is how I became a candidate for the fifth Lok Sabha election from Burdwan. My election office was in the office of the CPI(M) in Burdwan and all matters connected with the election were looked after by the party. Before my election campaign started, I did not even know the topography of all the areas in my constituency. My acquaintance with the grassroots workers in those areas was limited to those I had come to know during my father's campaign. I had no place to stay in Burdwan and I had to take on rent a small flat near Arati cinema hall. Amita came to Burdwan and, together with Namita, Sabita and my wife, joined in the campaign by visiting different households and meeting people. My daughters, who were in school at the time, also came to Burdwan and joined their mother, their aunts and party workers in the campaign.

In subsequent elections, along with my daughters, my grandsons Shashwata and Saurabh (sons of Pratap and his wife, Shakuntala, who is a Konkani girl and has learned Bengali very well), and my very young granddaughters (Surya and Trisha, daughters of Anuradha and her husband, Sugata Bhattacharya, an engineer) often participated in the campaigns in their own way. Anuradha, who stayed in Delhi, spent many days in my constituency. Anushila, who runs a cultural institute in Kolkata, spent a number of days with me during my election campaigns. Pratap too visited my constituency along with my two sons-in-law Sugata Bhattacharya and Debi Prasad Basu (a businessman and sports enthusiast), and some of my cousins, nephews and nieces. Of course, my election campaign on all occasions was run by the party, which was in full control of the election machinery.

I have been asked on several occasions how I could become a candidate of the CPI(M) when my father was a leader of the Hindu Mahasabha. Now that I have recounted the events, I believe those who expressed surprise will understand how I became a candidate for the Lok Sabha election in 1971. I was an independent candidate supported by the CPI(M) but I decided to take the symbol of the party as my election symbol and the party readily agreed.

I was by that time established as a fairly successful legal practitioner in the Calcutta High Court and connected with various cultural and professional institutions. I was the senior advocate of the Left Front government in the Calcutta High Court in 1969 but resigned to contest the election. I was also quite an active member of the Bar Library Club, Calcutta Bar Association, Supreme Court Bar Association, Bar Association of India, International Law Association, Indian Law Institute, Shri Aurobindo Society, Asiatic Society, All India Civil Liberties Council, Democratic Lawyers' Association, apart from being connected with various trade unions and employees' associations.

Novice that I was in running an election campaign, it was a relief that I did not actually have to take any major decisions relating to it. Everything was taken care of by the party. Being an independent candidate, I had asked party leaders about the financial contribution I had to make to meet election expenses. The party responded that once the party had supported my candidature, it was its responsibility and not mine to run a successful campaign. I made a small contribution to the party in addition to meeting the expenses of the car in which I travelled as well as the rent and running of our temporary household.

My first election meeting was held at a place called Galsi, about twenty miles from Burdwan. My election agent was Biswanath Sen. I was expected to speak at the meeting. I was extremely tense and tried to think of what to say. I was not sure whether Pramod Dasgupta remembered his promise that he would be present at the first meeting to be held in my constituency. I had, in fact, given up hope. But I will never forget the excitement and thrill I experienced when I learnt that Pramod Dasgupta was going to address the meeting. I realized how affectionate and concerned as a leader he was. He wanted to encourage me as a new candidate. He was aware that I was rather hesitant and valued his support. I remember feeling immensely grateful that he came all the way from Calcutta to join me on that momentous day. To begin with, I could hardly speak for about five minutes but Pramod Dasgupta put me at ease. He kept the audience spellbound. His introduction gave me tremendous confidence.

My experience during the election campaign was an eye-opener about how sincere and committed the party comrades were. I had to do nothing but attend public meetings and make brief speeches as per the schedule drawn up by the party. I have no hesitation in admitting that my election, and also that of my father during the third and fourth Lok Sabha elections, was due to the efforts made by the party, apart from the reputation my father had as a lawyer and a public figure. As far as I am concerned, my victory was the party's. The sincerity and the commitment of the leaders was something that should provide lessons to other parties also.

Because I had spent some money during my first election, Pramod Dasgupta decided that I need not pay any levy to the party during the term of the fifth Lok Sabha as other MPs elected on party tickets had to, though I did offer to pay.

Bholanath Sen, PWD minister in the Siddhartha Shankar Ray government in West Bengal, and a member of the legislative assembly from Bhatar constituency, which was a part of Burdwan parliamentary constituency, was the Congress candidate against me. I won by a margin of 64,080 votes, getting 56.72 per cent of votes polled.

I entered the fifth Lok Sabha in 1971 with great trepidation and a feeling of overpowering responsibility.

2

DEMOCRACY, DICTATORSHIP AND DISORDER

In the latter part of the fourth Lok Sabha, there were internecine problems in the Congress and it was divided into two groups. The ruling faction, under the leadership of Indira Gandhi, was known as Congress (R), while the other was known as Congress (Organization). During the period Indira Gandhi was in a minority in the Congress, the CPI(M) had extended support to her for several progressive measures taken by the government. A bill had been introduced in the Lok Sabha in 1970 to abolish privy purses and other privileges of princes. Although the Lok Sabha passed the bill, it was defeated by only one vote in the Rajya Sabha. An order was thereafter issued withdrawing recognition to the princes. This was challenged by the princes in the Supreme Court, which decided in December 1970 that the order was contrary to the spirit of the Constitution, arbitrary and illegal. The nationalization of banks in July 1969, which was acclaimed by all sections of the people, met with the same fate and was declared ultra vires. Indira Gandhi thereupon decided to dissolve the fourth Lok Sabha to seek a fresh mandate from the people, nearly fourteen months before its term was due to get over. She declared that reactionary forces were obstructing progressive measures only because her government wanted to ensure a better life for the vast majority of the people. As a result, public support for Indira Gandhi reached an all-time high.

With such populist measures, backed by the slogan of 'Garibi Hatao', Indira Gandhi appeared to have complete sway over the people of the country, who gave her a resounding victory in the election to the fifth Lok Sabha in 1971. Her party won 352 seats out of 518. The CPI, with only twenty-five members, was the next largest party, which meant that she had virtually no opposition in the House.

Tumultuous events unfolding in Pakistan, leading to the formation of Bangladesh, greatly added to Indira Gandhi's popularity. General elections had taken place in Pakistan in December 1970. In East Pakistan, Sheikh Mujib-ur Rehman and his party, the Awami League, had made the denial of the right of the Bengali people to use their mother tongue and the exploitation of the rich resources of East Pakistan by powerful elements in West Pakistan its main campaign planks. In an unexpected verdict, the Awami League won 167 of the 169 seats in East Pakistan, while Zulfikar Ali Bhutto's Pakistan People's Party (PPP) won only 88 of the 144 seats in West Pakistan. To prevent Sheikh Mujib-ur Rehman from coming to power, President Yahya Khan sought to nullify the results of the election. The Awami League called an indefinite general strike against this ill-advised move, which was crushed by the use of brutal force. The people of East Pakistan, who were agitating for self-determination and protection of their language, were, however, determined to face the military dictatorship bravely.

Because of the atrocities perpetrated on the minority community in East Pakistan, there was a large-scale exodus of Hindus to India, particularly West Bengal. It was estimated that more than eight million refugees made their way to India. The Government of India opened camps in several states to provide shelter to them. There was a speedy deterioration of the situation in East Pakistan and the Awami leaders in Calcutta formed a 'government in exile' in anticipation of dramatic political developments.

Indira Gandhi decided that a war was inevitable to save the people of East Pakistan. When Yahya Khan took the drastic step of bombing Indian targets, the Indian Army marched towards Dhaka. The war lasted for about two weeks. Lieutenant-General A.A.K. Niazi of the Pakistan Army surrendered to General Jagjit Singh Aurora of the Indian Army on 16 December 1971. To the credit of India, Bangladesh was liberated and became an independent country in an astonishing sweep of events.

India's role in the emergence of Bangladesh as a free nation made Indira Gandhi even more popular with the Indian masses. A section of the media reported Atal Bihari Vajpayee describing her as Goddess Durga, though he later disputed the report.

Apart from the Indo-Pak war, the massive influx of refugees from East Pakistan and the liberation of Bangladesh, the fifth Lok Sabha (1971–77) witnessed many historic events such as the Allahabad High Court judgment in the Indira Gandhi election case, the imposition of Emergency and its concomitant consequences – enactment of the draconian Maintenance of Internal Security Act (MISA), political detentions, censorship of the press, enforced family planning, the 42nd Constitutional Amendment, extension of the term of the Lok Sabha, among others. When I entered Parliament as a first-time member, I had no inkling that such a turbulent period of our democracy lay ahead.

In the fifth general election held in 1971, twenty-four candidates of the CPI(M) were elected to the Lok Sabha, nineteen from West Bengal, two each from Kerala and Tripura, and one from Andhra Pradesh. Among other Left parties, the CPI had twenty-five members, the Forward Bloc two and the RSP three. A.K. Gopalan was the leader of the CPI(M) Parliamentary Party in the Lok Sabha. Jyotirmoy Bosu was one of the party's prominent members in the House. He was elected from the Diamond Harbour constituency in West Bengal. He had been a member of the fourth Lok Sabha, too, representing the same constituency, and had already made a great mark as a crusader against black money, which controlled the economy, and as an active and efficient parliamentarian, raising diverse issues of improprieties or of corruption on the part of the ministers of the Central government headed by Indira Gandhi. Bosu was very effective in exposing skeletons in the cupboard of the Central government and I could sense that almost all ministers without exception were scared of him.

Although I was not a member of the party, I took my seat among the members of the CPI(M) group. The Lok Sabha secretariat considered me as one of the CPI(M) members of the Lok Sabha, as I had been elected on the party's symbol. I felt happy to have earned the confidence of the CPI(M) and tried to discharge my duties in keeping with the party's decisions. I also felt great satisfaction that the party, and particularly the leader of the parliamentary party, A.K. Gopalan, treated me with affection and encouraged me to take part in the proceedings of the House.

I was keen to learn how to be an effective MP and how to best raise important issues in the House and articulate people's causes. Not only did one need to have a proper knowledge of the rules of procedures and well-established conventions for the conduct of business but one also needed to utilize the opportunities that came one's way. I remained close to Jyotirmoy Bosu. He treated me as his pupil and taught me a lot. After the end of a day's session, I used to accompany him to his residence for a few hours every day. A large number of mediapersons and MPs used to be there, too, and my discussions with them helped broaden my horizons.

I often wondered how Jyotirmoy Bosu managed to get so much secret and confidential information about the functioning of the government, and its wrongdoings and misdeeds. He used to tell me that he had many sources, including some insiders in the Congress party and ministers of the government, who tipped him off so that he could not only raise issues of national importance but also embarrass these sources' detractors inside the House. I remember one day as we were entering the Central Hall, passing through the Coffee Board counter, a well-known minister crossed us. He hugged Jyotirmoy Bosu, casually enquired, 'Jyoti, how are you', and moved on. Bosu then brought out from his pocket a bunch of papers which the minister had left with him when they embraced each other. Those papers contained a lot of insights into the activities of some other ministers. This unique encounter revealed the weaknesses in the functioning of the Congress party and government.

In the initial stages of the fifth Lok Sabha, I did not give up my legal practice fully and tried to attend Parliament on as many days as possible in a week, combining them with my appearances in the Supreme Court and at the Calcutta High Court. During the weekends I also visited my constituency.

Being an MP gave me a unique opportunity of getting to know a galaxy of great leaders. A.K. Gopalan was an outstanding leader of the kisan movement and the working class and had been a great freedom fighter too. He gave new direction to the parliamentary activities of the party. Though he was soft spoken, members listened to him with great respect and attention. Other prominent leaders in the fifth Lok Sabha included Samar Mukherjee, Ahilya Rangnekar, Bijayakrishna Modak, Dr Saradish Ray, Rabin Sen and Sasanka Sekhar Sanyal. Stalwarts belonging to other parties included Hiren Mukherjee and Indrajit Gupta of the CPI, H.V. Kamath and P.G. Mavalankar. From the Congress, there was the redoubtable Indira Gandhi and Sardar Swaran Singh, Dr Karan Singh, Dinesh Singh, H.R. Gokhale, Mohan Kumaramangalam, Siddhartha Shankar Ray, Babu Jagjivan Ram, Y.B. Chavan, Gulzarilal Nanda and I.K. Gujral. I can never forget Madhu Limaye and Madhu Dandavate of the Socialist group, Piloo Mody of the Swatantra Party, Era Sezhiyan of the Dravida Munnetra Khazagham (DMK), Atal Bihari Vajpayee of the Jana Sangh, and Tridib Chowdhury of the RSP.

I rate Prof. Hiren Mukherjee, a senior and outstanding leader of the CPI, as the greatest parliamentarian I have come across during my entire tenure of nearly four decades. His commitment to the common people, his understanding of their problems and his command over language were unmatched. His speeches were enthralling. They always left me mesmerized. To me he was the true embodiment of what an ideal parliamentarian should be – precise and to the point, with in-depth knowledge of the selected subject, appropriate articulation, extremely respectful to the Chair and ever mindful of the rules and conventions of the House.

I was also greatly impressed by the well-prepared submissions of Madhu Limaye and the meticulous points of order raised by Era Sezhiyan, which created many awkward situations for the government. I had the distinct feeling that on occasions, the Speaker, Dr G.S. Dhillon, felt unequal to the task of regulating the proceedings, especially when Jyotirmoy Bosu and Madhu Limaye took the floor.

Observing these senior members and listening to their trenchant and insightful interventions communicated in a most forceful, yet dignified, manner inspired me to make my contributions to the House proceedings meaningful, impactful and memorable.

I made my maiden parliamentary speech on 24 May 1971 on the 1968–69 annual report of the University Grants Commission (UGC). Although I had prepared well, I was nervous. Initially, I was at a loss for words but quickly regained my composure. When I completed my speech, I was applauded by party leaders and other senior members, which encouraged me a lot. In my speech I pointed out that the report of an important commission like the UGC was being discussed two years after its presentation to the House, by which time it had lost all topical interest. It was nothing but an exercise in futility as the commission had by then submitted other reports without the benefit of the opinion of the House.

An explosive matter that generated great controversy in the fifth Lok Sabha was the Nagarwala case. It was alleged that Rustom Sohrab Nagarwala, an ex-army captain and intelligence officer, had telephoned the Parliament Street branch of the State Bank of India on 24 May 1971 and spoken to its chief cashier, Ved Prakash Malhotra, impersonating Indira Gandhi, instructing him to withdraw Rs 60 lakh and hand it over to a person from Bangladesh. Surprisingly, without trying to ascertain the genuineness of the telephone call, Malhotra handed over the amount to Nagarwala. After this, Malhotra met P.N. Haksar, secretary to the Prime Minister, and asked for a receipt. He was informed that he had been duped. The matter took a curious turn with the death of its investigating officer, D.K. Kashyap, in a car crash. Nagarwala was arrested and died in custody the same year, reportedly due to a heart attack. It was claimed by many in the Opposition that the fraud could not have been committed without the knowledge of the Prime Minister's office.

In 1971, the government promulgated an ordinance, only a few days before Parliament was convened, for maintenance of internal security. When Parliament met, the government introduced the Maintenance of Internal Security Bill to replace the ordinance. On 17 June 1971, I spoke on this important bill and commented on the constitutional impropriety involved. An ordinance, which is an executive legislation, should have been promulgated only if an extreme urgency justified it. No such justification could be provided by the government.

I strongly criticized the blatant misuse of the ordinance-making power of the executive and observed that

> ... soon after the ruling party came into power with the slogan of 'Garibi Hatao', all that they could and did banish from the country was personal freedom and individual liberty, instead of 'garibi' ... the bill is a scar on any civilized society believing in human freedom and personal liberty. In their hunger and greed for power, ruling parties show a tendency of becoming totalitarian. It was a shameless exhibition of hunger and greed for more power, when they took upon their hands this draconian Act, this piece of legislation, which does not provide even the semblance of security to an individual in this country. In the name of refugee influx, in the name of security of the state, which remained undefined, power has been given in the hands of petty mandarins, who are prone to act at the behest of the party in power. When the minister was moving the bill, he was trying to give a façade of reasonableness for this bill by indulging in vague generalizations and pious platitudes. I was pained to see that every member of the ruling party was supporting this blindly.

I pointed out how similar provisions in the Prevention of Violent Activities Act, 1970, had been misused in West Bengal, where, in the name of preventing so-called violent activities, the Act was used by an oppressive administration to arrest and detain its political opponents selectively and indiscriminately, without bringing the persons to trial. It was a glaring example of a ruling party finding itself alienated from the people, and instead of tackling the real problems faced by them, it sought to arm itself with almost unlimited powers to detain persons on trumped-up charges. I continued by asking, 'Has the situation in West Bengal improved? No, because the real reason is something else. After twenty-three years of misrule, there is complete degeneration of the youth. There is complete frustration because they have no future ... Instead of tackling the economic problem and the real problems of society, merely arming the government and the district and additional district magistrates with these arbitrary powers will not solve the problem.' I concluded by categorically opposing the bill. I stated, 'We are firmly of the view that it is going to be utilized against political opponents. That has been made very clear by the ruling party.'

The bill was, of course, passed in spite of strong objections, as the Congress had a majority in the House. Needless to say, the Act was misused. Unsurprisingly, the goodwill and the overwhelming support with which Indira Gandhi returned to power in 1971 soon evaporated because of the acts of omission and commission on her part and that of her government and her minions. What was also unprecedented was the phenomenon of a wholly non-constitutional authority – the Prime Minister's younger son, Sanjay Gandhi – wielding undiluted and unquestioned power over, as it were, the entire administration of the Government of India. Sanjay was projected as her representative as well as her chosen successor. He was brusque, extremely high-handed and tried to pose as the saviour of the nation.

At this time, it came to be known that Sanjay was very keen on setting up an automobile factory, though he had no experience or resources. To make his dream come true, he was given over 300 acres of land at a nominal price by Bansi Lal, the chief minister of Haryana, one of the Gandhi loyalists. The heir apparent was allowed to misuse the machinery of the government, and most Congress chief ministers and leaders, as well as senior bureaucrats, entered into an unseemly competition to fulfil his wishes. The Maruti factory was a monument to governmental misfeasance and the most talked-about act of nepotism of the era. The unsavoury development was raised in Parliament on several occasions by Jyotirmoy Bosu and Madhu Limaye, but the government and the Prime Minister barely reacted.

I came to know from a very reliable person, one of the top officers in the intelligence branch, that every morning at 7.00, senior officers, including him, had to report to one of the personal assistants of the Prime Minister at her residence and wait there, just in case Sanjay Gandhi wanted to meet them. They had to keep standing for hours, till they were permitted to return. Though it was very humiliating, they could do nothing about it. Even the finance minister faced the same ordeal, which gave his colleagues some cold comfort!

The slogan of 'Garibi Hatao' was evidently only for public consumption with no concrete, tangible action taken to remove poverty from the country. The people continued to suffer because of the failure of the government in all sectors – failure to provide food, employment, education, health care, even security. Worst of all, there was all-pervading corruption. The Prime Minister was quite content to leave all major 'initiatives' to her son, who played havoc with his programmes of population control through forced sterilization, forcible removal of slums and other reprehensible acts. Indira Gandhi herself displayed fascist tendencies, ensuring more and more centralization of power and placing party men loyal to her in important positions of governance. She misused intelligence agencies to keep watch over her political opponents, both within and outside the party.

Not satisfied with only a pliant administration, Indira Gandhi wanted a submissive Supreme Court, too, at her beck and call. One of the major issues, raised vigorously, related to the appointment, in March 1973, of Justice A.N. Ray of the Supreme Court as the Chief Justice of India, superseding Justice J.M. Shelat, Justice K.S. Hegde and Justice A.N. Grover, who were senior to Justice Ray. There were protests all over the country on account of the unjustified supersession of three eminent judges and the brazen violation of the well-established convention of appointing the senior-most puisne judge of the Supreme Court as the Chief Justice of India. The matter was raised in the House by Madhu Limaye. Participating in the debate, A.K. Gopalan mentioned that the supersession has 'justifiedly roused widespread criticism in the country and that the government had not given any cogent reason to throw away the convention established since Independence'. Though he referred to the elitist character of the judges as was displayed in the case of bank nationalization and abolition of privy purses, he maintained that such arbitrary action on the part of the government would only create an atmosphere of sycophancy among the judges.

S. Mohan Kumaramangalam, the minister of steel and mines (who was not connected with the decision of appointment, except as a Cabinet minister), was the main speaker on behalf of the government. He justified, in what has been described as an infamous speech, the act of supersession on the ground that the seniority of judges was not the most important principle to observe in matters of promotion. He referred to the confrontation between the Parliament and the government on the one hand and the court on the other, highlighting the Golak Nath case, where the Supreme Court by a narrow majority of 7:6 challenged the sovereignty of the Parliament to amend the Constitution; the decision of the Supreme Court invalidating the bank nationalization Act; and also the order whereby the government had withdrawn recognition to the princes. He rhetorically observed, 'Is it not good that we should have as Chief Justice of India a man who will be able to help to put an end to this period of confrontation, a person who will be able to ensure stability, certainty about the state of the law, a person who would be able to give a certain continuity, a certain permanence, to the approach made by the court to the important problems that come before it?' He tried to lend credibility to the government action stating that 'a duty is laid upon the government that not merely must we take into consideration judicial integrity, which we do, not merely the legal knowledge and skill, which we do, but also the philosophy and outlook of the judge. We are denounced for wanting committed judges as though we want the judges to commit themselves. We do not want any committed judges. No judge has to commit himself. But we do want judges who are able to understand what is happening in our country; the wind of change that is going across our country; who are able to recognize that Parliament is sovereign; that Parliament's powers in relation to the future are sovereign powers.'

I took part in the debate after what I called the arrogant intervention of the steel minister. Now when the matter had earlier come up before the House, the law minister, H.R. Gokhale, had tried to rationalize the appointment by relying on the recommendations of the Law Commission made about ten years ago, but which had never seen the light of day. The steel minister's intervention was clearly not based on the Law Commission's recommendation as he postulated that the government had absolute power to appoint the Chief Justice, deciding his suitability only on the basis of his political outlook and social philosophy.

I asked on what basis the government would select the Chief Justice of the country or the Chief Justice of any High Court or even a judge of a particular High Court for that matter, since the

Law Commission's recommendations had not been followed in the past. I wondered whether, in future, appointments would be made on the basis of the subjective satisfaction of a particular minister or of the Prime Minister. I argued:

> ... now this has to be done objectively. What are the objective standards? How does one find out a judge's political outlook? A judge is not supposed to hold any political views, at least not to air them in public. He is not supposed to proclaim his social philosophy openly and publicly. Then how does one ascertain it? Will there be a viva voce test in the presence of the Prime Minister and the law minister of India to know his political views and social philosophy to judge his qualification for appointment as Chief Justice of India? How do you find out what is his social philosophy? How do you ascertain his political outlook? That is why we say that this is not done to strengthen the judiciary, not to achieve what they conceive to be the real Directive Principles, for which the executive has never bothered. Through the judiciary, you cannot achieve the Directive Principles in this manner. The object is to have docile judiciary and a pliant judiciary. The theory now being propagated is that a judge, if he wants to continue in office, must give judgments which receive the executive's approbation. This is a theory we cannot accept, but this is being sought to be implemented ... We are being told of social philosophy and political outlook. Out of the judges who constituted the majority in the Golak Nath case, three were subsequently made chief justices, namely Justice Hidayatullah, Justice Shah and Justice Sikri. Justice Shah and Justice Sikri were also in the majority in the bank nationalization case and the privy purse case. All these three judges were part of the majority in the Golak Nath case. How were they appointed chief justices? Mr Justice Hegde was not a part to the Golak Nath judgment at all. He was not even a member of the bench then. Mr Justice Bhargava and Mr Justice Mitter who were in the minority ... in the Golak Nath case, were

in the majority in the bank nationalization case. In one case, Mr Justice Bhargava and Mr Justice Mitter were progressive and the same learned judges were reactionary in the other judgment. Is this the way you find out a reactionary judge or a progressive judge? Mr Justice Bhargava was also in the majority in the privy purse case, but he was in the minority in the Golak Nath case. They are supposed to be reactionary judges? Mr Justice Ray was a reactionary judge because he was in the majority in the MISA case? Mr Justice Mitter was progressive in one case and the same learned judges were both reactionary and progressive? Mr Justice Bhargava was also in the majority in the privy purse case, but he was in the minority in the Golak Nath case. Is he supposed to be a reactionary judge? Mr Justice Ray was a reactionary judge because he was in the majority in the MISA case? Mr Justice Shelat was a reactionary judge, Mr Justice Hegde was a reactionary judge and Mr Justice Grover was a reactionary judge because they stuck down this infamous law, 17A of MISA, which is a draconian law? You talk about social philosophy and Directive Principles. But you have enacted a law for detention of people without trial for three years, indefinitely. And you are talking of the social philosophy and social outlook of these judges who have struck down a draconian piece of legislation; they are being characterized as reactionaries. This is the attitude of this government. Mr Justice Ray delivered the leading judgment in the newsprint control case. The learned judge criticized very strongly the government's decision in the matter and struck it down, describing it as an arbitrary decision and executive high-handedness. The same judge suddenly becomes a reactionary in the newsprint control case? This is not the way we decide as to what is reactionary, who is a reactionary judge and who is a progressive judge. On the basis of one or two judgments, the executive will decide who will be the Chief Justice of India and which judge will be given the order of the boot because you do not like one particular judgment of his.

Mohan Kumaramanglam had flayed the decision of the Supreme Court in the Golak Nath case seeking to curtail the Parliament's power to amend the Constitution. Kumaramangalam spoke of the role of Justice Hegde of the Supreme Court, who, according to him, did not merit consideration for appointment of Chief Justice because of 'his political philosophy as could be discerned from his judgment'. Although we shared the view that the Golak Nath judgment had unfortunately curtailed the power of the Parliament to bring about the amendments to the Constitution, I could not accept the reasons he put forward. I submitted:

> We are entitled to say that some judgment is wrong but we should not necessarily impute motives to a particular judge and then say he was a reactionary on the basis of some observations in another judgment. You then pick and choose on the basis of your own predilections. There will be now competition among these judges to curry favour with the executive government. For instance, I have been raising this question, why do you offer job and assignments to retired judges? That is one of pernicious principles that have crept in the judicial set-up of this country to lure those judges – if you keep yourself in the good books of the government, your future even after retirement will be looked after. They will be parading before you with their certificates of social philosophy and political outlook to get appointments. Therefore, I submit that the reasons which have been put forward are not only contradictory, they are sterile. The real reason was to single out one judge for a very inconvenient and annoying judgment ... I need not elaborate. I am only sorry for Mr Justice Grover and Mr Justice Shelat because in order not to give the impression that a particular judge has been singled out, these two judges have also been clubbed with him. Otherwise, it would have been too obvious even to the votaries of Indira socialism and that is the real object of this supersession.

The years 1973 and 1974 were marked by recession, unemployment and price rise, which made life increasingly unbearable for the common people. The railway strike, which began on 7 May 1974, and involved more than 400,000 workers under the leadership of George Fernandes, president of the All India Railway Men's Federation, was an iconic protest against these developments. To counter this very successful and historic trade union mobilization, the government undertook a series of repressive measures.

It sought to break the morale of the workers by splitting them through special incentives and even took recourse to bribing some workers. The government also held that a strike in an essential service like the railways was an anti-national act, a sabotage, and that the workers had to be taught a fitting lesson. A large number of workers were dismissed without even an enquiry or a show-cause notice based on peculiar service rules, which provided for dismissal without a charge sheet. In spite of these efforts, the strike lasted for twenty-one days.

The railway strike was raised in Parliament by the entire Opposition, which fought a principled battle. However, it was clear that the government had lost all commitment to the people and their problems and viewed the entire working class as its mortal enemy.

In my capacity as a lawyer and an active supporter of the trade union movement, I felt that the illegal orders dismissing workers should be challenged in court. With the help of some well-meaning juniors, petitions were filed in the Calcutta High Court against the dismissal of more than 30,000 railway workers. My colleagues and I contributed towards the court fees and preparation of papers and documents, which was greatly appreciated by the workers. It was heartening that all the petitions were allowed, the dismissal orders set aside, and the workers reinstated by the railways.

In May 1974, more with a view to divert the attention of the country from the debilitating effect of the railway strike than anything else, the Prime Minister decided to give the go-ahead for the explosion of a nuclear device, marking India's entry into the nuclear world. This led to mixed reactions. A section of parliamentarians congratulated the government for taking this decisive step. However, the Left parties opposed it, pointing out that the prevailing economic situation did not justify India's attempts to become a nuclear power.

With pervading acts of corruption, mismanagement and high-handedness, people's misery was aggravated and discontent built up ominously in different parts of the country. These issues, raised in Parliament through no-confidence motions, were tabled and discussed in the Lok Sabha on 21 and 22 November 1973, 9 May 1974 and 23 and 25 July 1974 but the Prime Minister did not pay serious attention to them. She chose to give routine replies and contemptuously brushed aside the concerns of the Opposition.

Gradually the entire country became engulfed in demonstrations and protests against Indira Gandhi and her son's dictatorial regime. At the beginning of 1974, the students of Gujarat started an agitation called the Nav Nirman Movement, demanding the removal of the Congress chief minister of Gujarat, Chiman Bhai Patel, because of his anti-people activities and corruption. Unfortunately, the movement turned violent and the police sought to crush it by harsh measures. There was large-scale destruction of public property. The movement became so strong that the chief minister had no alternative but to resign and President's Rule was imposed in Gujarat.

The success of the Nav Nirman Movement in Gujarat encouraged students in other parts of the country to oppose the government's misdeeds. In Patna, students started an equally strong movement. In March 1974, they staged a march towards the assembly building, but were forcibly restrained by the police. This led to clashes which resulted in the death of three students. Many more were injured. When Jayaprakash Narayan came forward to lead the movement, it gained wider public support. He gave a clarion call for non-cooperation with the government and asked students not to attend schools and colleges. The entire state fell into turmoil. In spite of the exhortation by Jayaprakash Narayan, violence continued unabated. He addressed a massive rally at Gandhi Maidan in Patna on 5 June 1974, where he announced that the time was ripe for a 'Total Revolution'. In order to take the movement to other parts of the country, a conference of Opposition parties was called to strategize on the future course of action. The leaders pressed for the dismissal of the Bihar government and dissolution of other state assemblies. The Prime Minister was forced to hold a meeting with JP, but the impending crisis could not be averted.

On 6 March 1975, Jayaprakash Narayan held a public meeting at the Boat Club Lawns in Delhi in support of the movement. The meeting was a great success, in spite of the all-out efforts of the government to prevent people from attending it. After the meeting, a representation was submitted to the Speaker of the Lok Sabha, outlining several charges against the government and demanding dissolution of the Bihar assembly.

A great impetus was provided to the Nav Nirman Movement by Morarji Desai, who went on hunger strike demanding early elections in Gujarat, which had been placed under President's Rule. The government had to concede to the demand. In the election held in June 1975, the Congress was defeated and the erstwhile Opposition parties formed the new government in Gujarat.

On 12 June 1975, a red-letter day in the history of India's parliamentary democracy, the Allahabad High Court delivered its judgment on the election petition filed against Prime Minister

Indira Gandhi, challenging her election from the Rae Bareli constituency. In March, she had appeared in the same court to give evidence in the case before Justice Jagmohanlal Sinha on the election petition filed by Raj Narain on charges of corruption. It was established that the Prime Minister had misused governmental machinery for her election campaign and was also guilty of corrupt practices as she used the services of a government employee as her election agent. On that basis, the court declared her election null and void and she lost her seat in the Lok Sabha. She was also debarred from contesting an election for the next six years. The court, however, granted a stay of the order for twenty days to enable her to file an appeal and also for electing another leader of her party to hold the office of the Prime Minister. Indira Gandhi refused to resign and made it clear that she intended to continue in office. The Opposition expressed its strong objection and decided to hold rallies and demonstrations throughout the country demanding her resignation. However, the government, too, mobilized large numbers of people, who gathered near the Prime Minister's residence every day. She would address them stridently, contending that there was a sinister conspiracy afoot against her by reactionary forces. As expected, the crowds, tutored as they were, appealed to her to continue in office.

Justice Krishna Iyer of the Supreme Court disposed of the stay application made on behalf of the Prime Minister by directing the stay of the order of the Allahabad High Court. Indira Gandhi would be entitled to attend the Lok Sabha but would have no right to cast a vote, unlike other members of the House. The order of the Supreme Court gave a fillip to the demand of the Opposition parties for the Prime Minister's immediate resignation in the national interest. But instead of paying heed to the Opposition, the Prime Minister took recourse to an extraordinary step. She declared a state of Emergency under Article 352 of the Constitution on the plea that a 'grave emergency exists whereby the security of India is threatened by internal disturbances'. She apparently relied on the advice of a few of her loyalists like Siddhartha Shankar Ray – who was stated to have drafted the proclamation of Emergency – and her son Sanjay, who had become her closest political advisor. The President of India was woken up at midnight on 25 June 1975, and made to sign on the dotted line of the draft proclamation. He was informed that the situation was so serious that a Cabinet meeting could not be held to approve the proclamation. Early in the morning of 26 June, the people learnt from radio broadcasts that Emergency had been imposed in the country. To prevent any adverse reactions from the media, in a chilling move, the power supply of newspaper offices was disconnected. No newspaper could, therefore, be published on that day.

Just before the public announcement declaring Emergency, in a pre-dawn swoop, displaying stark desperation and vicious authoritarianism, almost all the prominent Opposition politicians and activists, including Jayaprakash Narayan, Morarji Desai, Choudhary Charan Singh, Acharya J.B. Kripalani, Atal Bihari Vajpayee, L.K. Advani, A.K. Gopalan, Jyotirmoy Bosu and Noorul Huda were arrested under MISA. Censorship was imposed on newspapers. Laws were enacted to curb the rights of journalists reporting proceedings in Parliament. All news that might bring 'hatred or contempt or excite disaffection' towards the government was restricted, effectively banning media publicity to criticism or any public protests. Unfortunately and surprisingly, the media capitulated.

On the evening of 25 June, I came to know from some sources that a number of Opposition MPs were going to be arrested, including Era Sezhiyan of the DMK, who was a very dear friend of mine. I persuaded him to leave his house on Dr Bishambar Das Marg, so that he could spend the night with an acquaintance of mine, named Rakshit, in Greater Kailash, south Delhi. Another friend, Erasmo de Sequeira, an MP from Goa, and I visited him the next morning along with Dinen Bhattacharya, an MP belonging to our party, when we learnt of the imposition of Emergency. The police had, in fact, gone to his residence with an arrest warrant but could not find him there. We stayed at Rakshit's place the whole day to avoid the police. To register our strong protest, we prepared a statement condemning the imposition of Emergency. Through the good offices of one of the senior journalists in Delhi, it was published in the foreign media as the national media did not want to have anything to do with it, for obvious reasons. Era Sezhiyan managed to avoid the police and reached Madras. We were relieved that he could avoid arrest and detention under MISA.

Dissent was suppressed overnight and a fear psychosis gripped the entire nation. The indiscriminately vindictive steps taken by the government made the people extremely apprehensive about their future. The world's largest parliamentary democracy was, in effect, converted into a police state. Indira Gandhi tried to justify her dictatorial action by alleging that the Opposition had deliberately planned, and was ready to adopt, extra-constitutional methods against her, contrary to basic norms of democracy.

The functioning of Parliament in a normal manner was not possible any more. Members of Parliament who spoke in the House were not supplied with copies of speeches that they were entitled to under the rules. Records of the speeches or proceedings in the House were not kept. Extremely regrettably, the Speaker, Dr G.S. Dhillon, did not stand up to safeguard the constitutional rights of the members and the dignity of Parliament.

A special session of Parliament was convened on 21 July 1975 to ratify the proclamation of Emergency. Leading members of the Opposition parties had been arrested and thus their strength in the House had come down considerably. The real import of

Emergency dawned on us when the House met at the usual time of 11 a.m. After the obituary references when the Speaker announced, 'Now, Papers to be laid on the Table', I was the first member to stand up and interject. I wanted to raise a point of order. A point of order relates to the interpretation or enforcement of the rules of procedure or such articles of the Constitution which regulate the business of the House, and which the Speaker can take cognizance of. Disappointingly, the Speaker did not allow me to raise the point of order, though I persisted. A sitting of the House should start with the Question Hour, but that was missing from the list of business circulated to members. The Speaker refused all points of order about the deviation from the accepted procedure raised by several members, merely saying, 'This is not a normal session. It is only a government business session'!

The design of the government became clear when the minister for parliamentary affairs, K. Raghu Ramaiah, sought leave from the chair to move a motion regarding the business to be taken up in that session and for the suspension of certain rules and procedure:

> This House resolves that the current session of Lok Sabha being in the nature of an emergent session to transact certain urgent and important government business, only government business be transacted during the session and no other business whatsoever, including questions, calling attention motions and any other business to be initiated by a private member be brought before or transacted in the House during the session and all relevant rules on the subject in the rules of procedure and conduct of business in Lok Sabha do hereby stand suspended to that extent.

When this motion was debated, several members from the Opposition protested about the blanket suspension of the rules of procedure, which was entirely uncalled for. Participating in the debate, I said, 'I consider this is nothing but a monstrosity being perpetrated on Parliament and thereby on the people of this country. In the name of an emergency session, following a spurious Emergency, the minimum functions of Parliament, which is a deliberative body, are being throttled, to put up a stance before the country that a so-called grave situation is prevailing.'

I reasoned that there was no reason for the Emergency of 1975, since there was already an Emergency declared in 1971 that had been approved by Parliament and that was still continuing. Emergency powers under the Constitution had already been acquired by and vested with the government in the context of the Bangladesh war. So where was the need for this Emergency? It was clear that this was intended merely to justify the arrests of Opposition leaders and the government's blatantly repressive actions. I reiterated that the motion, if adopted, would be a misfortune for the country and would convert Parliament to nothing more than a rubber stamp. As it was, the voice of the working people was being crushed, the press had been subjected to censorship and had become the extension of the Press Information Bureau of the Government of India, and now with this 'the limited role of Parliament, as a deliberative body and as a watchdog of the executive action, was destroyed in the name of the so-called Emergency'. I also urged that 'if we pass this resolution, we negate everything. We denigrate Parliament, we denigrate ourselves and we denigrate the people of this country.' I recalled Era Sezhiyan's words that Parliament was sought to be reduced to a 'muted museum'. The right to ask questions is of the utmost constitutional importance in a parliamentary democracy and this motion, if passed, would take away that right, thereby tying the hands of the people's representatives and stifling their voices. As I put it, 'You have made the Constitution your plaything.'

Indrajit Gupta, whose party, the CPI, had supported the Emergency, appealed to the government:

> Why cannot you wait until the end of August 1975, that is, the last day of the monsoon session, for passing this resolution? Why cannot you hold the regular monsoon session? Why are the minimum rights of Parliament being taken away? What are we here for? Are we here just for the purpose of raising our hands so that, whether there is Emergency or not, whether there is an individual Emergency or nation's Emergency, we have to go and run along and swim along with the current?

But all this was to no avail. The motion to impose a blanket ban on the operation of the rules of the House was eventually carried with 301 votes in favour and only 76 votes against it.

Then came the statutory resolution for the approval of the proclamation of Emergency. Of all the members of the Cabinet, it was the minister for agriculture – not the home minister, not the law minister, not the parliamentary affairs minister – who moved the resolution. Perhaps, it was done on purpose because of the stature of the agriculture minister, Babu Jagjivan Ram. In the discussion that followed, A.K. Gopalan strongly objected to the issuance of the proclamation, which had resulted 'in an extraordinary and most distressing situation in which thirty-four Members of Parliament are not here, not of their own volition, but because they have been detained without trial and with Parliament itself being reduced to a farce and an object of contempt by Mrs Gandhi and her party'.

A.K. Gopalan himself had been arrested and kept in jail for a week and he mentioned the inhuman treatment meted out to the detainees. He had in fact undertaken a hunger strike in jail against the way political prisoners were being treated. He mentioned that he had been released only because he was 'an old man who cannot speak loudly' while his younger and more vociferous colleagues Jyotirmoy Bosu and Noorul Huda continued to be detained.

In his stirring rejoinder, A.K. Gopalan articulated how the declaration of Emergency was not on account of a real threat to internal security but because of the judgment of the Allahabad High Court, the verdict against the Congress in the Gujarat elections, and Indira Gandhi's refusal to step down from office till the final verdict of the Supreme Court. He mentioned that the CPI(M) had over the last three years warned about the rise of the tendency towards authoritarianism and to totalitarian and one-party dictatorship, reflected in the slogan 'one leader, one party and one country' raised by a section of the Congress. He pointed out growing attacks on trade unions and democratic rights, the semi-fascist terror and rigging of elections in West Bengal, and how the continuance of emergency and special powers like MISA were simply a tool to keep the ruling party in power. He ended by saying:

> ... the measures taken by the government in the wake of the declaration of Emergency unmistakably show that the thrust is against the people. Whatever democratic rights were available to the people have been completely obliterated. Chapter III of the Constitution enshrining the Fundamental Rights has become a dead letter. Articles 14 and 22 have been suspended. Any person arrested need not be produced before a court. The news of his arrest, whereabouts and condition can be kept completely secret. He may be physically liquidated by the police and nobody need know anything about it. That is the position today. Meetings and demonstrations have been banned throughout the country. The people and the forces against which this semi-fascist terror and rigging were directed are not the right reactionary forces but the left democratic forces representing the workers, peasants, employees, teachers, students, refugees, women and poorer sections.

To A.K. Gopalan's contention, the Prime Minister could only say, 'So far as you are concerned, there has been no change because you have been calling me a dictator all these four years. So what is the change? I was a dictator before and I am a dictator now!'

Opposing the motion, Mohan Dharia, one of the Young Turks in the Congress, made a brilliant presentation, some of which is worth recalling:

> June 12 was a bad day for the Congress party. The rude shock came when Mrs Gandhi was unseated and disqualified to contest any elective post for six years by the Allahabad High Court. Though the judgment was unfavourable, it was perhaps the golden opportunity for Mrs Gandhi to establish moral leadership along with her political leadership in the country. With a view to respect the judiciary ... and to create ideal conventions for healthy democracy, [a] voluntary declaration by Mrs Gandhi to step down till the final ruling of the Supreme Court would have raised her prestige sky-high. I would, therefore, like to request the government to immediately withdraw the unwarranted Emergency, release the political leaders and workers and resume a national dialogue. I hope sanity will prevail and patriotic Congressmen and the Bhishmacharyas in the Congress party will no more tolerate any further *vastraharan* of the deity of our democracy ... This is not democracy, but hypocrisy.

The emergent session was brief and ended on 7 August 1975 after the government got all the necessary approvals it sought. Since the government had a majority, parliamentary sanction for its actions was obtained, though the government lacked any vestige of morality.

As A.K. Gopalan had mentioned in his speech, Jyotirmoy Bosu continued to be detained and was subjected to reprehensible atrocities. I am sure he was targeted specifically by the Prime Minister because of his consistent and successful efforts to expose the corrupt and anti-people activities of the government. I wanted to meet him in Hissar Jail but was not allowed to do so. When I came to know that he wanted me to appear before the Supreme Court on his behalf, I made a fresh request to the government to let me meet him as my client. After much persuasion and persistent follow-up, I met him at Hissar Jail with my junior Dilip Kumar Sinha. After keeping us waiting for a long time, he was brought from his cell, but the accompanying police and jail officers refused to leave us alone. As a lawyer, I was entitled to discuss the case with my client. Though the officers could only be present within 'seeing distance', they not only refused to permit me to talk to him privately but also recorded our conversation. Could there be a greater mockery of well-established rules and procedures in an independent country where law was supposed to be sacrosanct?

Jyotirmoy Bosu had been kept in complete isolation, in a solitary cell that had no window or door except for a small ventilator near the ceiling and an iron grill for a gate. When there was a dust storm, he had no protection. The cell was flooded when there was a downpour. To make the isolation complete, two thick blankets had been fixed on the gate and a kutcha brick and mud mortar buffer wall erected. For a number of days, no switches were provided for the lights in the cell. He had to put up with a bright light throughout the night, which attracted thousands of insects. Later, the bulb was removed. The fan hardly worked due to frequent voltage fluctuations and load-shedding. There were a number of open latrines and drains near the cell and the place was infested with flies. This gives an idea of the inhuman conditions endured by a well-known political leader of our country during the Emergency. The fate of other detainees makes one shudder.

A petition for a writ of Habeas Corpus was filed in the Delhi High Court on behalf of Jyotirmoy Bosu. When the matter came up for hearing, the government informed the court that the order of detention, which had been challenged in the petition, had been withdrawn. A fresh order was being made, which made the petition infructuous. A fresh petition to challenge the new order of detention had to be filed. The action of the government was nothing but a blatant ploy to delay the hearing of the Habeas Corpus petition. The same tactic was shamelessly adopted by the government again and again. As a result, Jyotirmoy Bosu was finally released only after Emergency was lifted.

Usually, a session of Parliament begins every year in the month of February with the President addressing both the Houses in the Central Hall, heralding what is called the Budget Session. In 1976, however, Parliament was convened early in January with the President's address. As is known, what the President delivers is a speech prepared by the government detailing its programmes, policies and plan of action for the coming days. It is debated extensively and the Opposition utilizes the opportunity to bring to light the lapses of the government. Participating in the debate on the motion of thanks to the President's address, on 7 January 1976, I questioned the government on its acts of commission and omission. The speech I made on the occasion has been reproduced in Appendix I.

Instead of responding to the points I raised in my speech, the government came up with more stringent measures and introduced draconian provisions in the MISA. I emphasized again, 'I oppose this bill, I oppose every word, every comma, semicolon, and full stop of this bill. This is a lawless law which is sought to be incorporated in our statute book and it will be a perennial, perpetual blot on the jurisprudence and the legal set-up of this country.'

India during Emergency had indeed become a prison house, with all democratic actions coming to a halt. A fear psychosis prevailed everywhere, which impacted the working of all constitutional bodies including Parliament, which functioned in a suffocating atmosphere, as well as executive functionaries. I remember when on one occasion I made a speech very critical of the Prime Minister, my good friend Dinesh Goswami (alas, he is no more), a very able member from Assam belonging to the Congress, came to me and said, 'Dada, what is the good of using such strong words; you know how vindictive the government is.' One could not but bemoan the surrender of the people of a vibrant nation like India without, as it were, even a whimper. The country had lost its freedom once more.

I had submitted my passport, which had expired, to the appropriate authority for renewal but Emergency intervened and it was not returned to me. I had received an invitation from a friend in England, and I wanted to go abroad to get away from the suffocating atmosphere that we all felt. However, I could not go, as I discovered that the return of my passport was being withheld on directions from the 'highest quarter'. I requested Siddhartha Shankar Ray, a known loyalist and a favourite of the Prime Minister, to help me get it back. I believe he spoke to Om Mehta, minister of state for home, who had the closest access to her. Mehta met me once in the Central Hall and requested me not to press for it 'as Madam was adamant'. Thus, during the entire period of Emergency my passport was not returned. When Atal Bihari Vajpayee became the foreign minister in the Janata government, I told him about the fate of my passport and I must recognize his prompt action. I received my passport the same evening, duly renewed, and delivered at my residence by an official of the foreign ministry. I realized that we had regained our freedom and I thanked Vajpayee for his decision and action, which I could not but appreciate.

As the country waited expectantly for the election to the Lok Sabha to be held in 1976 after the five-year term of the fifth Lok

Sabha came to an end, the government in its infinite capacity for mischief brought a bill before the House, described as the House of People (Extension of Duration) Bill, taking advantage of the provisions of Article 83 (2) of the Constitution, which gives power to Parliament to extend the duration of the House by one year at a time while a proclamation of Emergency is in operation.

Obviously, the Prime Minister had realized that she was doomed if she faced the electorate then. Thus, apart from nullifying the decision of the court disqualifying her, she also decided to postpone the election – another instance of her most high-handed and undemocratic tendencies – as a result of which the fifth Lok Sabha had a term of six years.

When the Bill came before the House on 4 February 1976, I strongly opposed it and said that the ruling party wanted to continue with a rubber stamp Parliament to suit its own political ends. I ended by saying that 'they are now trying to write a new definition of democracy under the leadership of one individual because they have equated an individual with the country and the country with an individual. Now democracy is of "X", for "X" and by "X".' The speech is included in Appendix I.

When elections were eventually held in 1977, Indira Gandhi and her party suffered a resounding defeat. The people of India had once again asserted their commitment to democracy and freedom.

3

COALITION CONUNDRUMS

In January 1977, the Janata Party was constituted by a merger of the Congress (O), the Jana Sangh, the Bharatiya Lok Dal (BLD) and the Socialist Party to take on Indira Gandhi's Congress in the election to the sixth Lok Sabha. The Congress suffered a serious blow when senior leaders like Babu Jagjivan Ram, Nandini Satpathy and H.N. Bahuguna left the party and formed the Congress for Democracy (CFD) before the election. Their decision almost overnight changed the suffocating situation prevailing since the imposition of Emergency. The CPI(M), the DMK and the Akali Dal agreed to join hands with the Janata Party to give a straight fight to the Congress and its allies – the CPI and the AIADMK – in the elections. The idea of a coalition of like-minded parties was floated and the creation of a national alliance for democracy and socialism became a priority for those who wanted to defeat the forces of chaos and disorder so assiduously cultivated by the Congress as a prelude to the imposition of another Emergency.

In view of the atrocities committed during the Emergency, the Congress had lost its popularity to a large extent, and this was reflected in the 1977 election. Out of 542 parliamentary seats, the Janata Party won 330 while the Congress got a meagre 154 (coming down from 352 in the fifth Lok Sabha), with 7 going to the CPI and 21 to the AIADMK. The Congress was almost wiped out in north India, where it won just two seats. What was dramatic was that both Indira Gandhi and Sanjay Gandhi lost in the election. In western India, the poll outcome was mixed. Only the four southern states saved the Congress, contributing ninety-two seats to its tally.

For the sixth Lok Sabha, the party desired that I contest the election, not from Burdwan but from the newly created Jadavpur parliamentary constituency comprising Jadavpur, Behala (East and West), Kabitirtha, Baruipur, Bishnupur (East) and Magrahat (West). It was more convenient for me because I could carry on my campaign from my house in Calcutta. I defeated Mohammad Elias of the CPI by a margin of 138,635 votes, having got 68.01 per cent of the votes polled. Incidentally, I had become a member of the CPI(M), as suggested by Pramod Dasgupta, in 1973.

The Janata government of 1977–79 marked a watershed in the political history of independent India, being the first attempt at a coalition government at the national level. Although non-Congress coalition governments had emerged in 1967, they were only state-level experiments with limited impact at the Centre.

The fledgling coalition experienced an initial crisis on the issue of who the Prime Minister would be. There were three aspirants: Morarji Desai, Choudhary Charan Singh and Babu Jagjivan Ram. Through the intervention of Jayaprakash Narayan and Acharya Kripalani, the crisis was resolved and Morarji Desai was chosen as the prime ministerial candidate, primarily because of his seniority and experience. The other contenders accepted the decision in the larger interest of the coalition. However, it left a trail of bitterness and sowed unwelcome seeds of discontent.

The two major constituents in the coalition, especially the Jana Sangh, felt that they were underrepresented in the Cabinet of nineteen, and that the Prime Minister's group was overrepresented. Tension simmered. George Fernandes, who was initially reluctant to become a minister, was denied the ministry of agriculture, which he wanted. The euphoria of the coalition appeared to be short-lived and the cracks it sustained at the outset turned out to be irreparable. Holding the coalition together turned out to be a major preoccupation. The government was frequently jolted by constant bickering and infighting and fell victim to factionalism, manipulation and personal ambitions of its leaders.

Bound only by anti-Indira Gandhi sentiments, the coalition was too disparate historically, ideologically and programmatically to be cohesive and effective. The Jana Sangh was communal in its outlook and maintained its organic links with the Rashtriya Swayamsevak Sangh (RSS). The Congress (O) was secular and essentially subscribed to the Congress ideology. The BLD was also secular but followed a pro-rich-peasant strategy and the Socialists were limited only to Bihar.

These dissensions in the Janata Party were aggravated by the fact that Charan Singh did not take kindly to Morarji Desai becoming the Prime Minister. Smarting under a perceived feeling of injustice done to him, he remained antagonistic to the Prime Minister throughout. The first open clash between Morarji Desai and Charan Singh involved Kanti Desai, the Prime Minister's son, against whom Charan Singh launched a tirade alleging impropriety and demanding an inquiry regarding his activities. The campaign of vilification by Charan Singh and the disagreement between the two leaders greatly affected the reputation and functioning of the government. In May 1978, Charan Singh, despite being the home minister, issued a statement strongly criticizing his government's policies, alleging surrender to capitalists and industrialists. Apart from his attack on the Prime Minister, he singled out the finance minister, H.M. Patel, and the industry minister, George Fernandes. Not being content with that, on 28 June 1978 he issued another statement criticizing his own government for its failure to put Indira Gandhi in jail. The next day, at an emergency Cabinet meeting, the Prime Minister was authorized by his colleagues to take action against both Charan Singh and his confidant, Raj Narain. Both were removed from the Cabinet.

Many Janata leaders tried to bring about a reconciliation between the Prime Minister and Charan Singh. In December, Charan Singh organized a well-attended farmers' rally in Delhi. Thanks probably to this assertion of his popularity and the efforts at reconciliation, Charan Singh was brought back to the government as finance minister in January 1979. He was also appointed as one of the deputy prime ministers along with Jagjivan Ram. But serious disagreements among the Janata constituents continued. A conflict arose on the question of dual membership. Non-Jana Sangh members of the Janata Party wanted members belonging to the RSS or with leanings towards it to sever their ties with the RSS. But the Jana Sangh members refused to do so. In July 1979, the Socialists became a separate group in Parliament, which amounted to a split in the Janata Party. Morarji Desai ceased to have majority support in the Lok Sabha.

The non-Jana Sangh constituents of the coalition fired their first salvo in Uttar Pradesh. In February 1979, the chief minister of Uttar Pradesh, Ram Naresh Yadav, dropped two Jana Sangh ministers from his Cabinet for alleged violation of the Janata election pledge of dissociating themselves from communal politics. This was interpreted by the Jana Sangh as a deliberate attempt to strike at the base of the coalition. The struggle took an ugly turn and in June 1979, Charan Singh resigned. Singh subsequently split the party with support from the Socialists, because of the refusal of the Jana Sangh members to relinquish their dual membership of the Janata Party and the RSS. Raj Narain, famous for having defeated Indira Gandhi, resigned and formed the Janata (Secular). The government suffered another severe blow when the Opposition parties attacked it for its complicity in many alleged misdeeds in governance. A no-confidence motion was brought by the Congress leader Y.B. Chavan in July 1979. Following resignations of ministers and secession of major Janata Party constituents, like the BLD and Socialists, the government was reduced to a minority one.

After the notice of the no-confidence motion was submitted, some members of the CPI(M), including Jyotirmoy Bosu and I, felt that it was necessary to do everything within our power to help the Desai government survive, so that the Congress did not come to power. But surprisingly, the party took a decision that its members should vote in favour of the no-confidence motion on the basis of the party's understanding and assessment of the performance of the Desai government. The CPI(M) had twenty-two members in the sixth Lok Sabha and many of them, including myself, felt that it was necessary that the MPs' point of view should be considered seriously by the party leaders. In that connection, I met Kanak Mukherjee, one of the most senior and respected leaders of the party and a member of the Rajya Sabha. She also felt upset about the party's decision to vote in favour of the no-confidence motion. Some others such as Krishna Chandra Halder, Dinen Bhattacharya and Sasanka Sekhar Sanyal also felt similarly. Along with Kanak Mukherjee, some of us met Pramod Dasgupta, secretary of the West Bengal unit of the CPI(M) and also a Politburo member, who was then in Delhi, and requested him that the party reconsider its decision as we felt that it would be suicidal and against the interest of the party to vote against the Desai government. Pramod Dasgupta said he could not do anything in the matter but could arrange a meeting of CPI(M) MPs with B.T. Ranadive, who was looking after parliamentary matters on behalf of the party. Accordingly, a meeting was arranged at the party's parliamentary office, then located at 12, Windsor Place. Jyotirmoy Bosu had prepared a note on the subject, which was, as we came to know later, sent to Ranadive before the meeting. Others did not have a copy of the note, in which it was understood that Jyotirmoy Bosu had given his views and suggested that the party should vote against the no-confidence motion. We had decided that Krishna Chandra Halder would speak on behalf of the MPs at the meeting. But at the very beginning it seemed to me that there was no possibility of the party reconsidering the matter. The meeting lasted hardly ten minutes. B.T. Ranadive observed somewhat sarcastically that it was good that Bosu had started reading Marxist literature. When Krishna Chandra Halder rose to speak on behalf of the others, he was asked what he understood of the political situation in the country. In reply, Halder could hardly say anything and just sat down. I was extremely disappointed but I can now divulge that some of us, including Jyotirmoy Bosu, had taken a decision to vote against the no-confidence motion and face the consequences because we felt that we could not act in a way that would strengthen the Congress in any manner. To sail with the Congress was totally abhorrent to us and, with our commitment to the party as loyal members, we could not reconcile ourselves to allying with the Congress and being responsible for the fall of the Janata government.

Meanwhile, as widely reported in the media, Morarji Desai had contacted Jyoti Basu, who was then in Switzerland. Basu informed him that unfortunately he could not do anything in the matter and it was for the Politburo to decide. However, finally we did not have to act contrary to the party's decision as Morarji Desai, apprehending that his government would lose the no-confidence motion, resigned on 15 July 1979.

After the fall of the Desai government, the Janata Party (Secular) under Charan Singh entered into an opportunistic alliance with the Congress and a new government was formed on 28 July 1979 with Charan Singh as Prime Minister. Y.B. Chavan was appointed as deputy prime minister. Subsequently, the AIADMK joined the ministry. But it did not last long. The Congress withdrew its support, and Charan Singh had to tender his resignation on 20 August 1979. He was left with the distinction of being the only Prime Minister of India who did not have to face Parliament.

Lok Sabha was dissolved on 22 August 1979. Charan Singh continued as the caretaker Prime Minister until 14 January 1980, when a new government under Indira Gandhi was formed. Indira Gandhi was back in power within three years from the time the people had unceremoniously ousted her and the Congress government.

Although short-lived, the Janata coalition did make some sincere efforts to comply with the election mandate of 1977. A reversal of the Emergency regime, the restitution of the rule of law and the swift dismantling of the structures of authoritarian control established by Indira Gandhi were among its signal achievements. The appointment of the Shah Commission and National Police Commission to look into the atrocities committed during the Emergency held much promise and had a far-reaching impact. The 1977 Industrial Policy Resolution sought to strike a balance between heavy and small-scale industries in order to strengthen the economy.

The government introduced a bill to repeal the Prevention of

Publication of Objectionable Matters Act, 1976, passed during the Emergency. The ban imposed on reporting the proceedings of Parliament by the press during the Emergency was also revoked. Participating in the debate on the bill, I said:

> We are glad that the Congress party has today realized the mistake which they have committed. Today they are giving their unflinching support to the repealing bill. It is really strange that they had mortgaged their conscience then. The people have thrown out those people responsible for this outrage on the freedom of the press and on the freedom of speech. The people have thrown them out as garbage into the dustbin of history. This will be a lesson for everybody. It shows all that the people's voice cannot be silenced forever.

The government held wide consultations with representatives of political parties on the 42nd Constitution Amendment Act. One of the most controversial and debatable pieces of amendments in the history of the Indian Constitution, the 42nd Amendment was primarily the handiwork of the Congress party and was undertaken during the Emergency when most members of the Opposition were in preventive detention and when a free and fair discussion on the proposed modifications was not possible. The overwhelming majority of the two Houses consisted of members of the ruling Congress and so it became largely a party affair rather than a product of national consensus.

The amendment introduced a number of changes. The main thrust was to reduce the power of the judiciary and legislature and strengthen the power and authority of the executive, particularly the Central government. It has been rightly described as an attempt to rewrite the Constitution. It sought to enlarge the amending power of Parliament so far as the Constitution was concerned, and reduced the power of the judiciary to question the laws made by Parliament in diverse respects.

The 42nd amendment made it obligatory for the President to accept the advice tendered by the council of ministers. It extended the terms of the Lok Sabha and state legislative assemblies from five years to six years. It strengthened the Centre vis-à-vis the state governments. It said that amendments could not be questioned 'in any court on any ground', and there shall be no limitation on Parliament's power to amend the Constitution 'by way of addition, variation or repeal'. The amendment was so extensive in nature and character that it has been described as a mini Constitution. It amended the Preamble, forty Articles and the Seventh Schedule, and added fourteen new Articles and two new parts to the Constitution.

One of the most pernicious provisions of the amendment related to Article 31. Laws in respect of antinational activity were sought to be protected. The provision was really intended to stifle political opposition and dissent as it contemplated passing of laws to control activities of political, social and cultural organizations.

Above all, the importance of fundamental rights was greatly devalued. Thus, the whole complexion of the Constitution was sought to be changed. No wonder then that, with the lifting of the Emergency in 1977, there was strident public demand that the 42nd amendment be scrapped.

Before coming to power, the Janata Party had advocated its complete repeal. However, after coming to power, it found some virtues in it. Certain sections of the House also appeared to think likewise. Taking strong exception to this, I exhorted:

> We have been insisting that as the 42nd Amendment Act represented a perverted notion, dictatorial attitude – and was introduced not for the sake of the benefit of the people – this government should keep its commitment to the people and repeal it altogether, because it is essential, according to us, that we should wipe out this aberration and the fraud on the Constitution of this

> country in its totality. According to us, this 42nd Amendment Act has been the antithesis of democracy.

Among the so-called positive features of the Act was Article 39A, inserted in Part IV of the Constitution as a Directive Principle of State Policy, which provided legal aid to needy people. Accepting that the absence of a provision for legal aid was a lacuna in the Constitution, I highlighted two interrelated issues. Even a people-friendly move is distorted if made part of a sinister attempt to exploit some imperfection of our Constitution in the short run to ruin it in the long run. Exposing this hidden agenda, I said:

> Our Constitution, unfortunately, is not a perfect one. We have not got the right to work. We have not provided for the right to subsistence wages, we have not got the right of free education in this country; many things have not been provided. But even whatever little rights were there for the citizens were shamelessly taken away for the purpose of one individual, one family and today you are saying that there were many good things there and we may retain them.

Another supposedly compelling argument advanced by the supporters of the 42nd Amendment Act was that it had incorporated the lofty ideals of socialism and secularism in the Preamble to the Constitution, which had to be retained. I opposed their contention and strongly denounced their covert designs by arguing that 'the amendment to the Preamble of the Constitution was nothing but a hoax on the people'. How was it possible to introduce socialism in this country by simply amending the Preamble? As far as I was concerned, the 42nd Amendment represented the blackest chapter in the history of India's democracy, and anything less than a total repeal of it would be tantamount to compromising with tyranny.

The true character of the 42nd Amendment Act was discernible in Article 31D, which attempted to provide for laws in respect of anti-national activities and abrogate all powers of the state and confer them on the Centre. I argued that 'Article 31D was a naked attempt to annihilate political opposition and dissent. All activities of political parties, trade unions and even social and cultural organizations could be brought under any law made under 31D. The object was to crush anybody who did not pay obeisance to the powers that be. It required a particularly vile mind to formulate a law like that to curb all the minimum and basic rights of the people of this country.' Interestingly, even the Swaran Singh Committee, constituted to formulate the design and broad contours of the Bill preceding this Act, was reportedly not in favour of Article 31D. This was pushed through, presumably at the behest, if not orders, of the top brass during the Emergency regime.

Such was the broad sweep of the 42nd Amendment Act that it did not leave even the judiciary untouched. I was particularly disturbed and argued as forcefully as possible for the independence of the judiciary, which I felt was 'the only institution which stood between dictatorship and democracy'. I argued that though we did not believe in the principle of the supremacy of the judiciary, and though it had its imperfections, it could not be denied that 'the judiciary has stood by the side of the people in their great distress ... by and large, during the last Emergency, the judiciary has served the people with great courage and devotion'. In fact, the independence of the judiciary was being tampered with under the garb of the supremacy of Parliament. But I was quick to refute such a misguided interpretation of the constitutional provisions. I contended, 'The supremacy of Parliament must be such that maintains the supremacy of the people. You cannot divorce the supremacy of Parliament from the supremacy of the people. We strongly feel that the attempt to interfere with judicial independence was something not good for the country.' This was also an effort to deprive the people of their fundamental rights by attacking its custodian.

However, the Janata government did redeem, to a large extent, its pledge to do away with the objectionable portions of the 42nd Amendment by enacting the 44th Amendment.

In another major development, the Privileges Committee of the sixth Lok Sabha was asked to inquire into a complaint against Indira Gandhi for her alleged misdemeanours in the fifth Lok Sabha on the ground that as Prime Minister she and others had created obstructions to the proper functioning of Parliament by taking recourse to intimidation and harassment of officials and institution of false cases. Indira Gandhi had, meanwhile, got elected to Parliament in a bye-election from Chikmagalur in Karnataka. The Lok Sabha debated the report of the Privileges Committee, which held her guilty but did not specify or recommend any punishment. However, on 19 December 1978, the House resolved to expel her and send her to jail till Parliament was prorogued a week later. Although the CPI(M) had agreed generally with the findings of the Privileges Committee, the members expressed their reservation about the decision to expel Indira Gandhi, as she had been recently elected as a people's representative and the order of expulsion would amount to negating the verdict of the people. Indira Gandhi spent a week in Tihar Jail. (Incidentally, the resolution of 19 December 1978 was rescinded by a resolution passed in the seventh Lok Sabha in May 1981 on the ground that the action taken was in violation of the principles of natural justice, though serious questions were raised about the maintainability of the motion to rescind. But the objections were negated by the Speaker, Dr Balram Jakhar.)

Contrary to the expectations of the Janata government, the eagerness shown to punish Indira Gandhi earned her a great deal of public sympathy and the brief jail stint made her a martyr of sorts. Vendetta is something the Indian people do not approve of, as has been demonstrated on many occasions. In any case, soon after the expulsion and arrest of Indira Gandhi, the glue that held the Janata Party lost its adhesive character and it collapsed into a shoddy mess under the weight of its own problems.

I expressed my disillusionment with the government when I said in the House in 1979:

> The ruling party has attained great notoriety for fighting among themselves instead of fighting poverty, unemployment, squalor, casteism, communalism and economic stagnation. It has shown an amazing complacency in assessing the political and economic problems facing the country. They are speaking of restoration of democratic rights, but it is the people themselves who have earned their own democratic rights and civil liberties and they have thrown away a fascist regime into the dustbin of history.

Little did I realize at that time that the very same regime would be back in power in less than a year!

The Janata experiment offered a ray of hope by doing away with the overwhelming dominance of one party. But the larger-than-life egos of its leaders who were not backed by cadres, their prime ministerial ambitions and the vengeful treatment of Indira Gandhi, bypassing constitutional proprieties, led to its premature demise.

It was a decade later that the next non-Congress coalition government was formed and, like the first, this too was short-lived. In the general election of 1989, as in 1977, there was a realignment of political forces with the Congress on one side and non-Congress parties – consisting of the Janata Dal led by V.P. Singh, who had resigned from the Congress, the Bharatiya Janata Party (BJP), the leftists and other regional parties – on the other. The Janata Dal, a new entity composed of various splinter groups of the erstwhile Janata Party, was the nucleus of the National Front, which was derided by Rajiv Gandhi as a 'national affront'! The National Front dislodged the Congress, whose strength came down from 404 seats in the eighth Lok Sabha to 197 in the ninth. Though the Janata Dal got only 141 seats, it was seen as a vindication of the struggle launched by V.P. Singh against the misdeeds of the previous government.

Even though the National Front did not have enough numbers to form a government on its own, it was invited to do so by the President, on the basis of the support extended by the leftists and the BJP from outside. It was a rare instance of the communists and the BJP making common cause, in the national interest.

It must be mentioned that because of the Ayodhya issue, the BJP emerged from the ashes, as it were, of the 1984 elections, where it had won just two seats. In raking up the Babri Masjid–Ram Janmabhoomi controversy, the BJP had appeared to be completely unmindful of the communal tension it would create. However, with its ascendance to the centrestage of national affairs, it was expected that the party would now adapt to the needs of pluralistic politics and mould itself as a nationally acceptable political entity.

It was, indeed, a display of the majesty and maturity of Indian democracy that while the single largest party with 197 seats accepted defeat with grace, declined with dignity the offer of government formation and decided to sit in the Opposition, the National Front, the second largest group, with barely 150 seats, formed the first minority government in independent India.

The Prime Minister, V.P. Singh, endeared himself to all with his emphasis on consensus and his call for value-based politics and social justice. The Left played a proactive role in creating a conducive climate, necessary for the smooth functioning of the government. There were weekly meetings at the Prime Minister's residence – which Indrajit Gupta and I attended on behalf of our respective parties, and Vajpayee and Advani attended on behalf of the BJP – where the various issues of governance and problems faced were discussed. The endeavour was to coordinate our strategies and work in sync on all major national issues.

But the experiment came undone rather hastily, by July–August 1990. Devi Lal, who was the deputy prime minister in the National Front government (although there is no such constitutional provision), created an acute embarrassment for the government on the issue of his son Om Prakash Chautala's involvement in large-scale and brutal violence in an election held at Meham, Haryana, in February 1990. This led to Devi Lal's exit from the Cabinet. This was followed by V.P. Singh's announcement of the extremely crucial decision to implement the report of the Mandal commission.

The Mandal commission had been appointed by the Morarji Desai government. The Janata Party had promised reservations in jobs for the educationally and socially backward classes, as recommended by the first backward classes commission, called the Kalekar commission, but did not fulfil that promise. Instead, it appointed another backward classes commission, headed by B.P. Mandal, to study the issue. The Mandal commission submitted its report to the President in December 1980, nearly a year after Indira Gandhi came back to power. It was tabled in Parliament two years later, in 1982. The Prime Minister, Indira Gandhi, had perfunctorily spoken in praise of the commission's recommendations. Thereafter, the two-volume report had been put on the backburner for reasons not known.

The Mandal commission report created a great and rather unexpected social upheaval. It was met with protests from the student community across the nation. Several states in north India in particular were caught up in the throes of violence. Military help was called in to maintain law and order. When the matter was taken up in the House, I said:

> I support reservation in jobs for the backward classes as recommended by the Mandal commission. We have to consider as to why after forty-three years of Independence, we have to speak of reservation in this country, even for Scheduled Castes, Scheduled Tribes and other sections of the people. We cannot deny that the situation in this country even after Independence, so far as poor and backward people are concerned – socially, educationally, economically – they have been the subject of more and more exploitation and all the resources of this country for over four decades have not been utilized for the purpose of true advancement of these sections of the people of this country.

The issue of merit is often brought to the fore very prominently in the context of reservations. I am not one of those who accepts that merit is only restricted to the upper castes. Many states in our country have followed a reservation policy for backward classes. It has stood the test of legal and judicial scrutiny.

I must admit that I was disappointed with the media reaction to the report of the Mandal commission. I found it somewhat difficult to comprehend. V.P. Singh was painted in dark colours as the chief villain responsible for tearing asunder the social fabric of the country. No longer was he regarded as an exemplary crusader for ethical and clean politics. The vicious and concerted campaign of calumny carried out against him was unparalleled in recent history. As I said in the House:

> I cannot but observe that in this case, the role could have been very usefully played by the media to inform the people of this country, to give the picture of both the sides as to what are the

> recommendations and objections and thus the people could have had a more objective look at the recommendations and could have decided for themselves. I do not know how the passions of a twelve-year-old boy can be roused to such an extent that he is threatening to commit self-immolation. I find photographs which came out in the newspapers where little boys, school-going children of eight to ten years, are deflating the tyres of buses. What do they realize about the Mandal commission and its implications unless they have been used by some people? I am very sorry to say that but I cannot help observing that. What are the parents, teachers and guardians doing? We do not find anybody trying to counsel patience and to have a talk, dialogue and discussion.

The anti-Mandal agitation and the attendant violence were of grave concern to Parliament. Speaking on the government's response to it, I made an earnest appeal to those connected with the movement to realize how a movement they had started was being highjacked by anti-social and criminal elements.

> We have appealed to the students and the government to hold discussions. Nothing can be achieved by confrontation alone and there is nothing that cannot be achieved with proper dialogue and discussion. Therefore, we appeal to the government and everybody, particularly the students, to be aware of the agent provocateurs. We have to consider this aspect seriously. The country is as much the young's as anybody else's. Therefore, the students should take an objective approach to this matter and respond to the Prime Minister's commitment to hold discussions and negotiations. Now, the Supreme Court has passed the stay order and at the moment, until the Supreme Court allows it finally, nothing can be implemented except the identification of the backward classes and listing them. This is the opportune moment when proper discussion, without pre-conditions and

> with an open mind, could be held, but certain basic postulates have to be accepted.

I couldn't help wondering how someone in the country's capital could say things like 'Gherao the MPs and MLAs who are supporting the Mandal commission's recommendations. Douse them with kerosene and burn them alive.'

Even as the country was reeling under violent anti-Mandal protests, L.K. Advani of the BJP announced a Rathyatra covering about 10,000 km to mobilize support for the Ayodhya Ram Mandir issue. There was no doubt that his fight was essentially against the Mandal issue, an attempt to counter the caste mobilization fallout of the Mandal recommendations with a communal mobilization. Unfortunately, the provocative speeches, espousing narrow-minded nationalism, made during the Rathyatra created a communally surcharged situation all over the country. Advani was arrested in Bihar. Thereafter, the BJP met the President and informed him that it was withdrawing support to the government. The President directed the Prime Minister to seek the confidence of the House. On that occasion, I raised certain issues which are as relevant today as they were in 1990. I said, 'The unity and integrity of the country is under a serious threat because of the communal flare-ups that had followed the Rathyatra.' I asked Advani pointedly, 'Do we want that the people of this country should fight among themselves on the basis of religion?'

> Is this the way we can maintain the unity and integrity of this country? Can we not stop fissiparous tendencies overtaking us? We cannot ignore that this is not a mere question of religion which is involved. Otherwise, we would not have seen the BJP's election symbol so much prominently displayed on the Rath. Obviously, the Ram Janmabhoomi–Babri Masjid issue will be the main plank of the BJP's election campaign in the next election. But is it for

> political reasons that the Rath was taken and the Rathyatra was started? ... This country has so many problems to face and solve. Let us dedicate our energies towards solving these major and basic issues and problems, not to drive a wedge among the people on the basis of religion in order to disturb communal amity and harmony, because only united people, united in all senses of the term, can bring the country out of this morass, which has been created by the previous government.

However, a split in the Janata Dal led to the government losing the motion of confidence. V.P. Singh had to bow out of office, grown in stature as a statesman, though he lost power as a politician. I greatly admired his integrity and his effort at providing a transparent government. Though there is no doubt that in principle I stand for the recommendations of the Mandal commission, maybe V.P. Singh's timing in implementing it was wrong. And of course, the media was stridently opposed to it and vilified V.P. Singh in a most scandalous manner. In fact, looking at how much the media was against him, I am tempted to say that he was probably right in what he did and the way he went about it!

V.P. Singh was followed by Chandra Shekhar as the Prime Minister. He had managed to get the support of the Congress, headed by Rajiv Gandhi, and a section of the erstwhile National Front. However, Chandra Shekhar's government, which lasted a mere three months, will occupy only a footnote in the political history of India for the singular distinction that it faced Parliament only once. I cannot recollect any development of consequence from that bleak period in parliamentary history. Opposing the motion of confidence moved by Chandra Shekhar as the Prime Minister, I said:

> I oppose this motion as the continuation of the so-called council of ministers with the grand number of two members, without

> even allocated portfolios, will mean the continued mockery and debasement of parliamentary democracy in this country. This government is founded on political immorality, constitutional impropriety and betrayal of the people of this country. This government is the product of political expediency where personal ambition and avarice and abject surrender to forces of authoritarianism have been given primacy over national interests and at the cost of secularism. The Prime Minister has said he wants to save the country from the aftermath of what, according to him, was the misrule of V.P. Singh's government and that is why he has come out and has taken the support of the Congress for the purpose of running the administration. I would ask him, why is it not the other way round? Why does not the single biggest party in Parliament have the political courage and honesty to take upon itself the responsibility of the administration and why Chandra Shekhar and his supporters did not decide to support that Congress government? They would have had a working majority. No explanation has been given for that. I would like to know as to what is the manifesto that Chandra Shekhar will implement? Will he implement the National Front manifesto on which he was elected or will he implement the Congress manifesto on which his opponent was defeated in the last general elections? We have to fight financial corruption in public affairs and we have to fight political corruption. Combination of persons and parties with no common policies and programmes will not solve any of the basic problems facing the country. This government has no political and constitutional basis and no mandate from the people. It must be ended here and now. I can assure the House that not a tear will be shed when this government goes as it is bound to go.

As I had predicted, this unholy alliance soon came apart as the Congress withdrew support to the government on the flimsy plea that intelligence people had been deployed in front of the residence of Rajiv Gandhi. Like Indira Gandhi in 1977, Rajiv Gandhi, the leader of the Opposition, opted to go in for elections rather than try and form a new government, thus drawing the curtains on the ninth Lok Sabha, which had a short term of barely one-and-a-half years.

A great tragedy unfolded in the run-up to the general elections to the tenth Lok Sabha. The assassination of Rajiv Gandhi on 21 May 1991 was an attack on India's unity and integrity. The perpetrators of the ghastly crime thought that by their cowardly act of eliminating India's leaders, they would shake the people's faith in their capacity to remain united as a nation. It was indeed a tragic loss to the country.

The third time a non-Congress coalition government was formed was in 1996 in the eleventh Lok Sabha with H.D. Deve Gowda as the Prime Minister following the defeat of the Congress led by P.V. Narasimha Rao. The coalition was a non-Congress and non-BJP one, led by what was called the United Front. Under Narasimha Rao's leadership, the Congress was nearly decimated in some of its erstwhile strongholds such as UP and Bihar. It became the single largest party following the general elections in 1996 but was short of the necessary numbers to form a government on its own. It paid a price for facilitating the biggest blow to the secular fabric of our polity on 6 December 1992. At the same time, the demolition of the Babri Masjid at Ayodhya by the Sangh Parivar headed by the BJP was fresh in everybody's mind and political parties of all hues were determined not to let it form the government. As a result, the BJP found itself in total isolation and no party came to support its claims to power. In keeping with the best constitutional traditions, the BJP, being the single largest party, was invited to form the government, but it was swept out of office after a paltry thirteen days as it failed to prove its majority. This led to the creation of the United Front – a broad non-Congress and non-BJP coalition consisting of fourteen parties, both regional and national, which came together on the vital principle of upholding secularism.

Though the CPI(M) was not a member of the coalition, having pledged outside support, Jyoti Basu was offered the prime ministership. The party declined the offer. Jyoti Basu and I were not averse to the idea. The decision of the party was later rightly described as a historic blunder. The party's refusal to accede to the request of the National Front parties to participate in government and its decision to not permit Jyoti Basu to become Prime Minister – in spite of the fact that as a matter of political strategy it has been taking part in electoral politics – were monumental mistakes, which not only disheartened a large number of our party workers but many progressive-minded citizens of the country. I was not a member of the party's central committee then and I do not know what transpired there but it was known that the other parties had requested the members of the central committee to reconsider the matter because, given the difficult times the country was going through, it was necessary to have a leader of commanding presence like Jyoti Basu as Prime Minister. He was at the time one of the tallest leaders of the country and the most well-known CPI(M) leader, with impeccable credentials and considerable experience in running a coalition government in West Bengal for nearly twenty years at a stretch and with great success. It was a matter of regret that the country, where large sections of the people are denied facilities and opportunities of a civilized existence, lost the great opportunity of having a leftist leader of the stature of Jyoti Basu as Prime Minister. Their hope was shattered by the CPI(M)'s quite intractable decision. With Jyoti Basu at the head, the coalition government at the Centre – consisting of major anti-Congress parties, who by and large believed in socialistic and progressive policies – could have brought about a sea-change in India's political firmament and also in its administrative ethos.

The ostensible reason behind the party's stand, as far as one can understand, was that the CPI(M) would not be part of a government in which it did not have a majority. This was totally untenable, as such a situation would hardly ever prevail except in the three states of West Bengal, Kerala and Tripura, where too at present the party's position is extremely tenuous, because of various wrong policies adopted by it. It seems a distant dream, if at all, that the CPI(M) would ever have such a commanding position in the country as a whole as to be able ever to secure a majority on its own in the Lok Sabha. It seems that the leaders at the Politburo level have never understood that in India the real power rests with the Central government, in view of our constitutional provisions. In our parliamentary set-up, it is essential to be able to acquire power at the Centre to bring about basic changes in the country's governance which could benefit the people at large. No party can really serve the people effectively in a democratic set-up and in a vast country like India only through agitations or movements or by criticizing the government's policies and programmes.

What was required at the time – after the disastrous policy followed by the Congress during the regime of Narasimha Rao, of opening the country's economy to foreign multinationals – was the adoption and implementation of policies and measures to strengthen the country's self-reliance and its own financial base and economy for the benefit of the country as a whole. By fighting against the baneful influence of foreign multinationals, sincere efforts would have been made to lead the country on the way to self-sufficiency, based on comprehensive land reforms and pro-people measures which would have immensely benefited India's rural economy and also workers, peasants and the vulnerable sections of society. The formation of a government under the leadership of Jyoti Basu in 1996 would have given a new life not only to the CPI(M) but to the entire Left and progressive forces in the country.

Large sections of members and supporters of the party also believed that the policies and programmes, particularly on economic issues, that would have been followed by a government under Jyoti Basu would have had a tremendous impact on the country's politics as a whole, and also in ameliorating the miseries of the common people. It would have created a new atmosphere of hope and faith among the masses while strengthening the frontal organizations of the Left parties substantially.

Jyoti Basu's experience in heading a coalition government was well established and well acknowledged. The fact that the other parties made an earnest request to the CPI(M) to reconsider its decision showed the great respect they had for Jyoti Basu and his leadership and I remember the immense disappointment expressed by those leaders when the party refused to reconsider its decision, which, according to me, not only affected the party's future but slowed the country's progress by a few decades.

It was a matter of great sadness that a majority of Jyoti Basu's colleagues in West Bengal, who had known, at first hand, the quality of the leadership and guidance provided by him as chief minister, and how he had been able to create an atmosphere of enthusiasm among the common people of West Bengal, also voted with the misguided majority.

A political party taking part in elections in a parliamentary democracy only with a view to criticizing the government's policies, programmes and performance in the legislature, while permanently remaining as a party in the Opposition, is anathema to democratic polity. The CPI(M) issues manifestoes during the elections, which contain its political assessments and formulations and promises to the electorate, on the basis of which the party expects to receive support for its candidates. The party did not realize that it could not expect the people to continue to support its role only as a critic. Apart from being a critic of others, a political party must also prove its sense of responsibility to the people by actually trying to implement the policies, programmes and promises contained in its manifesto. The question is one of commitment to the people and to parliamentary democracy. On many occasions following the rejection of the Congress by the people, one had expected that the Left parties would be able to fill up the vacuum created in India's body politic. But that was not to be because they hardly showed any interest in the governance of the country as a whole, whenever such an opportunity arose. And that has, to my mind, made the people – except in the three states where the party has a mass base and where the organization has remained strong – realize the futility of giving any electoral support to the party.

India's Prime Minister has been given wide powers and occupies the most important position in India's constitutional and administrative set-up. It is not as if Jyoti Basu could have brought about any basic and fundamental change forthwith, but he would have inspired his colleagues to implement policies and programmes which would have been in favour of the common people of the country and not for the benefit of a handful of them. At least the economic policy of the country would have seen fundamental changes in the right direction, in the interest of the deserving masses.

The main protagonist of the party's policy of non-participation, as I understand, has been Prakash Karat, who has been able to persuade his comrades against participating in the government except in the three states. Unfortunately, it has helped neither the party, nor the teeming millions of our country. Given that advice of leaders like Jyoti Basu was rarely taken note of, it is not surprising that today we find the party greatly reduced in strength not only in the Lok Sabha but throughout the country. The result of the fifteenth Lok Sabha election of 2009 in West Bengal and Kerala, the two major states in which the party exists, has been nothing but a total debacle for the party. It came as a great shock to Jyoti Basu and all members and supporters of the party. The result of the municipal elections in West Bengal held in May/ June 2010 has further demonstrated how the party continues to suffer because of the distorted policies followed by the central leadership, which has lost all sense of history and even the ability to comprehend the real problems facing the party and issues agitating the people.

In the scenario created by the party's refusal to permit Jyoti Basu to be the Prime Minister, H.D. Deve Gowda, a dark horse, became the Prime Minister on 1 June 1996, with outside support of the Congress and the leftists. The CPI joined the government with Indrajit Gupta becoming the home minister. My speech during the debate on the motion of thanks on the address of the President when Deve Gowda was the Prime Minister, on 25 February 1997, has been reproduced in Appendix I.

The Congress, however, pulled the rug from under the feet of the coalition partners and Deve Gowda could remain Prime Minister only up to 21 April 1997, less than eleven months. Thus, the government had hardly any time to implement the programmes of the United Front. Congress president Sitaram Kesri proposed that the Front should change its leadership, and Inder Kumar Gujral became the Prime Minister on 21 April 1997. However, his government too was short-lived. The Congress probably felt that it would come back to power if a fresh election was held. How wrongly they assessed the situation. The eleventh Lok Sabha lasted only eighteen months, from 15 May 1996 to 4 December 1997, and we had three Prime Ministers during this period – A.B. Vajpayee for thirteen days, H.D. Deve Gowda for just over ten months and I.K. Gujral for about seven months. Gujral continued as the caretaker Prime Minister till 19 March 1998, when the twelfth Lok Sabha was constituted, which brought the BJP to power.

Since then coalition governments in one form or other have been formed in the country. I believe that the emergence of coalition politics and coalition governments is a reflection of India's diversity and cultural and linguistic plurality, and its acceptance as a viable system of governance is suggestive of the maturity of our parliamentary polity. Of course, there are certain pitfalls, like a lack of cohesion and agreement among the coalition partners, the preponderance of regional parties with petty regional agendas pulling in different directions. However, today there is also a realization among the academia and the intelligentsia that coalition politics reinforces our federal polity. Under coalition politics, the regional identities of the states have been further enhanced and their aspirations have been reflected more effectively and meaningfully. Coalition politics also enables the individual states to maintain their distinctiveness without compromising national unity and integrity. Regional parties now have their own space in the political set-up, not merely in their limited territorial spheres but also in national politics because of the prevalence of coalition governance.

4

THE CONGRESS AFTER EMERGENCY

A MANDATE WASTED

In the election following the collapse of the Janata government in 1980, Indira Gandhi returned to the centre stage of Indian politics after three years in the wilderness. The Congress won 353 seats in the Lok Sabha. The people of India demonstrated their resolve not to be taken for granted by anybody. They showed that wrongdoers or non-achievers on either side of the political divide would be dealt with suitably. After the excesses of Emergency, one could not have thought that Indira Gandhi would be able to stage such a remarkable comeback. However, the bickering within the Janata party and overall non-performance of both the Desai and the Charan Singh governments – in spite of many welcome steps taken by them to weaken, if not destroy, the edifice of Emergency

– disillusioned and frustrated the people. Tellingly, her party's election manifesto declared that 'the Indian National Congress (I) is the only party and Indira Gandhi is the only leader who can save the country after its recent traumatic experience'.

Soon after assumption of power as Prime Minister, Indira Gandhi sought to monopolize power and made several attempts to destabilize non-Congress governments in the states by misusing the office of the governor. The dismissal of N.T. Rama Rao's government in Andhra Pradesh was one such shameful effort. In August 1984, the governor of Andhra Pradesh, Ramlal, dismissed NTR's government and made Nadendla Bhaskara Rao, finance minister in the government and an erstwhile Congress man, the chief minister. Following a huge hue and cry in the media and an extraordinary mobilization of the people and of various opposition parties, Indira Gandhi was forced to remove Ramlal as governor. Ramlal's successor, S.D. Sharma, reinstated NTR as chief minister in September. In the Lok Sabha, I impressed on the government:

> We are all for removal of distortions in our electoral system ... But we have no faith in the politics of destabilization. Such attitude must be abandoned lock, stock and barrel. Otherwise, there is no chance of having a proper electoral system in the country. We protest against any attempt to create difficulties for democratically elected and lawfully constituted governments in the states. Sometimes by denying the funds, sometimes by depriving the people of the state of food supplies and other essential commodities, sometimes by withdrawing plan proposals, the Centre creates difficulties for the states. How can they possibly be expected to function properly if all the time they have to resist (such) attempts by defection or with the help of black money which some parties have in abundance apparently? Therefore, I submit that if any progress has to be made in the context of electoral reforms or strengthening the federal

> structure of our polity, the ruling party at the Centre has to make it absolutely clear that it would not encourage defections and that it should not be a party to defection and destabilization of duly elected governments.

Instead of reforming the electoral system, the government enacted repressive laws such as the Essential Services Maintenance Act (ESMA) and the National Security Act (NSA), without taking the views of the Opposition into consideration. The ESMA was widely believed to meet the conditions imposed by the International Monetary Fund (IMF) to sanction a large loan India was negotiating at the time. The Opposition introduced an adjournment motion in November 1981 to discuss the issue of the IMF loan as we came across widely published reports that the Indian representative on the IMF had given an assurance that 'Parliament would not be allowed to act as a constraint on the IMF loan agreement'. Speaking on the occasion, I said, 'This sort of an agreement has never been entered into. The people in this country do not know about it. The Parliament has been bypassed. It is an affront to Parliament and it is compromising Parliament's powers and authority.' These views were ignored by the government.

The ESMA sought to impose severe restrictions on workers' democratic right to protest by bringing several activities under the ambit of essential services. The discussion on the ESMA bill was marked by flippancy and lack of seriousness, and not a single point I raised were replied to. In my decade-long experience in the House, I had never seen an important debate, on a subject agitating lakhs of people, being dealt with by the home minister of the Government of India in a way the ESMA bill was. The Opposition was trying to voice the sentiments of a very large section of the country. We knew that this bill would be passed despite our objections. The least we expected the government to do was listen to the submissions we had to make, whether they liked them or not. The bill was thoroughly exposed to be anti-labour, anti-working class, anti-people and anti-national. We put up a resolute fight against the bill and gave numerous amendments to most of the obnoxious clauses and I remember that the House had to sit till late in the evening to dispose of the amendments. I said emphatically, 'We oppose every word, comma, semi-colon of this bill. Therefore, this House and the people outside should reject it.'

Sardar Zail Singh was the home minister of India at the time. Once, during a debate in the House on the above bills containing various anti-people draconian measures, I described the home minister as the police minister of the country who had no concern for the people. This enraged Sardar Zail Singh immensely and he hit back at me, alleging that I belonged to a rich family and did not understand the problems of the common people and of the farmers, and that he belonged to a family of farmers, which of course had no relevance to the debate. Satya Sadhan Chakraborty, who was then deputy leader of the CPI(M) in the Lok Sabha (representing South Calcutta constituency), stood up and said, 'Indeed, Somnath Chatterjee is an enemy of his class, because as a successful lawyer he should have been with the bourgeois parties but instead he has joined the party of peasants and workers and that shows he is an enemy of his own class.' It was quite an interesting interlude during the debate and I mention this only to show that MPs have the ability to come up with a humorous retort.

The government enacted another black law, the National Security Act, in late 1980, reminding us that Indira Gandhi had not lost her authoritarian streak, in spite of the sordid experience of the Emergency. Among other draconian provisions, the Act provided that 'the central government or the state government may, if satisfied with respect to any person that with a view to preventing him from acting in any manner prejudicial to the security of the state or from acting in any manner prejudicial to the maintenance of public order or from acting in any manner prejudicial to the maintenance of supplies and services essential to the community it is necessary so to do, make an order directing that such person be detained'. Since the government had sufficient numbers to get away with whatever it decided, the Opposition could only register its protest as loudly as possible, lest future generations accuse them of being guilty of silence. Calling the bill a 'monstrosity', I said:

> Today is another dark day for the freedom-loving people of this country. It is a matter of lasting shame that this august House, which should be the bastion of personal freedom, civil liberty and democratic rights of the people of this country, is involving itself today in the process of denuding the people of their minimal rights. What we find today is that we have been asked to legitimize an aberration and an outrage, an evil law and a savage law.

We knew that the government wanted more powers in its hands and we had experienced how ruthlessly it had used these powers against democratic movements and political opponents.

By this time, Punjab was boiling over because of the imbroglio created by the misguided policies of the Congress. Stern action was unavoidable to address the problems but unfortunately this came in the form of military action at the Golden Temple in 1984, which had very serious repercussions. The government came to Parliament after the military action with a bill to set up special courts for terrorist-affected areas in Punjab and Chandigarh. On the occasion, I said:

> The Prime Minister spoke of the healing touch after the army action. If the government has thought this to be one of the instances of providing a healing touch, I think they are sadly

> mistaken. I remember I was in the House in 1971, when MISA was introduced and passed with acclamation by the ruling party. And, many of the ruling party members themselves became victims of the same Act subsequently. Therefore, do not be under any illusions. Today, you may be in the good books of the powers that be, but you may not continue to be so. These are matters which will rebound on the life of the ordinary people of this country.

I asserted that the Opposition opposed terrorism and terrorist activities and emphasized that it had for years been demanding proper action, primarily political initiatives coupled with administrative measures, in Punjab. We had opposed the special amendment to the National Security Act in April 1984, which stipulated more rigorous and draconian provisions for Punjab. Instead of addressing the problem through political initiatives and administrative measures, the government was hell-bent on introducing systems that would further alienate the already aggrieved people of the beleaguered state. I requested the government to adopt a new and humane approach towards the Punjab problem.

But the government went ahead with its ill-conceived policies and the country had to pay a heavy price for them. The tragic assassination of Indira Gandhi by her own bodyguards, in retaliation for military action in the Golden Temple, closed a blood-soaked chapter of deep strife in Indian politics, even as the country lost a charismatic leader.

Even as the nation was engulfed in grief and a crisis of confidence, another tragedy was unfolding, particularly in and around Delhi, where the Sikh community was attacked by violent mobs allegedly in retribution for the Prime Minister's assassination by her Sikh bodyguards.

A new Prime Minister had to be immediately sworn in. There are well-established constitutional conventions pertaining to this, which were ignored. Rajiv Gandhi, Indira Gandhi's sole surviving son who had been inducted into politics after the tragic death of Sanjay Gandhi, and had also become an MP, was sworn in as the new Prime Minister by President Giani Zail Singh without even a resolution from MPs of the Congress Parliamentary Party.

The young prime minister showed great promise in trying to usher in the twenty-first century. It was on that optimistic note that the country faced the general election in late 1984. The Congress won an unprecedented 404 out of 545 seats, which could appropriately be called a 'brute majority' in Parliament.

I stood for the election from Jadavpur in Calcutta, but was unsuccessful, primarily because of the sympathy wave for the Congress. Without in any way giving an excuse, I would like to mention the sustained campaign of vilification unleashed against me on totally concocted allegations and misrepresentation. I had never before faced such slander and nor would I do so in any other election thereafter. I acknowledged my defeat and I believe I was the first person to congratulate Mamata Banerjee, to whom I had lost by less than 20,000 votes. It remains the only time I have lost in an election in my entire parliamentary career. I was, however, back in the Lok Sabha in December 1985.

Saradish Ray, who represented Bolpur in the Lok Sabha, passed away less than a year after the general election in 1984. In the ensuing bye-election, I was nominated to contest as the CPI(M) candidate. My rival was the once-powerful Siddhartha Shankar Ray. I polled 339,078 votes, while Ray polled 240,079. In fact, I got more votes than the winning candidate of Jadavpur a year earlier.

I took oath as a member of the eighth Lok Sabha on 19 December 1985. Coincidentally, I had lost the last election on 19 December 1984! It is indeed rare for a candidate who loses an election to contest in a bye-election. It had happened with Indira Gandhi in the sixth Lok Sabha. My friend Madhu Dandavate quipped that it was a strange spectacle to have two members from the same constituency in the Lok Sabha. The victorious candidate was there along with the vanquished – albeit now I was representing another constituency.

The Opposition was in total disarray in 1984, with its numbers having been reduced drastically. The CPI(M) had twenty-two members in the House, the Janata Party had ten, the CPI six and the BJP only two. None of these parties qualified to be recognized as the opposition party. Ironical as it may sound, it was a regional party, the Telugu Desam Party (TDP) from Andhra Pradesh, which, with thirty seats, was recognized as the opposition party. The reason for the TDP's strong showing was the unconstitutional dismissal of the NTR-led TDP government at the behest of the Congress at the Centre. (The TDP government had had to be reinstated thereafter.) The move boomeranged on the Congress, which managed only a few seats from the state despite the sympathy wave that swept the party to power in 1984. The prominent leaders of the Opposition included Indrajit Gupta, Geeta Mukherjee, Chitta Basu, Madhu Dandavate, Jaipal Reddy, Basudeb Acharia and Saifuddin Choudhury.

Prime Minister Rajiv Gandhi was the darling of the masses as well as the media and enjoyed the enviable image of a clean and charming young man with the best of intentions. His speech at the centenary celebrations of the Congress in Bombay in 1985 endeared him to the intelligentsia, which had become cynical of the politics of hypocrisy and sycophancy promoted by Indira Gandhi. In this celebrated speech Rajiv Gandhi decried the role of power brokers in the Congress. He alleged that they had taken the party away from the masses. He appeared intent on ridding the party of the ills that plagued it. It is, however, another matter that by the end of his term as Prime Minister, he too had succumbed to the very power brokers he wanted to eliminate.

The Terrorist and Disruptive Activities Act (TADA) was passed in 1985, in spite of our opposition. Going against all norms of justice, common law was overturned as the accused was now presumed guilty till proved innocent! This was done in the name of fighting terrorism in Punjab, but the Act was made applicable all over India. Since TADA is no more in the statute book, I will not dwell on its unsavoury aspects.

One significant achievement of the Rajiv Gandhi government was the anti-defection legislation. I had advocated this legislation way back in 1971 when I was a member of the Jagannatha Rao Committee on Electoral Reforms. However, a major defect of the anti-defection law as passed by the Rajiv Gandhi government related to the provision that entrusted the presiding officer, the Speaker, with a quasi-judicial function, which in many cases he or she might not be equipped to perform. It was also going to be difficult for presiding officers to remain totally impartial, as their decisions would impact their political future. The role of many Speakers adjudicating such cases has been questioned and there have been some who have kept proceedings pending for unduly long periods, in effect, making them infructuous.

Another drawback of the anti-defection law was that it made the Speaker answerable to the courts. According to the Constitution, the Speaker's rulings and directions while presiding over the House cannot be questioned in a court of law. The anti-defection law weakened the position of the Speaker, leading to a conflict between the legislature and the judiciary, as in the Borobabu Singh case of the Manipur Assembly. Here, as observed by Justice J.S. Verma in the Kunjilal Dubey Memorial lecture in 2007, 'an employee of the secretariat challenged in the court an administrative act of the Speaker on the ground of violation of his fundamental right. The Speaker refused to honour the court's order made on judicial review. This led to a contempt proceeding, which also was ignored by the Speaker. The Supreme Court was constrained to direct the personal appearance of the Speaker in his capacity as the administrative head of the secretariat to uphold the majesty and the rule of law. However, as soon as the Speaker appeared in the court and its order was obeyed, the court promptly discharged the notice and closed the matter, observing that it was only concerned with obedience of the court's order...' This matter raises quite a few disturbing issues.

By the middle of the term of the eighth Lok Sabha, Rajiv Gandhi's sheen was beginning to wear off. In 1986, price rise assumed alarming proportions. Several protests were reported from across the country. To demonstrate solidarity with the protesting millions, the Opposition decided to boycott the President's address at the start of the budget session that year.

And it was not only the common man who was falling out with the Congress. The intelligentsia, which had warmed up to Rajiv Gandhi in the initial stages, shook its head in disbelief as the government began to pander to communal elements with an eye on the vote-bank. The Muslim Women's (Protection of Rights on Divorce) Bill was one such retrograde step. The origins of the bill lay in the Shah Bano case, a milestone in the Muslim woman's search for justice. Shah Bano, a sixty-year-old divorcee, went to court seeking maintenance from her husband who had divorced her. The court ruled in her favour: she was held entitled to maintenance from her ex-husband under Section 125 of the Criminal Procedure Code (with an upper limit of Rs 500 a month) like any other Indian woman. When the Islamic orthodoxy termed the verdict an attack on Islam, the Congress, unwilling to stand up to these conservative elements, caved in. It enacted the Muslim Women (Protection of Rights on Divorce) Act, 1986. The most controversial provision of the Act was that it gave a Muslim woman the right to maintenance for the period of *iddat* (about three months) after the divorce, and shifted the onus of maintaining her to her relatives or the Wakf Board. The Act was seen as discriminatory as it denied divorced Muslim women the right to basic maintenance that women of other faiths had recourse to under secular law.

In my address to the House I accused the government of trying to create confusion among the Muslims by insinuating that the Supreme Court had decided the way it had only because of the religious profile of the persons who constituted the bench. As such it was casting aspersions on the impartiality of the court. I warned that the bill would tear apart the very fabric of our national life. One could not tackle forces of communalism and fundamentalism by surrender and appeasement. The Opposition cautioned the government that the bill would provide Hindu fundamentalist forces in this country an excuse to raise their heads. We were proved right. The BJP saw the Act as 'appeasement' of the minority community and discriminatory to non-Muslim men, because they were still bound to pay maintenance under Section 125, CrPC. The Ramjanmabhoomi movement gathered steam primarily because the Act created an impression among the Hindu majority that the Muslim minority was being appeased. I pointed out how a vast section of the people, Muslim women who require sustenance, who require succour, had been denied their minimum right. Needless to say, the appeal fell on deaf ears.

From 1987 onwards, things started taking a dangerous turn as the President and Prime Minister were not able to see eye to eye; in fact, they were not even willing to see each other! It was widely reported that the Prime Minister, going against well-established tradition, had stopped briefing the President. The lack of communication and the resultant strain in the relations between Giani Zail Singh and Rajiv Gandhi became obvious in the context of the infamous Postal Bill, which would have given the government unlimited freedom to intercept private mail in the name of internal security. Giani Zail Singh, in a remarkable show of determination, refused to sign the bill, presumably in deference to public opinion. The President, we came to know, was meeting leaders of different parties. I got a call from him, I reckon as the leader of the CPI(M) in the Lok Sabha. The President seemed greatly disturbed and felt that his office might have been bugged. He hinted at that and took me out to the Mughal Gardens, away from everybody else, to express his views on the development and what he proposed to do. I mention this just to show how an atmosphere of distrust was created.

Around this time, there appeared in the media a letter purportedly written by Giani Zail Singh to Rajiv Gandhi, expressing his deep dissatisfaction about the way the President was being treated by the government. The Opposition was seized of this issue. Members gave notices to the Speaker, Dr Balram Jakhar, to raise the matter in the House. However, the Speaker consistently maintained that 'the name of the President could not be allowed to be used in any manner to influence discussions on the floor of the House'. I believe this was a wrong position given that the President was a part of Parliament and had raised an issue concerning the important matter of the discharge of the Prime Minister's duties and his attitude towards the head of the state. The Opposition was convinced that the Speaker was acting under pressure from the ruling party. We were deeply dissatisfied and decided to express our feelings. The only effective protest was moving a motion for the removal of the Speaker. An extreme step, no doubt. At the desire of the Opposition parties, it fell to me to move the resolution which came up for discussion in the House on 15 April 1987. I said:

> I beg to move that this House having taken into consideration the rulings of the Speaker of the House, including the one on 19 March

> 1987 on the question of privilege denying to the members the right to raise vital constitutional and procedural issues and burning problems, the Speaker has ceased to command the confidence of all sections of the House and therefore resolves that he be removed from his office ... with anguish but no animosity, with seriousness, but no motive except the purest one and impelled by a sense of duty, we are constrained to move this resolution against the Speaker ... though not against Dr Balram Jakhar, the person, for that matter, a loveable one.

Since I moved the motion, I had to explain the reasons behind my action. I told the House:

> [A] sense of duty, like wisdom and patriotism, is not the monopoly of the ruling party. We on this side are also active participants in the parliamentary processes. We cannot be silent spectators of the near consistent and almost coordinated attempts to denude Parliament of its authority. We should be failing in our duty to posterity if we do not voice our protest and that too emphatically. It is a sad day for all of us that we perforce say that the Speaker is privy to the attempt. Freedom of dissent and freedom of debate are the hallmarks of parliamentary democracy. I should imagine that the floor of the House is the most obvious place to dissent through debate. But once access to the floor is restricted or closed, suffocation, if not annihilation, of the entire system will be the obvious consequences. We, on this side, are second to none in our respect for the august office of the Speaker. He has a very vital role to play not only in maintaining the dignity of this House but also to protect and strengthen the great and important position it occupies in our constitutional set-up. Parliament is not the exclusive property of the ruling party. The Opposition is an integral part of the entire system in parliamentary democracy...

The motion was defeated due to the huge majority the ruling party had in the House.

Shortly after this episode, the Bofors gun was fired, sending waves across our political spectrum. The revelation came in the form of a Swedish Radio broadcast in April 1987 that bribes had been paid in connection with the sale of the Bofors gun to the Indian Army. Instead of coming clean on the issue, the government appeared determined to create impediments to every attempt of the Opposition to know the truth. Its stand kept shifting, raising deep doubts in the people. For the first time in our democracy, charges of corruption hinted at the possible involvement of the top authority in the government. A frustrated Opposition moved a no-confidence motion against the Rajiv Gandhi government in 1987.

Speaking on the no-confidence motion, I said:

> The Opposition in the House is charged with the duty to the nation to get this government out of power, so that the people can be saved from the rampage of a corrupt and, at the same time, inept and inefficient administration. It is in discharge of that solemn duty, and to articulate the mood of the millions of our countrymen, that we have been compelled to move this motion, which gives expression to the true feelings of the people of this country and to demonstrate that this House ... no longer correctly represents the people's views and their urges and aspirations.

Of course, given the government's majority, the motion failed.

The Bofors issue dominated the attention of the nation and media from 1987. This put the government in a tight spot, which thought that the most effective way of tackling the problem was by repression. Towards this end, the Defamation Bill was introduced in 1988. The bill sought to make an offence 'the publication of imputations falsely alleging commission of offence by any person'. The statement of objects and reasons said that 'freedom of speech should not degenerate into a license' and put the onus upon the accused of proving that no defamation was caused. The government rushed this through the Lok Sabha as the Opposition had quit the House by then, in protest against the government. The media criticism became so strident and embarrassing that the government was forced by the weight of public opinion to abandon the bill even after it was passed by the Lok Sabha. The Defamation Bill achieved the dubious distinction of being the only bill in our parliamentary history to be withdrawn by the government after its passage by the Lok Sabha.

As elections were approaching, the government hit upon the amendment of the Constitution to bring down the minimum age for voting from twenty-one to eighteen, a measure I had been advocating since 1972. This was touted as a major electoral reform, without touching any of the other major issues. I welcomed the reduction of the minimum age for eligibility to vote. But so far as the ruling party was concerned, I said, 'This so-called concession is nothing but a desperate attempt to ingratiate itself to the young people who are suffering under the maladies of the anti-people policies of the government ... today the young people are the largest unemployed people in the country. The government thought of this with the vain hope that the young people will vote for them in the next elections.'

In protest against the government's involvement in the Bofors scandal, the opposition members submitted their resignation letters en masse to the Speaker on 24 July 1989. The Speaker promptly accepted them much to the relief of the ruling party, which greeted our resignations with thumping of desks. The government's anti-democratic credentials showed up sharply as the ruling party carried on with a Parliament consisting only of members of the ruling party.

As a direct fallout of the Bofors issue, the Congress lost the election to the ninth Lok Sabha, which was constituted on

2 December 1989 and continued till 21 June 1991, and during which V.P. Singh and Chandra Shekhar were Prime Ministers.

The Congress came back to power following the general election held under the tragic shadow of the senseless assassination of Rajiv Gandhi at Sriperumbudur on 21 May 1991 by the LTTE. The dastardly terrorist attack, which extinguished a life of great potential, shocked the country. The nation as a whole mourned his loss.

The 1991 general election threw up a fractured mandate. The Congress, which emerged as the single largest party with 232 seats, formed the government. Narasimha Rao, who was neither a member of the Lok Sabha nor of the Rajya Sabha, was sworn in as the Prime Minister on 21 June 1991. It was for the first time in the history of independent India that a person who was not a Member of Parliament was appointed as the Prime Minister. Narasimha Rao had not contested the general election on health grounds. He was, however, subsequently elected to the Lok Sabha in a bye-election.

The Prime Minister led a combination of disparate forces in government and there were no coherent plans or programmes. Throughout his tenure, the Prime Minister was preoccupied with trying to save his government from being overthrown, rather than redressing the grievances of the people. Many treated him as a lame-duck incumbent.

At the foundation of good governance lies consensus. A minority government is not expected to take unilateral decisions on issues of far-reaching significance and alter the economic architecture of the country. To the Opposition's utter dismay, the government seemed bent on working against the country's long-standing policy of self-reliance and mixed economy. Within a couple of months of assuming office, Narasimha Rao virtually mortgaged the country's interests to international financial forces for some 'tainted lucre'. My apprehensions, as also those of many others, were not exaggerated, in view the track record of such forces in destabilizing the politico-economic systems in many underdeveloped and developing economies.

The 1992-93 Budget was the final nail in the coffin. We contended that the Budget was nothing but a faithful implementation of the fiats of the IMF and the World Bank that compromised India's economic sovereignty. The market economy of the Western world became the mantra of the government. The Nehruvian development model was projected as anti-growth and tossed out unceremoniously. The finance minister, Dr Manmohan Singh, was projected as a messiah by the government, though for the common people the government was the harbinger of financial doom.

In its push for so-called economic reforms, the government decided to ignore the contribution made by Public Sector Undertakings (PSUs) to national development. Shares of PSUs were sold for a song. Sick PSUs were referred to the Board for Industrial and Financial Reconstruction (BIFR), which recommended many of them for closure. On behalf of the party, I opposed the indiscriminate sale of PSU shares to those who had no concern for the interest of the country and its working class. Unfortunately, the Prime Minister seemed to be unconcerned.

It was not the loosening of bureaucratic control and end of licensing that I was against. I am all for healthy competition and would have been happy to see India competing on her own terms in the world economy. It was the unseemly haste with which the Indian market was being opened up to multinationals that was impossible to understand. Instead of generating employment opportunities for the people and strengthening the economy, the government's actions led to a state of helplessness and hopelessness.

The solution to India's economic crisis did not lie in the IMF or the World Bank prescriptions, but in restricting non-essential imports and increasing exports. What was also required was implementation of land reforms, dispersal of the ownership of industrial capital and introduction of labour-intensive technology that would *use* labour and *not* replace them. Such reforms would have increased the purchasing power of the common man, bolstered the domestic market and brought about agricultural and industrial growth. But none of this was attempted.

A series of scams that rocked the regime demonstrated the inefficient and unethical functioning of the government. Of these, by far the biggest was the securities scam triggered by Harshad Mehta. The scam strained the Indian economy and ruined thousands of small investors. It was an appalling shame that public funds of over Rs 3,500 crore were lost without a trace. To make matters worse, it unfolded at a time when the country was passing through one of its most trying times, economically. The most disquieting aspect was the ease with which the scam was committed. Banks had recklessly made ample financial resources available to share brokers. Harshad Mehta, the public face of the scam, had direct access to the highest echelons in the finance ministry and, in a short time, amassed a huge amount of wealth. The Opposition had expressed serious reservations when the index of share prices had shown an unusual increase in 1991 but the government was euphoric and insisted that the boom was due to its liberal policies. The fraud was of such great magnitude that the commerce minister, P. Chidambaram, was forced to resign. The CBI was assigned the investigation of the scam. An ordinance was promulgated on 8 July 1992 providing for the establishment of a special court to try offences relating to transactions in securities.

There was a demand in the House for a Joint Parliamentary Committee (JPC) to go into the securities scam. I congratulated the Prime Minister for accepting the demand. The JPC handed in a unanimous report on 21 December 1993. It observed that foreign banks had been facilitated in their efforts to violate the laws of the land and that the Reserve Bank of India (RBI) and the ministry of finance were also involved in irregularities in security transactions. The RBI's excessive accommodation of foreign banks had made them arrogant. They were thus able to emerge as the biggest players in the scam. The report, however, left it to the government to punish the guilty and take remedial action to prevent such scams from recurring.

After the JPC's findings became public, the government had to take moral and political responsibility. The Opposition demanded the resignation of the finance minister. I have great personal regard for Dr Manmohan Singh and I appreciated his principled stand of submitting his resignation on 24 December 1993. Of course the Prime Minister did not accept it. Unfortunately, not a single person was charge-sheeted or even found guilty for the scam.

No action was taken in respect of the Bofors scandal, too. Members had expressed serious doubts during the 1992 budget session of Parliament about the progress of investigation in the Bofors case. Though the CBI had registered a case, there were apprehensions that the government was thwarting proper investigation. Handing over of a note by the External Affairs Minister Madhavsinh Solanki to his Swedish counterpart, during a visit to that country in February 1992, was nothing but an effort to sabotage the case. What was shocking was that the minister could let himself be used thus.

It will not be out of place to make a mention of the Vohra

Committee report in this context. A committee under the home secretary, N.N. Vohra, was set up by the government on 9 July 1993 to take stock of activities of crime syndicates, mafia organizations and similar outfits, which had developed links with and were reportedly being protected by government functionaries and political personalities. The Vohra Committee, in its report presented to the government on 5 October 1993, found that the mafia was virtually running a parallel government, rendering the state apparatus irrelevant. Surprisingly, the government kept the report in deep freeze for a long time and no serious action was taken on it. It only hurriedly appointed a nodal agency of officials before the Parliament was to discuss the matter on 28 August 1995, which achieved nothing of note.

The Hawala case was yet another serious corruption issue the country had to face during this regime. In 1991, there was evidence to show that vast sums were received from sources abroad and disbursed by hawala racketeers to Kashmiri terrorists, militants, politicians and bureaucrats. The government took three years to come to a mere prima facie conclusion to this effect. In November 1994, the Supreme Court rightly expressed its concern on the matter and said there was significant inaction on the part of the government. Because of the court's censure, proceedings were initiated against some bureaucrats and officials of PSUs, who, it was divulged, had given favours to industrialists or business houses. It was difficult to believe that the Prime Minister did not know there were allegations against many of his ministers for being part of the hawala transactions and for harbouring criminals. The Opposition strongly felt that the Prime Minister had failed in his duties.

In fact, he himself was accused of purchasing MPs. In July 1993, the Opposition initiated a no-confidence motion against Rao's government because the Opposition felt that the government did not have sufficient numbers to prove a majority. It was alleged that Rao, through a representative, offered millions of rupees to members of the Jharkhand Mukti Morcha (JMM), and possibly a breakaway faction of the Janata Dal, to vote for him during the confidence motion. The Supreme Court, to our great concern, unfortunately held that no action could be taken against MPs even if there was evidence of bribery for casting votes, because of the immunity provided by the Constitution. The moot question was how did Narasimha Rao, who could not enthuse the people of this country to give him a majority, manage a majority in the House? An allegation was also made that the voting on the no-confidence motion on 28 July 1993 was managed in a particular manner because of what the Prime Minister had said about the Jharkhand issue, assuring due consideration of the demand for a separate state. Narasimha Rao was described by many, particularly the media, as the fountainhead of corruption.

But by far the government's darkest hour was the demolition of the Babri Masjid on 6 December 1992. To my mind, it was the most concerted onslaught on our cherished principle of secularism. Though the heinous act was committed by the BJP–VHP combine, duly facilitated by the state's BJP government led by Kalyan Singh, the connivance of the Central government was undeniable. When this concerted, barbaric, uncivilized and anti-national act, striking at the root of our secular structure, was being committed, the Prime Minister was happily asleep and his home minister, S.B. Chavan, unconcerned.

As soon as I got the information regarding the attempt to damage the mosque, I rang up the Prime Minister but he was not accessible as he was resting! I then called the home minister and told him what was happening but he said he was already aware of it. The chief minister had assured him that the situation was under control. Within four to five hours, the entire structure was razed to the ground. A makeshift structure was set up and deities brought there. The objective of the fundamentalists was smoothly and successfully achieved and the Central government did nothing to prevent it. In fact, it almost looked as if it passively encouraged the demolition.

I had earlier suggested to the government to acquire the land around the disputed structure and hand it over to whoever was entitled to it, after an adjudication by way of a negotiated settlement or by a judicial determination. The VHP and the Bajrang Dal had, in July 1992, started construction work on the 2.77 acres of acquired land around the disputed structure in Ayodhya but the government had turned a blind eye to it. This happened despite the 15 July 1992 interim order of the Lucknow bench of the Allahabad High Court restraining the contending parties from undertaking or continuing any construction activity on the acquired land. The chief minister of Uttar Pradesh, Kalyan Singh, had assured the National Integration Council (NIC) that his government would protect the Babri Masjid structure and make all efforts to find an amicable solution to the dispute. The state government had also given an undertaking in the court, backed by letters from some prominent members of the BJP and the VHP, that the kar seva would be symbolic in nature and would not involve any construction activity in violation of the court orders. Yet, a large number of people were allowed to gather at the disputed location to perform kar seva.

I had requested the Prime Minister to maintain the status quo in all aspects. He had been assured full cooperation by the Opposition so long as he did not compromise with the integrity of the country and did not surrender to the forces of fundamentalism. Yet, the Babri Masjid was destroyed. The dispute was not only about a mandir or a masjid; it affected the very foundation of our existence, the very principle of unity in diversity. The BJP tried to divide the country on religious lines and the government was clearly unable or rather unwilling to do anything to prevent it. Thousands of innocent people lost their lives as a direct result of the sacrilege committed by the BJP–VHP combine. I have been a strong critic of Article 356 throughout my political life. However, because of the threat posed to the nation and its harmony, on 3 December 1992, I urged the government in the House to take recourse to the power it had under the Constitution and save the country from disintegration.

I remember vividly that a few days after the dastardly crime was committed, Sharad Pawar invited some of us belonging to the Opposition to his residence in New Delhi and showed us a film on how the mosque was demolished by hordes of fanatics and fundamentalists with great glee and rejoicing, in a well-planned manner, and how many BJP leaders witnessed the desecration without making any effort to stop it. Some of the leaders were subsequently named as accused in the FIRs. The Liberhan Commission set up to investigate the demolition has taken seventeen long years to come out with its findings, which severely indict the BJP leaders but surprisingly give a free chit to Narasimha Rao, when he was the one man who, if he really wanted to, could have stopped the demolition and the carnage that ensued.

I had expected that during the debate on the no-confidence motion against the government on 17 December 1992, Atal Bihari Vajpayee would condemn the sacrilege committed. It was disappointing that a senior leader like him did not utter a single word of condemnation although initially he had expressed regrets as the leader of the Opposition about the ghastly incidents that had tarnished the secular credentials of our country permanently.

I held the Narasimha Rao government squarely responsible for the outrage on our secular fabric. Its policy of appeasement and surrender to the forces of communalism had greatly encouraged the BJP. I was appalled that Narasimha Rao chose to talk to a few chosen sadhus and mahants about a solution. Such a sensitive and complex problem could have been solved only by adopting a secular approach and not by pampering those whose avowed objective was to espouse the cause of the people belonging to a particular religion at the expense of another. The complicity of the government and its collusion with fundamentalist forces led to one of the darkest phases in post-Independence Indian history that will forever remain a blot on our collective conscience. The Prime Minister should have apologized to the people for this unforgivable lapse. The action of the divisive and fundamentalist forces pushed the nation to the brink of a catastrophe. I demanded that an assurance be given that all steps would be taken to rehabilitate the innocent people who had suffered and that those responsible for the destruction of the mosque would be brought to book.

I have always believed that 6 December 1992 was a day of national shame and I demanded on the floor of the House that the mosque be rebuilt exactly at the place where it stood. I also wanted a complex symbolizing national integration to be set up at the site. Since then, MPs who believe in the secular basis of our polity, observe the day as a day of national shame and affirm their determination to fight against religious fanaticism and fundamentalism.

P.V. Narasimha Rao's regime saw the introduction of the MPLADS (Members of Parliament Local Area Development Scheme), a scheme to which my party was strongly opposed. When it was announced by the Prime Minister on 29 December 1993, as the leader of the CPI(M) I protested on the ground that it was morally and politically improper and would create a number of administrative difficulties. I also mentioned that it would only end up pampering the MPs. A number of MPs resented the fact that I had objected to the scheme. It made me unpopular with them. However, I stuck to my objection and whenever the issue came up I opposed it but to no avail. Some of my apprehensions were proved to be justified as, during the fourteenth Lok Sabha, a number of MPs were found to have taken recourse to serious improprieties including corruption in the implementation of the scheme. The annual amount provided to each MP has now risen from Rs 5 lakhs to Rs 2 crores, which, among other aspects, gives an unjustified advantage to a sitting MP during an election vis-à-vis his opponents. The way the scheme has operated has not only given rise to undesirable developments but has also seriously disturbed and upset the proper implementation of various state and district plans, the execution of which was considerably delayed or not carried out in the rush to assign unmerited priority to projects under MPLADS.

The tenth Lok Sabha was also witness to the motion for removal of Justice V. Ramaswami, a judge of the Supreme Court of India, for his misdemeanours. I moved the motion on 10 May 1993 with a great sense of responsibility only to uphold the sanctity of our judiciary and the Constitution. It was for the first time that such a motion was being moved in the House.

A judge has to set standards of the highest morality, rectitude and honesty in all his actions and behaviour. If any charges or allegations are made against a person occupying a high position, it is in the fitness of things that he himself invites an inquiry and investigation into the allegations and charges so that his reputation, as well as the reputation of the authority he represents, remains unaffected.

In the first quarter of 1990, some newspapers reported about the huge expenditure said to have been incurred by Justice Ramaswami, Chief Justice of the Punjab and Haryana High Court at the time. On 20 July 1990, the Chief Justice of India advised

Justice Ramaswami to desist from discharging judicial functions so long as the investigations continued and his name was cleared on this aspect. On 29 August 1990, the Chief Justice sought the advice of three judges of the Supreme Court on the question 'whether the involvement of Justice Ramaswami in proceedings in relation to administrative decisions and other alleged administrative acts and omissions as the Chief Justice of the Punjab and Haryana High Court would render it embarrassing for him to function as a judge of the Supreme Court'. Justice Ramaswami refused to recognize such jurisdiction.

Under these circumstances, MPs had a solemn duty to protect the Constitution. On 27 February 1991, 108 members submitted a notice for a motion to present an address to the President of India for the removal of Justice Ramaswami under Article 124(4) of the Constitution, listing eleven charges against him.

The notice of motion was admitted by the Speaker, Rabi Ray, on 12 March 1991. Under the Judges (Inquiry) Act, 1968, the Speaker constituted a committee consisting of Justice P.B. Sawant, a sitting judge of the Supreme Court, Justice P.D. Desai, Chief Justice of the Mumbai High Court, and Justice O. Chinnappa Reddy, former judge of the Supreme Court, to investigate the grounds on which the removal of Justice Ramaswami was sought. The committee gave full opportunity to Justice Ramaswami, but the judge, instead of accepting the findings of the committee, levelled charges against its members. He went so far as to use disparaging language against the committee, the judges, the Speaker and MPs. The committee, therefore, had to investigate the matter without any cooperation from him.

After carefully scrutinizing and considering the documents received from various sources and all other material aspects, fourteen charges were framed by the committee against Justice Ramaswami, alleging conduct amounting to wilful and gross misuse of office, wilful and persistent failure or negligence in discharge of duties, habitual extravagance at the cost of public exchequer, moral turpitude, using public funds for private purpose and bringing the high judicial office to disrepute.

Justice Ramaswamy refused to accept the findings of the committee and alleged that it had framed charges on the basis of false allegations and that the members of the House were vindictive. It fell on me to move the motion for impeachment, the first ever moved in India. The Opposition leaders wanted me to move the motion probably because of my legal background and I believe we were able to make a most convincing case against the judge. The judge was represented in the Lok Sabha by his counsel, Kapil Sibal. Sibal made a lengthy submission that was followed by a debate. Through his counsel, the judge indulged in the rhetoric of confusion and deliberate distortion of facts. The House was told many untruths and some half truths. In my reply to the debate on the motion on 11 May 1993, I appealed to the members to vote for the motion as voting against it, I felt, would tarnish the image of the judiciary. I also believed that the judiciary would be denigrated if Justice Ramaswami continued to occupy his seat on the bench. There would be a question mark on the future of the judiciary if he was exonerated because of political considerations. It involved the question of having a clean judiciary, an independent judiciary and a judiciary which enjoyed the faith of the people and which would not be subjected to any pressure or inducement or laxity in the standard of behaviour.

Yet, the motion failed as the Congress abstained from voting and thereby protected a tainted judge. It appeared that members of the party hailing from Tamil Nadu, the state to which the judge belonged, had raised the bogey of action being taken against a Tamil judge and persuaded the party as a whole not to take action against him. Significantly, not a single member of the House voted against the motion or in favour of the judge. The Congress members having abstained from voting, the requisite majority could not be had. After the securities scam, the demolition of the Babri Masjid and the communal riots, here was an opportunity for the government to redeem itself but it chose not to do so. I consider the defeat of the motion for the impeachment of Justice Ramaswami as the defeat of our Parliament. The Congress played a most inglorious role in the episode and compromised with the requirement of fullest judicial probity on some political and chauvinistic grounds whose effect is still being felt as nowadays there is a proliferation of complaints regarding absence of judicial honesty and rectitude.

It speaks volumes of the wisdom of the Indian people that they threw out the Congress in the next general election. People had had enough of misrule and corruption at the highest levels of government. The Narasimha Rao regime will be remembered for taking corruption and ineptitude to a new high, much to the detriment of the nation as also the Congress.

5

THE DIVISIVE NDA YEARS

For me and many other right-thinking Indians, the years 1996 to 2004 were traumatic due to the ascendance of communal forces and the failure of secular forces to provide a stable government. The pro-rich policies of Narasimha Rao's government had brought untold miseries to the people. There was a general sense of apathy and helplessness, both among the masses and the intelligentsia. The threat of the country disintegrating into chaos and turmoil, thanks to the rise of communalism, appeared frighteningly real.

The 1996 election manifesto of the CPI(M) cautioned about the danger posed by the communal forces. It said:

> Never since the partition of the country have communal forces mounted such an offensive as has been witnessed during the last five years. The communal forces, in recent period, once again seek to mount an offensive, spreading deeper the poison of hatred

> against minorities in order to garner more votes. The Vishwa Hindu Parishad has issued a blueprint for a Hindu Rashtra, while whipping up the campaign for the destruction of mosques in Kashi and Mathura. Considering the fact that the BJP had emerged, in the last elections, as the major Opposition, it still represents the most consolidated danger to the very unity and integrity of our country. It is out to destroy the very social fabric that composes India.

In fact, the leftists remained vociferous critics of the BJP and the Sangh Parivar's policy of dividing the country on communal lines. It wasn't surprising then that L.K. Advani would go on to say that no party, except one, was 'untouchable' for the BJP, and that party was the CPI(M). I am proud that I remained an untouchable for Advani and the BJP because of my commitment to secularism.

The general election of April–May 1996 threw up a piquant situation as no single party was able to secure a clear majority. The BJP emerged as the single largest party with 161 seats. From only 2 seats and 7.74 per cent of votes in 1984 to 161 seats with a vote share of 20.29 per cent in 1996, the BJP's growth was impressive, yet disturbing. But the BJP was not yet in a position to form a government on its own.

There were genuine fears and apprehensions that fundamentalist forces would take over the country's political and social structures. The Congress Working Committee (CWC), in its meeting on 12 May 1996, passed a resolution pledging support for a secular government at the Centre. The Third Front was also resolute in its stand not to permit the BJP to form the government. As mentioned earlier, on 13 May 1996 it unanimously endorsed the name of Jyoti Basu, the chief minister of West Bengal, as its candidate for the post of Prime Minister but the CPI(M) did not agree.

The need of the hour was to form a secular government in order to keep the communal forces at bay. The efforts of the National Front–Left Front (NF–LF) combine with 180 members finally resulted in the unanimous selection of H.D. Deve Gowda, the chief minister of Karnataka, as the leader of the National Front and it staked a claim to form the next government. The President was informed on 14 May 1996 and the Congress party was requested to provide support from outside.

As such, the President's invitation to Atal Bihari Vajpayee on 15 May 1996 to form the government was a bolt from the blue and a great setback to all of us, for we were sure that secular forces would be able to form the government. The Congress party's failure to inform the President in time about its decision to support Deve Gowda created this unfortunate situation. I am not sure whether the delayed action was deliberate or not.

The Vajpayee government came to power on 16 May 1996, almost by default. Here was a party forming the government with less than 30 per cent of seats and 20 per cent of votes, thus making a mockery of the principle of majority rule, which is central to parliamentary democracy. As directed by the President, the government had to prove its majority support on the floor of the House on 27 and 28 May 1996.

I did not expect Vajpayee to stake his claim to government formation thanks to an electoral fortuity, as his floor managers, with all their efforts, could manage only 194 seats for him. Vajpayee knew very well that he did not have the majority and thus there was no constitutional or moral basis for him to accept the invitation of the President. The only reason I could think of was the BJP's lust to come to power by any means, even if only for a few days. The government was a constitutional aberration and deserved to be voted out. Since the government lacked majority support, I requested that the motion for a vote of confidence be put to vote without any discussion.

I had no doubt whatsoever that Vajpayee would go down in India's parliamentary history as the Prime Minister with the shortest tenure. It was shocking that a person of his eminence while speaking on the motion of confidence came across as a devout RSS functionary and not as the Prime Minister of the nation. I have great respect for Vajpayee personally. But hearing him that day, I was convinced that he had become captive of the saffron brigade. He used the opportunity not to address the members of the House and persuade them to vote in his favour but to the people outside the House. Vajpayee tried to divide the people and create mistrust among them on the basis of religion, only to retain power.

Since the BJP government was formed without majority support, immediately after assuming office, it got busy in political manoeuvring and crude attempts to transform its minority status to a majority one. It tried to present a spectre of civil war, disintegration and collapse of internal security in its effort to virtually blackmail the members. A section of the media was also utilized towards this end. Ministers made promises and policy announcements knowing fully well that they lacked any constitutional authority to do so. The BJP stooped to the lowest level, politically and morally.

The continuance of the BJP government was an insult to the people and amounted to the weakening of the secular fabric of the country. The government tried to project a simulated secular image and gave an impression that there had been a change in its heart and priorities as it no longer raised issues like the construction of the Ram Temple in Ayodhya. It was nothing but a deliberate effort to mislead the nation. The BJP's election manifesto had clearly stated that 'on coming to power, the BJP government will facilitate the construction of a magnificent Sri Ram Mandir at *Janmasthan* in Ayodhya which will be a tribute to *Bharat Mata*'. The Prime Minister, in his address to the nation on television, also said, 'If the problems related to religion are not resolved for a long period of time, then the result is what happened in Ayodhya.' It was a veiled threat directed at the minority communities. I could not think of a more shocking approbation of one of the most heinous happenings in the history of our country.

On 27 May 1996, before the discussion on the motion of confidence moved by the Prime Minister started, the members were told by the government benches that there would be no luncheon recess and that the debate on the motion would continue until it was completed. But suddenly during the debate, around one o'clock, we were informed that there would be a luncheon recess, and that the debate would resume after the recess. After the House rose during the recess, we came to know that an urgent Cabinet meeting was being held during the recess to approve the counter-guarantee to be given in favour of Enron in respect of the Dabhol Power Project. Significantly, by that time, from the proceedings in the House, it was abundantly clear that the government would definitely fall because it was in a hopeless minority.

Here, it is necessary to briefly state what the Enron issue involved. Enron, an American energy company, was setting up a massive power plant at Dabhol in Maharashtra. The project was initially developed by the National Thermal Power Corporation (NTPC), a government undertaking, and was to be the first of the coastal gas-based power plants in the country. The project was initiated in 1992 by NTPC. But ultimately Enron became the major owner of the Dabhol project in which the Maharashtra State Electricity Board (MSEB) had a 15 per cent share and the rest was owned by powerful multinationals. Ignoring all objections, the power sector in India was opened up to private foreign investors. Enron entered into a memorandum of understanding with MSEB to set up the project as a joint-venture project. Dabhol Power Company and MSEB had signed a power purchase agreement in December 1993. Enron lobbied with the Government of India, the US government and other financial institutions like the World Bank for financial assistance for the project. However, the World Bank found the project economically unviable and thus did not finance the same as the cost of production of power would be extremely high. Many other negative aspects of the project were also highlighted by the World Bank and it became highly controversial. There were serious allegations of malfeasance and corruption connected with it.

In 1995, there was a change of government in Maharashtra after the elections and an alliance of the Shiv Sena and BJP came to power. The new government appointed a committee, known as the Munde committee, to review the project. In its report the committee criticized not only the process through which the project had been developed but the terms of the deal as well, and concluded that there was lack of transparency and that Enron had been given undue favours and concessions. Based on this evaluation, in August 1995, the Maharashtra government decided to halt the construction and cancel the project and initiated legal proceedings to nullify the agreement on the ground that the same was vitiated by fraud and misrepresentation. However, in November 1995, Rebecca Mark, chairperson of Enron International, held what seemed to be a crucial meeting with the leader of the Shiv Sena, which resulted in resumption of negotiations between Enron and the state government. On 8 January 1996, the Maharashtra government announced that it would accept a revised agreement whose terms were finalized on 23 February 1996. Thereafter, the legal proceedings initiated by the Maharashtra government were withdrawn. The Dabhol project remained extremely controversial and almost everyone in the country aware of the project realized that both the original agreement and the revised agreement of 23 February 1996 were against national interest. The revised agreement expanded Phase

I of the project by proposing larger generation of power. The MSEB was committed to buying 90 per cent of the plant's output as well as covering the risk of currency fluctuations. Thus, the proposed expansion increased the financial risk to the state under the revised agreement.

The project continued to remain controversial and the Maharashtra government itself considered it to be contrary to the national interest and to the interest of the state, which is probably why they revised their stand and decided not to pursue it.

By the time the Lok Sabha resumed discussion on the motion of confidence after the luncheon recess, some members came to know that the government – which was certainly going to be defeated and had no political, far less moral, authority to take any decision without having proved its majority as it was required to do to continue in office – had decided on the luncheon adjournment only so that it could during the recess surreptitiously hold a Cabinet meeting and ratify the controversial counter-guarantee to be given to Enron. The government had neither the authority nor any justification to take such a decision, keeping the Parliament totally in the dark, entering into a subterfuge regarding its proposed action of ratifying the counter-guarantee in favour of Enron, which was totally against the interest of the state of Maharashtra and the country. But the hopelessly minority government of Atal Bihari Vajpayee took the dubious decision, which clearly exposed that they were even prepared to act against vital national interest by trying to take advantage of being in power temporarily. The whole episode of the ratification of the counter-guarantee in favour of Enron was nothing but a scandal where the people's representatives were deliberately kept in the dark, if not hoodwinked.

During my intervention in the course of the debate in the House, I referred to the serious impropriety committed by the government and described its action as nothing but an affront not only to the House but also to the President, because he had desired that the government should prove its majority, which meant that before taking any important decision, it had to establish its credentials and its right to remain in power. My 27 May 1996 speech on the motion of confidence in the council of ministers headed by Atal Bihari Vajpayee has been reproduced in Appendix I.

I was convinced that nobody would regret the demise of the BJP government, given its potential for misdeeds and its fundamentalist and communal character. A government composed of religious obscurantists was not competent to solve the problems the country was faced with. While replying to the debate on 28 May, Vajpayee, who was aware that he did not have the required majority, announced his decision to resign and the motion of confidence was not put to the vote of the House. The Vajpayee government went down as the shortest one in the history of Indian democracy.

What had disturbed the majority of members of the House and many well-meaning people in the country was that a political party which was not in majority – and which never even expected to get a majority unless it took recourse to improper means possibly through horse-trading – should have been invited to form a government, and that without offering proof of majority would take decisions for which it had neither constitutional mandate nor the mandate of the House. The fact that the government lasted only thirteen days and that Atal Bihari Vajpayee acquired the distinction of being the Prime Minister for the briefest period in India's parliamentary history till then clearly established the mockery of the formation of such a government and the political immorality of the party in pretending before the President that it would ultimately get majority support in the House.

The Deve Gowda and the Gujral governments that succeeded the Vajpayee government could not last long due to the adversarial attitude of the Congress, which once again let down the secular forces by withdrawing its support to the governments and forcing early elections.

In the general election of 1998 for the twelfth Lok Sabha, a BJP-led alliance came to power. Vajpayee was able to send a list of only 240 members to the President while staking his claim to form the government. Members of the AIADMK, the Marumalarchi Dravida Munnetra Kazhagam (MDMK) and the Trinamool Congress (TMC), who were supposedly alliance partners, were missing. For three to four days, the second biggest alliance partner of the BJP, the AIADMK, and its other allies, refused to send a letter of support to the President. It finally reached him only after hard bargaining. We could not find out what exactly transpired. The threat to the multi-religious, multi-ethnic and multi-linguistic character of our society re-emerged. The BJP manifesto was based on the RSS slogan of 'one nation, one people and one culture'. Minority communities were required to follow the Indian tradition or Hindutva as understood and interpreted by the BJP.

The National Democratic Alliance was an opportunistic, political combination, masquerading as partners. The alliance was fragile and the BJP's claim of people voting for a pre-poll alliance led by it was nothing but a myth. If indeed there was a common basis for the alliance, its constituent partners would not have had separate manifestoes, as was the case. For me, the earlier thirteen-day Vajpayee government was a constitutional aberration and I had expressed my wish to see Vajpayee as the permanent ex-Prime Minister of the country. Unfortunately, I was to be proved wrong!

In the national agenda, which I called a 'national tamasha', the BJP omitted the main issues of its manifesto, like the building of a Ram temple at Ayodhya, abrogation of Article 370 and the uniform civil code as it had done in the 1996 presidential address. I wanted the Prime Minister to give his views on this when he sought the support of the House for the confidence motion moved on 27 March 1998. I wanted him to disclose the commitments the BJP had made to its alliance partners. I was not against the Prime Minister making any special arrangements for or giving benefits to any state. I was happy that he believed in making the states of India strong so as to make a strong India, which I have been seeking all along. However, I was afraid that if the BJP government continued in power, apart from the common people, it would be catastrophic to Vajpayee himself as he was never completely sure when the rug would be drawn from under his feet!

My speech delivered in the House on 27 March 1998 has been reproduced in Appendix I.

The 1999 presidential address to members was a great disappointment. It neither provided any direction nor made an assessment of the performance of the government. The Prime Minister seemed perpetually worried about the frowns and smiles of his allies. The allies kept heaping demand upon demand and the government was caught up meeting them. Its survival depended on their 'goodwill', after all. I recall a cartoon at the time which had Vajpayee saying, in desperation, '*Arre bhai, haathi, ghodha, gaadi, jo bhi maange, de do. Sarkar to chalana hai aakhirkar.*' How correctly it reflected the prevalent political scenario!

Price rise and the mishandling of the public distribution system (PDS) aggravated the already murky situation. The government launched a deliberate attack on the federal and democratic set-up of the country by imposing President's Rule in Bihar. It was intriguing that the BJP, from the time of the election, had been talking of President's Rule in the state. How could a duly elected state government be dismissed just because one did not like it?

It was also wrong to appoint a party functionary, S.S. Bhandari, who wore his RSS links as a badge of honour, as the governor of the state in complete disregard of constitutional proprieties. The only objective of this appointment was to destabilize the popularly elected government of Bihar. The dismissal of Rabri Devi and the imposition of President's Rule on 12 February 1999 was a crude attempt to humour the BJP's ally, the Janata Dal (United).

Engaged as it was full-time in appeasing its allies, the government simply did not have the time or the will to tackle the perennial problems of poverty, illiteracy, unemployment, lack of health care, etc. It sidelined the Lokpal Bill – which sought to bring elected representatives under the scope of investigation for corruption – which it had promised to enact, and hobnobbed with the former Congress minister Sukh Ram, who was embroiled in many scandals. Shockingly, Sukh Ram was made deputy chief minister of Himachal Pradesh where the BJP was in power. In another arbitrary move, the Parliament was not informed about the dismissal of the chief of naval staff, Admiral Vishnu Bhagwat. He had been appointed chief of naval staff on 30 September 1996 and was sacked on 30 December 1998 under Article 310 of the Constitution of India. This was after the Cabinet Appointments Committee appointed Vice-Admiral Harinder Singh as deputy chief of naval staff. Refusing to accept the Cabinet order – on the grounds that Harinder Singh had sought to foment communalism in the armed forces, and questioning his competence and commitment to duty – Admiral Bhagwat went public with his opposition to the government's decision. The government said that a series of actions from Admiral Bhagwat 'were in deliberate defiance of the government'. The dismissal resulted in an outcry throughout the country. Admiral Bhagwat himself appropriately described it as a 'politico-military coup'. The defence minister, George Fernandes, went on TV to defend the decision!

Given Admiral Bhagwat's severe indictment of George Fernandes, which was probably unprecedented in the history of the Indian armed forces, major political parties demanded the resignation of the defence minister and also a high-level enquiry. I raised the issue in the House on 9 March 1999 and observed:

> ... it is very surprising that the Parliament of India cannot discuss an unprecedented event ... Is the dismissal of the naval chief a usual and routine matter? Can the Parliament not discuss it? ...
>
> We have seen several versions coming out in the papers. Many statements have come out ... Hon'ble defence minister has made statements which have appeared in the press outside the House. He has also given an interview on television. Hon'ble Prime Minister has referred to this dismissal outside the House. I feel the Parliament of India will be failing in its duty if it does not refer to this matter ... and discuss it with all the seriousness it demands ...
>
> The former naval chief has even held a press conference, we find from the newspapers, in which serious allegations have been made as to how such a decision was taken. He has made allegations of improprieties. He has made allegations of corruption in defence deals. Does not the government feel obliged to come before the House and take the House into confidence and tell the country through this House as to what has happened and what is the response of this government? A very serious charge has been made by the defence minister that the former naval chief had become a security risk.
>
> ...with regard to that, there is not a single response. What has the government or the defence minister said in reply to Shri Bhagwat's press conference?

The government also failed to devolve powers to the states, contrary to the commitment made in the national agenda which the BJP and its twelve partners formulated for the country's governance. The state electronic media was blatantly misused to promote the vested interests of the BJP, effectively making it a publicity wing of the party. Most seriously, a decision was taken to close down eight PSUs of West Bengal. Members, irrespective of their political affiliations, and the chief minister of Bengal requested the industry minister to defer this drastic move and make efforts for their revival. It was ignored only because the PSUs were located in West Bengal, a state ruled by a leftist combination, which was the most strongly opposed to the BJP and its anti-people policies. In comparison, if there was any request from its allies, howsoever unreasonable, the government almost always bent over backwards to oblige.

With no concrete achievements to show, the government went for pyrrhic victories. It conducted a series of nuclear explosions in Pokhran on 11 and 13 May 1998 and justified them on the grounds of national security. The explosions were hailed as an 'emotional national assertion'. The leader of the Opposition was not consulted before taking such an important decision. I did not consider this an achievement of the government by any stretch of imagination as was made out, but that of our brilliant scientists. The government very conveniently highjacked what was a scientific achievement. It had been India's policy not to sign the Nuclear Non-proliferation Treaty (NPT) while striving for general and complete disarmament. I was genuinely apprehensive that in response to our explosions Pakistan would also follow suit, which might lead to an arms race in the subcontinent. My worst fears were realized. During the discussions in the House on 28 May 1998, we were informed that Pakistan had indeed successfully conducted a series of nuclear explosions. To bolster a totally unfit government, a potentially dangerous situation was created endangering the security of the entire nation. Of course, recent revelations by a leading scientist closely associated with the nuclear explosions, K. Santhanam, who described the explosions as a 'fizzle', have raised serious doubts about the effectiveness and the genuineness of the whole exercise.

In spite of strenuous efforts, the government was not able to keep its flock together. One of the major partners in the alliance, the AIADMK, which had been quite reluctant from the start and kept on needling the BJP at frequent intervals, withdrew its support on 14 April 1999. The President thereupon asked the government to prove its majority on the floor of the House. The Opposition was not responsible for the situation in any way and it was unwarranted on the part of the Prime Minister to suggest that the Opposition had let the country down. The BJP conveniently forgot that it too had withdrawn support to the V.P. Singh government in 1990 without suggesting an alternative. Again, when the Congress had withdrawn support to the Deve Gowda government, the BJP had openly joined hands with it.

The government was defeated by a single vote on 17 April 1999. The twelfth Lok Sabha was dissolved on 26 April 1999 and Vajpayee's government continued as a caretaker government until the thirteenth Lok Sabha was constituted on 10 October 1999.

Between May and July 1999, when Vajpayee headed the caretaker government, a serious armed conflict, which has gone down in history as the Kargil war, took place between India and Pakistan. It began after it was detected that Pakistani soldiers and Kashmiri militants had crossed over the line of control (LoC) on the Indian side. The LoC serves as the de facto border between the two countries. The Indian Army rose to the occasion and fought valiantly in the most difficult terrain and ultimately emerged victorious. I need not go into the details of the Kargil war as it is part of our recent history. The victory of the Indian Army roused a great sense of patriotism throughout the country. There was an outpouring of sentiments of national pride and the Indian people enthusiastically hailed the great victory of the Indian Army.

Regrettably, but not surprisingly, the BJP sought to utilize such feelings of patriotism and national pride for its own narrow political interest. A well-orchestrated propaganda was carried out to credit the victory in the Kargil war only to the leadership of Vajpayee, and national sentiments were sought to be roused in favour of the party. It was projected that the rule of the BJP-led government had resulted in the victory of the Indian Army. Thus, an unfortunate and serious armed conflict between two neighbouring countries, in which our jawans – many of whom had laid down their lives for the sake of the country – had displayed exemplary courage and patriotism, was utilized as election propaganda by the BJP.

And sure enough, such propaganda helped the NDA government under the leadership of Vajpayee to come back to power in the general election held in September–October 1999, much to the chagrin of all secular forces. The Telugu Desam Party, with twenty-nine members, supported the government from outside. Atal Bihari Vajpayee was once again sworn in as Prime Minister.

To everyone's disgust, the NDA seemed to be a revolving door. Ministers went out and came in and it seemed it did not really matter who was out or who was in. Secularism was given an indecent burial. As in the previous tenure, there was price rise, people were mired in poverty, farmers were neck deep in misery, with numerous cases of suicide by farmers, small-scale industries were in disarray and yet, distressingly, the government was unconcerned. Instead of reviving PSUs and taking care of the workers, they were sold off at throwaway prices. The government made the country subservient to foreign economic policies and programmes. Everything foreign was valued, while Indian companies went into liquidation. Citing a commitment to the World Trade Organization (WTO), the government set in motion the process of undermining what had been built up over the years with the toil of Indians.

The government's scorecard reflected a sorry list of failures. Some of us in the Opposition made sincere efforts to evolve a consensus on the women's reservation bill. But the government clearly lacked the will to have the bill passed. The government enacted the draconian Prevention of Terrorism Act (POTA) with the ulterior motive of misusing it against political opponents. In the case of Bofors, with which the BJP had targeted the Congress when it was in the Opposition, the government filed an incomplete charge sheet, raising doubts as to whether it had any intention of unearthing the truth. In the Babri Masjid case, there was deliberate delay in bringing the culprits to book. All the investigations were completed in 1993 but it was strange that even six years later and after filing of the charge sheet, the case was not disposed of. The home minister, L.K. Advani, was one of those charge-sheeted. The prosecutor and the accused were the same! The Opposition was justified in demanding that the Prime Minister make his government's position clear on this blatant impropriety. When charges were filed against Bihar Chief Minister Lalu Prasad in the fodder scam, all sections of the House had sought his resignation. In the interest of fairness and credibility of the government, all the Central ministers accused in the Babri Masjid case should also have tendered their resignations without any prompting but they did not do so.

On 13 December 2000, the Lok Sabha discussed a motion under Rule 184 calling upon the Prime Minister to drop from his council of ministers three ministers – L.K. Advani, Murli Manohar Joshi and Uma Bharti – against whom prima facie charges had been established with regard to their involvement in the demolition of the Babri Masjid. The Opposition was not passing any judgement on the merits of the case or giving any opinion when they moved this motion. Instead of giving the matter the serious consideration it deserved, the Prime Minister avoided the Lok Sabha. Not only that, he made certain statements that greatly troubled the Opposition as well as his allies. As a result, the House could not function for several days. Vajpayee could have rejected the Opposition demand for the resignation of the accused members of his Cabinet or he could have said that he did not find anything against them. But he asserted that the demolition was the manifestation of national feelings and national sentiment, or 'rashtriya bhavana', as he termed it. Whose 'bhavana' was Vajpayee referring to? It was only a small section of the majority community. Further, he said, 'I have not supported the demolition of the mosque, but what is of importance is how the temple should be constructed.' Vajpayee was known to be a moderate and many of the allies had reposed their faith in him because of his so-called liberal outlook. Inexplicably, he adopted a stance that was opposite to his professed views. I was not sure whether he had to wear a 'mukhauta' (mask) for political expediency but I was certainly taken aback by this volte-face. The Prime Minister by exonerating the charge-sheeted ministers interfered with the due process of law.

It was disconcerting that the construction of the Ram temple was discussed during a three-day meeting of the dharmasansad at the Kumbha Mela in January 2001. I knew this was meant to be addressed to the most fundamentalist and obscurantist forces in the Sangh.

The attempt by the Vishwa Hindu Parishad (VHP) to get a darshan of the idol on 17 October 2001 was part of the calculated scheme to rouse communal passions in the upcoming election in Uttar Pradesh. Ayodhya was no longer a matter of religion. It had definitely become a political issue. L.K. Advani had no hesitation in admitting that he was in Parliament because of the

Ram Janmabhoomi movement and that the increased strength of the BJP was due to the success of his Rath Yatra in 1989.

The Prime Minister then went on to announce the creation of a cell in the Cabinet Secretariat to find a solution to the crisis regarding the Ram Janambhoomi issue before 12 March 2002. It was a strange move as the matter was meant to be resolved either by the court or through mutual agreement. The Supreme Court had ordered that only the priest had access to the sanctum sanctorum to perform rituals for the deity, and devotees were not allowed to offer prayers in the prohibited area. Allowing some people into the disputed site in March 2002 was a violation of the order and I had expected the Supreme Court to take action for its contempt.

The observation made by Vajpayee that there was a temple at the place where the mosque stood was another attempt to influence the decision of the court. The Supreme Court had made it clear that only upon final adjudication of the matter, the question of dealing with the land, either disputed or undisputed, could be taken up. The decision of the government to approach the Supreme Court to change the status quo was questionable and done with the intention of favouring fundamentalist forces. Since elections were approaching in different states, the BJP wanted to utilize Hindutva as a major plank. We were vehemently opposed to this ugly policy of dividing the people and the country on the basis of religion and demanded the withdrawal of the petition from the Supreme Court.

The breakout of communal violence in Gujarat following a fire in the Sabarmati Express on 27 February 2002 near Godhra railway station left a long-lasting and deep scar on our psyche. The Prime Minister said that events in Godhra and the rest of Gujarat had brought shame to the entire nation. The Opposition unanimously condemned the incidents. What happened in Gujarat was not an aberration; it was part of a calculated and reprehensible state-sponsored pogrom against innocent people. Chief Minister Narendra Modi reportedly said that every action would have a reaction. This was a condemnable attitude. Processions were held, seeking revenge for the incident at Godhra, which had claimed fifty-eight innocent lives. The police were heavily outnumbered, and in many instances were ordered to fall in line with the diktats of the communal government of Gujarat to turn a blind eye to the rioting mobs. The army was kept in a stand-by position. Even after thirty hours of the incident at Godhra, the army was not called in to handle the situation, which spiralled out of control. It was unnerving to realize that Gujarat had become the laboratory for imposing Hindutva of the despicable BJP and VHP variant.

I was a member of the all-party parliamentary delegation that visited Gujarat in the wake of the riots. We were given a death toll figure of 618 plus 58 of Godhra. So far as missing persons were concerned, the figure was over 2,000. We saw heart-rending scenes at the relief camps. The 30,000 affected persons in the camps had their houses destroyed, looted, their families maimed, raped and killed only because they professed a particular faith. They were herded in like animals and had lost all sense of security or hope of justice.

The state government's culpability was amply evident also from the fact that examinations were forced on the students who were languishing in relief camps. I got letters from different camps seeking my help. I requested the government to heed the students' request but this was rejected.

There was not a semblance of law and order in the state. Minorities and those who were opposed to the BJP had no protection from well-planned murderous assaults on them. The local administration was busy fomenting trouble and encouraging murderers and those who indulged in loot and arson. I remember receiving a frantic telephone call from the CPI(M) office at Bhavnagar. Those present there narrated how rampaging mobs were threatening them. Finding no way out, I talked to L.K. Advani to intervene and protect the people at the CPI(M) office. I believe it was only because of his intervention that the police stepped in and saved them. I telephoned Advani and conveyed my thanks to him. But it exposed the deliberate refusal of the state government to deal with the law and order situation in the state on its own.

On 30 April 2002, I appealed to the Prime Minister to rise above his party affiliation and fulfil his responsibilities and obligations towards the people of India, irrespective of religion and faith. It was not too late and the situation could be redeemed. I asked him to show the way so that we would be able to once again hold our heads high and reassert our civilizational claim of celebrating unity in diversity. The Gujarat government should have been put on notice under Article 355 of the Constitution for having failed to control internal disturbance. It was essential to bring the guilty to book, restore law and order and ensure that relief and rehabilitation measures were extended to all affected families. I demanded the removal of the chief minister, appointment of a sitting Supreme Court judge to ascertain the truth within the next three months and implementation of all the recommendations of the National Human Rights Commission immediately.

Appendix 1 contains some extracts of my speeches made in the House on 11 March 2002 and 23 July 2002. They demonstrate the extent to which the shameful events unfolding in Gujarat exercised my mind.

The Prime Minister simply refused to devise a strategy to save the people of Gujarat. He waited for weeks to go there. When he did, he visited only one or two camps and made perfunctory noises about the chief minister's 'rajdharma'. Oddly enough, the Prime

Minister went on to give a certificate to Narendra Modi stating that he was in fact performing his rajdharma! I recalled Vajpayee had once said, 'It is no secret the Sangh is my soul.' At a meeting of overseas Indians in New York in September 2001, he had said, 'I may or may not be Prime Minister tomorrow, but no one can take away my right to be a swayamsevak.' His insensitive and non-statesman-like comments in the wake of the Gujarat riots revealed that he was more a leader of the Sangh than of India.

It has now been revealed by Jaswant Singh – who was unceremoniously and peremptorily expelled from the BJP in August 2009 – that on a flight on his way back from Gujarat, where he had visited some camps, the Prime Minister was extremely sad and wanted to take steps for the removal of Narendra Modi as the chief minister of Gujarat but because of the opposition of L.K. Advani, the then deputy prime minister, he could not take the decision. It was only partisan political interests that protected a chief minister from the consequences of his sins of commission and omission, a chief minister who was clearly guilty of total inaction, if not complicity, in the killing of innocent people of his state, just because they professed a different religion. The home minister's tacit support and the Prime Minister's inaction amounted to condoning the chief minister, whom the entire nation wanted to be punished. It also amounted to condoning the acts of inhuman torture, killing of innocent men, women and children and large-scale destruction of property. Surely the Prime Minister himself did not perform his rajdharma by compromising with his conscience at the instance of his deputy. His failure to take proper action against the erring chief minister shocked the whole nation.

As part of the determined endeavour to impose Hindutva on the country, a policy to saffronize the system of education was engineered by the BJP. This was extremely disturbing. Never before had such an attempt been made, striking at the country's ethos, its culture and tradition. I appealed to those in the NDA who had secular credentials to ponder how their support to the BJP was being exploited and how the future of the nation was being sold to the forces of divisiveness, darkness and backwardness.

Education was the most important vehicle for their ideological thrust. The clear intention was to use it as a tool of indoctrination. The human resources development minister, Murli Manohar Joshi, played a key role in this exercise. Ample resources of the government were utilized for the purpose. These were transferred from research and development to areas that suited the Sangh Parivar to perpetuate their hegemony. Astrology and Vedic mathematics were introduced in universities and in the national curriculum framework prepared by NCERT without requisite consultations. There were many other stark examples of the overzealousness to elbow out liberal ideas. Saffron supporters and sympathizers were appointed as heads of institutions of national and international repute. The representative of the RSS in the US was appointed as adviser in the Indian embassy in Washington to look after NRI interests!

In 2001, the sale of 51 per cent shares of a profit-making Bharat Aluminium Company Limited (BALCO) to a blacklisted company, M/s Sterlite Industries, caused a huge stir. While the disinvestment commission had recommended selling 40 per cent shares of BALCO, it was raised to 51 per cent without going back to the commission, and the blacklisted company now became the company's majority shareholder. Digvijay Singh, the chief minister of Madhya Pradesh, where the unit was located, had strong reservations about the sale. MPs were entitled to know how the sale was effected. But what could be expected of a government which instead of having a minister for investment had a minister for disinvestment?

For the government, the rationale for privatizing or not privatizing a PSU was not based on whether it was making a profit or not but whether it was in a strategic sector or in a non-strategic sector. If it was in the non-strategic sector, it was ripe for privatization. I had no idea what the criteria were for deciding a strategic sector. How could one say that the petrochemical sector was a non-strategic sector? I had protested against the disinvestment of profit-making PSUs like Hindustan Petroleum Corporation Limited (HPCL) and Bharat Petroleum Corporation Limited (BPCL). The decision to disinvest in PSUs like Air India and VSNL on the ground that they were non-strategic PSUs was shocking as these were among the navratnas, the nine jewel performers in the public sector! Centaur Hotel in Mumbai was transferred to a private party which, within six months, made a whopping profit of Rs 34 crore by a second round of sale. The disinvestment minister was perhaps the only salesman in the world who ran down the product he was going to sell, before he actually sold the product. I often asked the government to come clean on how much money from the amount realized from disinvestment was utilized for the social sector or for meeting the budgetary deficit or for the benefit of the workers. I did not get any satisfactory replies. There were also serious allegations about the methods adopted in valuation and in selection of bidders. It was incumbent on the government to disclose how many PSUs were restructured and what assistance was given to them out of the funds realized from disinvestment. But the government preferred silence. Even though the government talked about a 'safety net' for workers, VRS (voluntary retirement scheme) was the only policy that was thought of, and which was often used as a tool to coerce them to leave their organizations. I had reiterated that if some loss-making PSUs could not be revived because of obsolescence of technology and lack of demand for their products, it was better to redeploy the workers. I requested that case-by-case studies be made and workers and the state governments be taken into confidence before closing down PSUs if they could not be revived. This was not done.

During the NDA regime, one of the most serious acts of corruption and wrongdoing in which senior politicians, bureaucrats, army officials and middlemen in defence deals were involved was exposed by *Tehelka*, an Indian weekly, on 13 March 2001. The modus operandi of Operation Westend, as the sting operation was called, was to use a spy camera and record negotiations and deals entered into in respect of defence matters. During 2000 and 2001, two dedicated journalists, Aniruddha Bahal and Mathew Samuel, undertook an exercise in audiovisual investigative journalism to expose corruption in defence procurement. The videotapes released showed Bangaru Laxman, then president of the BJP, colluding with top army officials in shady defence deals. He was shown accepting cash and asking for further payment in US dollars. The then Samata Party president, Jaya Jaitley, was filmed discussing funds for facilitating defence deals. On 13 March 2001, tehelka.com released a forty-two-page transcript of the tapes on the internet, which was then telecast. After the tapes were made public, the defence minister, George Fernandes, resigned. Jaya Jaitley resigned from the presidentship of Samata Party and Bangaru Laxman was removed from the presidentship of the BJP. The army also set up a court of enquiry, which filed a report on 31 May 2001 recommending that action, ranging from court martial to suspension, be taken against officials found guilty.

There was a strong demand in the Parliament for appointment of a JPC to investigate the matter but the government ignored the demand and appointed an inquiry commission headed by Justice Venkataswami, a sitting judge of the Supreme Court. The terms of reference for the Venkataswami commission contained, inter alia, a clause which provided as follows: 'To inquire into all aspects relating to the making and publication of these allegation and any other matter which arises from or is concerned with or incidental to any act, omission or transaction referred to in sub-clauses (a) and (b) above.'

Thus, the terms of reference clearly exposed the government's intention to implicate those who made and published the reports. That is why the government had been so keen to avoid a JPC probe and had appointed a single-member commission. Such terms of reference had never been included in any inquiry ever before and A.G. Noorani, well-known constitutional expert and lawyer, commented in the *Hindustan Times* of 31 July 2002:

> Never in the half century of the Commission of Inquiry Act, 1952, had anybody been asked to probe into the credentials of those who had made the charges. The focus was on the message, never the messenger. If this move is allowed to pass muster, the press will be effectively muzzled. Any time it publishes an expose, the government will retaliate by setting up inquiries not only into the truth of the charges, but also into the motives, finances and sources of the Journal which published them.

The manner in which the Venkataswami commission discharged its duties is proved by the fact that tehelka.com was accused by the commission of fabricating allegations and carrying out a biased and motivated campaign at the behest of the political foes of the government and held that the government's lawyers were empowered to go into all aspects relating to the making and publication of the allegations. The commission demanded thousands of papers, travel expenses, etc. from *Tehelka*, which compelled *Tehelka* to engage a number of lawyers to defend itself and spend 30,000 man-hours on commission-related work. Consequently, the website and the journal ceased to function. The government not only targeted *Tehelka* through the commission but also opened different fronts to launch a fierce counterattack against *Tehelka*, which was accused of financial irregularities. It jailed many of its journalists and its chief financial supporter. The website closed down in 2003.

Justice Venkataswami tendered his resignation as chairman of the commission on 23 November 2002 and the government appointed Justice S.N. Phukan, a retired judge of the Supreme Court, as head of the single-member commission. The Phukan commission submitted its report during the fourteenth Lok Sabha (2004–09) and the UPA government placed it on the table of the House on 14 May 2005 with intimation that the government had rejected the report, which was stated to be incomplete since it had not addressed all the terms of reference and that any finding on any issue without investigating the main charge of corruption would necessarily be an incomplete one. The UPA government entrusted the inquiry to the CBI, which has registered several cases against, among others, Bangaru Laxman and many defence officials.

The Tehelka episode clearly showed to what extent the government could exercise its power and be vindictive in the face of serious allegations of corruption involving high functionaries, political as well as defence.

After the Tehelka episode came to light, George Fernandes (who was also the convenor of the NDA) resigned as defence minister and publicly announced that he would not assume office until he was exonerated by the commission. His principled stand was generally appreciated but during the pendency of the inquiry, before hardly any progress had been made, the Prime Minister brought Fernandes back again into his Cabinet as defence minister. Not only it was against Fernandes's announcement when he had taken up the attitude of injured innocence, the re-induction of the minister into the government during the pendency of the inquiry was to my mind a most condemnable act. The Opposition decided that the reappointment of Fernandes was grossly improper and unethical. It boycotted Fernandes in the House and whenever he made any statement or tried to answer any question, the entire Opposition walked out of the House to register a very dignified protest. I believe that the political morality of the ruling clique in India in those days had reached rock bottom.

The government was by now neck deep in scandals and the financial position of the country was indeed precarious. The Unit Trust of India's (UTI) decision on 2 July 2001 to suspend both sales and repurchases of US-64 units for a period of six months up to December 2001 – ostensibly to arrest redemptions and restructure the scheme – caused great anxiety among the people. It was odd that when the value of the unit went down, the finance minister, Yashwant Sinha, stated that the government could not be held responsible for a statutory corporation. I asked for his resignation for this blatant lack of accountability.

The government failed on many other fronts, too. And for a party that prided itself on its nationalist rhetoric, whose home minister modelled himself as an 'Iron Man' following in the footsteps of Sardar Patel, by far the most glaring failure lay in its inability to provide a sense of security to the common man. Terrorist strikes became a common feature and showed the government in a poor light. India had been a victim of terrorism for decades. But during the NDA regime terrorists seemed to be able to make daring strikes at will, which belied the BJP's claims of standing for a strong state.

The hijacking of IC-814 to Kandahar on 24 December 1999 brought to the fore the urgency of combating terrorism. The incident also marked a new low in the fight against terrorism as the government meekly surrendered and released three hardcore terrorists, who were safely escorted to Kandahar by none other than the country's foreign minister, Jaswant Singh, after a Cabinet meeting which L.K. Advani has repeatedly stated he kept himself away from. Of course, in the light of the damning revelations made by Jaswant Singh after his unceremonious ouster from the BJP in 2009, it now transpires that Advani might have been 'economical' with the truth! In any case it is inconceivable that the country's home minister will not be privy to a decision of such magnitude pertaining to internal security.

The killing of thirty-five persons by heavily armed militants on 21 March 2000 in Chittisingpora, Jammu and Kashmir, sent shockwaves across the country. The Prevention of Terrorism Ordinance, 2001(POTO), was promulgated on 24 October 2001 reportedly to meet the challenge posed by the upsurge of terrorist activities, intensification of cross-border terrorism and insurgency. Even the allies of the NDA were not consulted in the matter. Almost the entire Opposition, particularly the Left parties, strongly opposed the promulgation of an ordinance containing draconian provisions, which was to be used against political opponents.

Despite the ordinance, however, the government failed to prevent the daring terrorist attack on Parliament on 13 December 2001, the first time in the history of India that the Parliament was targeted by terrorists. It is a different matter that security forces valiantly repulsed the attack and eliminated five terrorists. When the dastardly incident happened, I was inside the House along with a large number of members. One shudders to think what would have happened if the terrorists were able to enter the chamber and start dictating terms, holding the members and the entire country hostage. Making a reference to the attack on 14 December 2001, the Speaker said, 'This is not an attack on Parliament only but on the very freedom of the country. The entire nation has stood as one against such attacks in the past and I am sure it will do so again.' A resolution was unanimously adopted condemning the cowardly attack.

I was appalled that no detailed information on the attack was forthcoming from the government. We had to rely primarily on media reports. As the Prime Minister and the home minister had often hinted at a possible attack on the Parliament, obviously, they had some information through intelligence sources. Shockingly, the attack was used only to berate the Opposition for not supporting POTA. No steps were taken to prevent the deadly terrorist attack. On 15 March 2002, I stated in the House that for such a serious lapse, both the Prime Minister and home minister owed an explanation to the country, but it never came.

There was actually no urgency in promulgating POTA. If the government had taken the Opposition into confidence, an acceptable law to deal with terrorism could have been decided upon after due deliberations. I asked the government to tell us how many terrorist groups were busted and how many terrorists were proceeded against under POTO. The ordinance had clearly failed to prevent incidents of terrorism and the record of prosecution under this law was dismally minimal. To me, therefore, there was thus no justification for POTA. Nobody could challenge our patriotism only because, on behalf of the Left, I expressed our opposition to POTO. I asked Vajpayee to point out if we had ever refused to support the government's stand on terrorism.

The Prevention of Terrorism Bill, 2002, was introduced in the Lok Sabha on 8 March 2002 to replace the ordinance. The bill defined acts of terrorism that were punishable and contained provisions for punishment for such terrorist acts. But its provisions were only meant to curb the activities of democratic forces and of opposition parties. The NDA, it seemed, could not govern except through the use of anti-people laws. Taking part in the debate on the bill in the House on 18 March 2002, I wanted to know from the government as to how many incidents were prevented by the use of POTO and in how many cases had prosecution taken place or had even been initiated. I also demanded that the government tell the House about the number of foreign terrorists as well as Indians who had been apprehended and prosecuted successfully. Of course, all those queries remained unanswered.

The bill was passed in the Lok Sabha on 18 March 2002. When the Rajya Sabha rejected the motion on 21 March 2002, the government called a joint sitting of both the Houses and ensured that the bill was passed on 26 March 2002. While participating in the debate during the joint sitting, I stated, inter alia, that:

> this joint sitting is being held ... because of the intransigence of this government in imposing on the democratic people of this country a most draconian piece of legislation ... people like us consider this as nothing but a declaration of war on the ordinary people. We know the real victims of this legislation, as has already been seen, will not be the die-hard terrorists because you are unable to catch hold of them; it will be used against your detractors, political detractors and particularly against the minorities, as we have already seen. The object of the bill was not to tackle terrorism but to carry out a virulent propaganda and to weaken the edifice of the Constitution and that was why it could not prevent a single terrorist act.

As I said in the House, I was apprehensive that the legislation would be used, as we were certain, against the detractors of the government, and particularly against minorities and not against terrorists. As it transpired, the Act failed to prevent terrorist attacks on innocent bus passengers and on the army camp at Kaluchak near Jammu on 14 May 2002 as well as the massacre in Kasimpura, Jammu, on 13 July 2002, and the attack on Amarnath pilgrims on 6 August 2002. Internal security had all but collapsed and the government's stated policy of 'zero tolerance' of terrorism stood exposed as a complete failure.

In another instance of the government's poor scorecard, the summit-level talks between India and Pakistan held at Agra on 15–16 July 2001 ended in failure in spite of genuine good wishes and longing for peace, tranquillity and good neighbourly relations between the peoples of India and Pakistan. Again, the government ignored the Opposition totally in the build-up to the talks. It was only five days before the summit that the government invited the opposition parties for a discussion on it. I knew it was only a formality. Anyway, I endorsed the proposed talks and said military rule in Pakistan should not be a reason for not talking to them. It was also unrealistic to say or assume that Pakistan would not take up the Kashmir issue and restrict itself to addressing important issues pertaining to economy, trade and cultural relations. Since both the countries were nuclear powers, it was all the more important to engage with each other and avoid any confrontation that might escalate to an all-out war.

The Prime Minister's suo motu statement in the House on the Agra summit on 24 July 2001 did not add anything to what was already known from media reports. It appeared that even an agenda was not fixed for the important summit, nor were details of the persons accompanying Pakistan's President known.

It was believed that because of the unpreparedness and the evident unprofessional manner in which the talks were conducted, the government failed to arrive at even a joint statement. Nothing was known about whether there was any agreement regarding the joint statement and the issues on which the two sides differed. President Pervez Musharraf left the country around midnight without even a handshake.

The situation in Iraq greatly agitated the Opposition. The US openly threatened war against Iraq in spite of the UN Security

Council resolution to the contrary. India should have reacted very strongly as Iraq had been one of our steadfast and closest friends and it was supplying us a huge quantity of oil, which was actually being eyed by the US. In a meeting of the leaders of political parties in March 2003, I suggested that a resolution be passed in the House condemning the US position. A majority of leaders supported my suggestion but it was not to the liking of the government. But as the Opposition put up a strong principled stand at the meeting called by the Prime Minister, he had no other option but to accept our demand, much to the discomfiture of his foreign minister. To our satisfaction, the House unanimously adopted a resolution on 8 April 2003 calling for the immediate cessation of hostilities and quick withdrawal of coalition forces from Iraq.

One of the infamous legislations, as my party and I described it, introduced during the NDA regime and which became a law, regrettably with the support of the major opposition party, namely, the Congress, was the Representation of the People (Amendment) Bill, 2003.

Our Constitution provides for a federal structure for our political set-up, with power – legislative and administrative – divided between the Centre and the states, and also a bicameral legislature, namely, the Lok Sabha, directly elected, and the Rajya Sabha, to which members are elected by different legislative assemblies. One of the essential qualifications of a candidate for election to the Rajya Sabha is ordinary residence in the state from which one seeks to get elected.

To get elected to the Rajya Sabha, a candidate often takes recourse to registering himself as a voter in a state other than to which he belongs. This is done by transferring his residence to the state from which he hopes to get elected. Obviously, this is aimed only at acquiring residential qualification to contest for a

Rajya Sabha seat. This procedure is resorted to by those for whom membership of the Rajya Sabha is believed to be essential. Barring the Left parties, almost all other parties, including the Congress and the BJP, indulge in this for obvious reasons.

Like the method of voting in all democratic elections, namely by secret ballot, the election to the Rajya Sabha, in which only MLAs can take part, was also by secret ballot. Leading parties like the Congress and the BJP found that in elections to the Rajya Sabha, some of their MLAs defied the whip and secretly voted against their party candidates for reasons other than political, often for candidates representing the corporate sector. Obviously, their votes had been purchased by some rich non-party candidate. The problem primarily lay with these parties which had in the first place selected undesirable candidates, who were totally untrustworthy and unfit for election as MLAs, for which the Constitution of India was not responsible.

With its infinite capacity for mischief, the NDA government, in close understanding with the Congress, brought forward a bill to amend the Representation of the People Act, 1951, to provide for a resident of any state to become a candidate for election to the Rajya Sabha from any other state, totally contrary to the requirement of being an ordinary resident to qualify as a candidate. Further, to deal with corrupt MLAs, the bill proposed to do away with secret voting and provided for open voting so that MLAs could not indulge in cross-voting.

In effect, to enable a handful of potential candidates to enter the Rajya Sabha, the bill sought to strike at the basic structure of a federal set-up and also at the well-established system of secret voting prevalent in all civilized democracies.

The Left parties strongly opposed this obnoxious and undemocratic measure but they could not prevent the pollution of our constitutional set-up because the major parties acted in concert with each other to pass the legislation to the eternal shame of our parliamentary institution.

On behalf of the party, I spoke against the bill when it came up for discussion in the Lok Sabha on 6 August 2003. My speech has been set out in Appendix I.

However, in what is undoubtedly a tragic development and signifies a bankruptcy of morality and ethics of our political formulations, important leaders of the Left parties have also entered Rajya Sabha taking advantage of this black law, which the parties had very strongly opposed on well-accepted principles of constitutional law and morality.

I always believed that to fight the anti-people policies and programmes of a virulently communal party like the BJP effectively, it was necessary that all secular parties pool their strength in meeting the challenges to the nation. The non-BJP parties had unfortunately not been able to work together either inside or outside the House and were deeply divided among themselves, which only helped the BJP-led government to carry on with their anti-people and fundamentalist programmes and activities. The Congress and the Samajwadi Party (SP), two major parties, were at loggerheads and their leaders were not even on speaking terms with each other. I felt that efforts should be made to bring them closer, so that anti-BJP forces would not fritter away their energies by fighting among themselves when united action was more important.

As the leader of the CPI(M), I felt that for effective coordination among the major secular parties, it would be worthwhile to make an attempt to bring them together, so that important issues concerning the nation could be discussed. With that objective, I invited the leaders of the Left as well as major secular parties, including the Congress and the SP, to attend a meeting on 21 November 2001 at my residence at 21 Ashoka Road, New Delhi.

I am happy that leaders of major parties responded favourably to my invitation. Among others, Jyoti Basu, Sonia Gandhi, Shivraj Patil, Mulayam Singh Yadav, Sharad Pawar, Chandra Shekhar and Deve Gowda attended the meeting. At the meeting, which was followed by dinner, discussions took place in a friendly atmosphere on the prevailing situation in the country and there was some unanimity of views on the importance of the secular parties working together on vital issues common to all. Although no final decision was taken, leaders of various parties at least sat together and held discussions on the challenges facing the nation. The ice was broken. I was happy that some progress was made.

Towards the later part of the NDA rule I had the satisfaction of being able to convince leaders of different parties in the Opposition to have floor coordination among themselves while raising matters in the Lok Sabha. So far, opposition groups had been engaged in trying to outdo each other in convincing the Chair of the importance of their respective issues, which only helped the ruling party as they conveniently ignored the multiple issues raised by various factions in the Opposition. As leader of the CPI(M), I discussed the matter with leaders of different parties and groups and suggested that during the session we should meet at least once a week and decide upon the matters to be raised for which all of us would give similar, if not identical, but separate notices to the Speaker. I was greatly encouraged with the favourable response to my suggestion. When I met Sonia Gandhi, the leader of Opposition, in her office in Parliament House, she enthusiastically welcomed the proposal and agreed to work together on matters on which all opposition parties would agree. She told me that she would send the deputy leader of the Congress legislature party to the meetings of the opposition parties and groups which would be held for the purpose. And this was done.

Having had such an encouraging response, which I believed was partly due to the discussions held at my residence on 21 November 2001, I called a preliminary meeting of all the leaders of the opposition parties and groups in the CPI(M) office in Parliament House, which was attended by leaders or representatives of all of them. At that meeting, it was decided that during the session of the Lok Sabha, the leaders or their representatives would meet at 9.30 a.m. every Tuesday in the CPI(M) office to decide on effective floor coordination and also to identify the important issues that would be raised in the House during the week. We all agreed that for each day, one most important issue would be raised for which all parties and groups would give notice to the Speaker, unless some party had some other extremely important matter to raise, for which it would give a separate notice. We would also decide which party would raise which issue on a given date, so that all parties had due opportunity.

This arrangement worked really well and all of us were encouraged with the result. I have no doubt that the ruling clique became considerably defensive because opposition parties had begun to work unitedly on vital issues. If a walkout had to be undertaken, we decided in the House itself among us and jointly took the decision. I was happy that in spite of many differences among the parties and groups in the House, there was a sincere desire to work together in a coordinated manner, which made the role of the Opposition more meaningful and effective, and the ruling party as well as the Chair had to take serious note of issues raised jointly.

This arrangement continued very successfully during the thirteenth Lok Sabha and I am obliged to the leaders of the various opposition parties for their willing cooperation, which strengthened the Opposition as a whole.

There was no dearth of issues to be raised in the thirteenth Lok Sabha. The NDA rule meant more miseries for the people because of the government's comprehensive failure on all fronts, its anti-people economic policies like senseless disinvestment, pervading corruption, escalating terrorist activities and because of its anti-minority and growing pro-Hindutva stand. Opposition parties realized the necessity of working together. I believe that such united action unnerved the government. And it was this that made them decide to bring the Lok Sabha election forward although they had a comfortable majority, so that Opposition unity did not materialize outside the House also.

I was convinced that the vast majority of our people who had to face the consequences of the misgovernance of the NDA government would not vote it back to power in spite of the BJP's aggressive 'India Shining' campaign. The results of the 2004 general election proved me right.

6

IN THE CHAIR

A ROLLER-COASTER RIDE

For the fourteenth Lok Sabha election held in 2004, the CPI(M) selected me as its candidate from Bolpur parliamentary constituency. I got 66.56 per cent of the votes polled and my majority over the Trinamool Congress candidate was 3,10,305. In fact, for the first time a party candidate from Bolpur got a majority of votes in all the booths in Santiniketan, the university town where Visva Bharati, the university founded by Rabindranath Tagore, is located. Interestingly, just before the election, a sustained campaign of vilification and misinformation was carried out against me by some vested interests involved with the real estate lobby and a few so-called intellectuals of Santiniketan and Kolkata on the ground that by allowing development of the area, and particularly some housing complexes in my capacity as chairman of Sriniketan Santiniketan Development Authority

(SSDA), I had gone against the ethos and the culture of Santiniketan and Visva Bharati. Some of my well-wishers felt greatly disturbed and were worried that I might fare miserably in Santiniketan. Understandably, I was very happy and felt vindicated when the election results clearly proved that the voters of Santiniketan had resoundingly rejected the motivated campaign against me.

The national verdict, however, was splintered. The Congress and its pre-poll allies – the UPA (United Progressive Alliance), comprising the Congress, the Rashtriya Janata Dal (RJD), the Nationalist Congress Party (NCP), the Lok Janshakti Party (LJP), the People's Democratic Party (of J&K), the Republican Party of India (RPI-Athawale), the DMK, the PMK and the JMM – got 221 seats. With outside support from the Left, the government was sworn in on 22 May 2004.

Though Sonia Gandhi was unanimously chosen by the UPA as its leader, she declined the prime ministership in an emotion-packed gathering of Congress MPs in the central hall. She suggested Dr Manmohan Singh's name as Prime Minister. A common minimum programme was adopted on 27 May 2004. The CPI(M), against my views expressed in the central committee, decided to extend outside support only, and agreed to take part in the UPA–Left coordination committee meetings. It was another inexplicable decision of the party, which has considerably weakened leftist politics and the Left parties. It demonstrated their lack of courage to take on and discharge responsibilities of governance.

Sometime in the latter half of May, H.S. Surjeet, general secretary of the CPI(M), informed me that a request had been made to the party by the Prime Minister and by the chairperson of the UPA that I should be the Speaker. I recalled that in the ninth Lok Sabha, when V.P. Singh was Prime Minister, Madhu Dandavate of the Janata Dal had suggested my name as Speaker. The party had refused to accept it. I told Surjeet that I had not given the matter any thought as it was wholly unexpected. It was for the party to take a suitable decision. The chief minister of West Bengal, Buddhadeb Bhattacharjee, telephoned me later and conveyed that the Politburo had discussed the matter at its meeting in Kolkata and agreed to my assuming the office of Speaker. I accepted the charge, conscious of what it entailed.

On 29 May 2004, I was nominated by the President as the pro tem Speaker of the House. The most senior member of the House, with the longest tenure is, by convention, appointed the pro tem Speaker. His or her main function is to preside over the first few days' proceedings, during which the members take their oath, until the election of the Speaker. The minister of parliamentary affairs, Ghulam Nabi Azad, accompanied me to Rashtrapati Bhavan on 2 June 2006 to make my affirmation as a member of the House. The Prime Minister also attended the ceremony.

Assumption of Office of Speaker: My Vision

My career as a parliamentarian reached its climax on the day I was elected the Speaker of the Lok Sabha, 4 June 2004. There were many firsts attached to the occasion. For the first time in the history of the Lok Sabha, eighteen nomination papers were filed in favour of one candidate. Leaders of all the parties had either nominated me or seconded my nomination. It was not merely an uncontested election, but a unanimous one. It was the first time a pro tem Speaker was elected as Speaker and also the first time that a member from a Left party occupied the office. The significance of the historic moment was not lost on me. I felt extremely humbled and wondered whether I really deserved the support that I received and hoped I would be able to rise to the occasion to discharge adequately my responsibility as the presiding officer of the most important elected body of our country, which is also the largest working democracy in the world.

On my election I was felicitated by the Prime Minister, Dr Manmohan Singh; the leader of the house, Pranab Mukherjee; the leader of the Opposition, L.K. Advani; the chairpersons of the UPA and NDA and leaders of other parties. The entire House assured me of full cooperation. My reply to the felicitations, reproduced in Appendix I, outlined my vision and raised many key issues that resonated throughout the tenure of the fourteenth Lok Sabha.

At the orientation programme for the newly elected members of the Lok Sabha organized by the Bureau of Parliamentary Studies and Training on 18 August 2004, I reiterated that being a representative of the people was not about powers and privileges. It was a very demanding and challenging job. A legislator was essentially a leader. What was important was to have a realistic role perception and work tirelessly to fulfil that acknowledged role. We should, at every step, ask ourselves whether our conduct befits the stature of this great institution and as trustees of the people. I advised my colleagues that they should make a distinction between a speech on the floor of the House and a political speech on a political platform. A speech in the House should be focused, supported by facts and figures, throw light on the issues being discussed and, most importantly, be guided by public interest. In the true democratic spirit, members should be good listeners, too. Democracy is a system of alternatives. This fact enjoins on us to display a high degree of tolerance. Every effort should be made to utilize the available opportunities in the House and its committees by making the best use of the Constitution and rules of business, which should be thoroughly understood. The greatness of Parliament lies not just in its majestic building, but is derived from and sustained by the quality of debates that take place inside it and the traditions of discipline and decorum that are set. Its greatness is determined by the progressive laws enacted, purposeful discussions held on critical issues and how they are perceived in moulding the future of the nation, without at any time ignoring the citizen, who is at the centre of our polity. I appealed to them again to respect the authority of the Chair without which it would be difficult to conduct the proceedings of the House in an orderly manner. I expressed the hope that the members would discharge their duties with dedication and commitment and conduct themselves in an exemplary manner.

That the fourteenth Lok Sabha turned out quite differently is the source of my greatest dissatisfaction and disappointment. In moments of agony, I described it as the worst phase of my political career. My valedictory speech on 26 February 2009 mirrors the highs and lows of a tumultuous phase in our parliamentary history and seeks an honest introspection on the future of democracy in our country.

A few weeks after I assumed the office of Speaker, I shifted from 21 Ashoka Road, where we had stayed for nearly twenty years, to 20 Akbar Road, the official residence of the Speaker. I initially wanted to continue to stay at 21 Ashoka Road but it was pointed out that 20 Akbar Road could not be allotted to an MP. But, with five bedrooms, it was too a large house for two persons. Fortunately for my wife and me, around that time my son-in-law, Sugata Bhattacharya, an engineer, who had been working with an Italian engineering concern at Chennai, and where he and his family were based for about five years, decided to take up a position offered to him by Larsen & Toubro in New Delhi. My elder daughter, Anuradha, and their daughters, Surya and Trisha, had to shift to Delhi. They proposed to stay at their apartment in Dwarka but my wife and I insisted that they stay with us. We could persuade them and happily for us they came to stay along with us. Surya, my elder granddaughter, took admission in the

School of Planning and Architecture in Delhi. Trisha rejoined Delhi Public School (DPS), Vasant Kunj.

The Speaker's house comprises not only a large building but also very spacious lawns that were frequently visited by a large number of peacocks. All of us used to eagerly wait for them. My son, Pratap, a busy barrister practising mainly in Kolkata, and his wife, Shakuntala, came to Delhi and stayed with us, as well as my younger daughter, Anushila, and her husband, Debi Prasad Basu, as and when they could spare time. Our grandsons, Shashwata and Saurabh, sons of Pratap, both extremely intelligent and now working in the USA, and our dearest granddaughter-in-law, Tarana (Shashwata's wife), would come and stay with us but very rarely. We also had a number of other visitors, some of whom were our close friends and relations, and my wife was very happy when we had welcome guests.

Presiding over a Fractious House and Its Fallout

Soon after I was elected Speaker, some senior school students called on me. I asked their spokesperson about which profession she wanted to take up later in life. What she said has haunted me since. 'Sir,' she said, 'anything but a politician!' I asked her the reason, as her response greatly shocked me. According to her, politicians were generally crooks and corrupt and they did not behave properly even when elected as MPs.

For my part, I was determined to work relentlessly to improve the image of Parliament and its members. I held the scales evenly for all sections of the House and did not discriminate among members on the basis of their political affiliations. As I had stated on assumption of office, I believed in the imperative of a strong Opposition in a legislative body for the effective functioning of the parliamentary system of governance. The primary duty of a watchful and alert Opposition was to highlight the deficiencies in the performance of the government. However, to be impactful the Opposition must be committed to the basic principles of parliamentary democracy, acknowledging the important role of the Parliament. The Opposition should not indulge in criticism for the sake of criticism but play a constructive role and be conscious that parliamentary democracy must be attuned to the most important task of strengthening the nation and sustaining the unity of the people and integrity of the country.

I had the conviction – with hindsight, rather misplaced – that having known most of the leaders of different parties over a long period, especially leaders of the opposition parties, I would not encounter major problems in managing the House. There were thirty-seven parties in the House, more than in any previous Lok Sabha, and if I may venture to say, none with as vociferous an Opposition as in the fourteenth.

Having been in the Opposition in the House since 1971 till the end of the thirteenth Lok Sabha, I was aware of the problems and difficulties faced by the Opposition, especially the smaller opposition parties. As the leader of the CPI(M) for nearly fifteen years, I had felt that the party did not get its due share of time and opportunity to raise important issues but neither I nor any member of the party ever raised doubts about the presiding officer or cast aspersions on him – as sadly happened to me.

Some of my predecessors, particularly the ones immediately preceding me, had on many occasions participated in meetings of the highest decision-making bodies of their respective political parties. I, as leader of the CPI(M), had not questioned this. Soon after my election, when the members of the central committee wanted to convey their greetings, I went to the A.K.G. Bhavan (the party headquarters in Delhi) to meet them and stayed there for not more than ten minutes. I was told later that some television channels had showed me entering the party office, without indicating how long I was there and for what purpose I had gone there. A press conference was held by a BJP leader within an hour of my visit and it was demanded that because of this 'impropriety' I should resign as Speaker. The leader of the Opposition, L.K. Advani, 'advised' me that I should not have gone to the party office. I found the double standards of the BJP patently hypocritical.

It was a matter of grave concern that over the years a feeling had arisen among parties that disturbing the proceedings in the House would be politically advantageous to them. The confrontational attitude of the parties towards each other exacerbated this unhealthy situation and greatly tarnished the image of the Parliament. The loud signal sent out was that the smooth running of Parliament was not critically important in the scheme of things. Disturbances and disruption of proceedings became the norm from the first session itself, and the media was awash with these negative reports.

I came to know that opposition parties had decided to boycott the meetings of different committees to protest against some decisions of the government. I was extremely upset because the committees would, in effect, be non-functional without the participation of the opposition members. Under the circumstances, I wrote a letter to L.K. Advani on 24 July 2004, which I quote verbatim as it gives an insight into how I treated the Opposition:

> Dear Advaniji,
>
> I am extremely grieved to learn that your party may not attend BAC (Business Advisory Committee) meetings and may not join the Standing Committees. This has come as a great shock to me. I earnestly beseech you to please reconsider your decision, if it has been taken...

As Speaker, I am only concerned with the functioning of the House. I am sure all issues for running the House can be resolved with a spirit of cooperation and goodwill. On my part, I am fully conscious that I cannot ever discharge my duties without your kind cooperation, which I most sincerely seek.

I am keen to constitute the committees without any delay. You are fully aware of the importance of the proper functioning of the Standing Committees and it is essential that the members of the Opposition should take active part during the deliberations and in the preparation of the important reports. In some of the committees, my friends from your party will preside and without them they cannot function.

I once again appeal to you to please see that the House and the committees function normally and as early as possible. On my part, I once again assure you my fullest consideration, as far as my authority extends.

With personal regards,
Yours sincerely,
Somnath Chatterjee

After a few days, the boycott was withdrawn. I was informed by Sushma Swaraj of the BJP that my letter had not come to Advani's notice earlier. Swaraj told me, and I was reassured to hear it, that had this been the case, the boycott would have been forthwith called off on the same day.

At a meeting convened by me on 23 November 2004, presided over by the chairman, Rajya Sabha, and attended by the Prime Minister, the leaders offered their cooperation for the smooth conduct of the proceedings of Parliament, which was very heartening. However, I was pained that these assurances did not find reflection in the actual business of the House. On 16 December 2004, I was constrained to observe from the Chair:

> Since my assumption of office, I have tried humbly to the best of my ability to discharge my onerous duties. I have been earnestly requesting the leaders of all the parties for their help in running the House and also seeking guidance from them. In spite of the assurances the House could not function yesterday after the Question Hour. I was accused of indulging in 'tanashahi'. The Chair does not have any prestige. It has become totally irrelevant. It is a matter of agony for me to occupy this chair, which I had never expected to do, far less solicited. If members are not happy I would have no regrets in leaving. I was happier facing the chair than occupying it. If the Parliament did not function, what is the future of parliamentary democracy in this country?

Nonetheless, I did not give up my efforts. In addition to the joint meeting with leaders in Parliament House, prior to each session, I invited the leaders of the main opposition parties, the leaders of the Congress, other parties in the NDA and the UPA separately, to my official residence for discussions on the major issues they wanted to raise and in what particular manner. Media reports called it my version of 'dinner diplomacy'. Much was made of the fare served and how it went down with different leaders, especially the fish prepared when Sonia Gandhi attended!

I would also meet the leaders at 10.30 every morning during the sessions in the Speaker's committee room. Mine was an open-door policy. Such concerted efforts for close coordination with parties for smooth running of the House had never been made in the past, if I may say so. Access to the Speaker too had not been as easy.

I, however, would not go beyond the remit provided in the Constitution for the Speaker. If I was expected to act as an arbiter between the government and the Opposition, and if the main opposition party wanted me to resolve its problems with the government, I was not ready to assume that unwarranted role.

On 5 May 2005, I observed from the chair that the 'Speaker's duty is to see that the House performs in accordance with the rules and procedures of business, so that the objectives for which the Lok Sabha has been constituted are fulfilled'. I pointed out that it would be 'an unwarranted exercise of power of the Speaker if he meddles into the political affairs or the political formulations of any party or group of parties, and seeks to intervene'.

Members of the Opposition had suggested that I should have written to the Prime Minister on the issue of what they termed 'the grievances of the Opposition against the government and the treasury benches'. I observed that 'it would have been an intrusion by the Speaker into an arena which should be left to the political parties to decide and resolve'. At the same time, I also made it clear that it was not my duty to go out of the way to support the government or to bail it out of difficult situations and that the ruling coalition should expect to remain in power so long as it continued to have the majority support in the House.

I would like to narrate an incident to underscore that I did not make empty promises to the Opposition about giving them suitable opportunities to enforce governmental accountability. On the eve of the fifth session, L.K. Advani indicated that he wanted to table an adjournment motion on the issue of infiltration from Bangladesh to Assam. I had no objection to allowing the discussion. He was pleasantly surprised because he did not think that I would concede to an adjournment motion so early in the fourteenth Lok Sabha. An adjournment motion is treated as a motion of censure against the government, almost like a motion of no-confidence, and is rarely admitted. If approved, the government is expected to resign.

When I informed the leaders of the Congress of my intention to admit the adjournment motion, they reacted with great surprise and concern. I explained that an adjournment motion would give an opportunity to the government to discuss an important issue fully. It was, after all, the duty of the government to establish that it had the support of the majority of the House. But the leader of the House and his senior colleagues, who obviously had their own reservations, did not seem to quite agree.

I admitted the notice for the adjournment motion on 26 July 2005. There was a thorough discussion with effective participation by all parties. The Opposition did not press for a vote after the debate and the motion was rejected by what is known as a 'voice-vote'. At the end of the day's proceedings, the Prime Minister, the leader of the House and the chairperson of the UPA conveyed to me that they had been wrong in their earlier reservations. They appreciated my view that the debate had, in fact, provided the government an opportunity to deal with a complex matter in depth and place its position to the people of the country.

In the same vein, I encouraged opposition members to give notices for calling attention motions, which permitted up to five members to raise a particular issue of importance on which the concerned minister was required to make a statement. Members giving the notice were allowed to seek clarifications on these statements. I knew from experience that such motions were extremely helpful for the members. I allowed 115 calling attention motions during my tenure, which is the highest to date in a single Lok Sabha tenure!

During the NDA regime a resolution had been passed that Question Hour would not be disrupted under any circumstances. Vajpayee, as Prime Minister, had severely criticized those who disturbed the Question Hour. This resolution, to my utter disappointment, was violated most brazenly during the fourteenth Lok Sabha. Notices for suspension of Question Hour were received with unwelcome frequency. Members would unreasonably insist that they would not wait even for an hour till the matters they wanted to raise were taken up in the House. This resulted in the loss of valuable opportunities to hold the government accountable – which was a great shame. Of course, as I often remarked, it was a bonus for the ministers not to be grilled by the Opposition! Behaving like 'super-Speakers' in the House and indulging in unbecoming conduct seemed to have become the order of the day. I was dismayed that members perhaps did not realize the consequence of this ill-advised trend.

The matter regarding corrective and disciplinary action against erring members, according to the rules, was often brought up by leaders of parties in the media and civil society. But when it actually came to enforcing the rules, I found that much of this enthusiasm evaporated. I knew it would be almost impossible to act without the support of the leaders. The mayhem one witnessed in many state assemblies was not what I would have liked replayed in Parliament. In the latter half of the budget session of 2008, a privilege notice was brought against thirty-two members for disturbing the House. However, an all-party meeting requested me not to take it up. I now realize that I should not have invested so much faith and trust in the promises of proper conduct, which were unfailingly trotted out to me by the leaders.

Out of 1738 hours and 45 minutes, the fourteenth Lok Sabha wasted 423 hours because of disruptions and adjournments due to disorderly scenes. This amounted to 24 per cent of the time of the House, which constituted an all-time alarming record. The cost to the public exchequer was unacceptable and justifiably drew a lot of trenchant criticism from all quarters. Harping on holding sittings of Parliament for at least 100 days in a year was meaningless if members could not conduct themselves in a befitting manner in the days that the House actually did sit.

I do not recall any occasion where I disallowed a discussion on an important matter that was admissible under the rules.

In fact, I repeatedly asked the leaders of opposition parties to indicate important matters that they would like to bring up. On the controversial land acquisition issue of Nandigram for setting up a chemical hub in West Bengal, which was a matter primarily relating to the state government, I permitted a discussion on 21 November 2007 because it had assumed national importance. I, in fact, advised the leaders on how the motion could be appropriately formulated to enable the discussion, by integrating the Government of India's policy pertaining to special economic zones (SEZ) in it.

I claim with confidence that I did not take any partisan decision though allegations, which were greatly exaggerated by the media, continued to be made. The first member I directed to cut short his speech was the leader of the CPI(M) in the Lok Sabha, Basudeb Acharia. The first walkout against my decision was staged by members of the CPI(M). There were other instances, too, where I took action against my comrades for violating rules. How much more impartial can a Speaker get?

I confess I have an unfortunate impression about the main opposition party, the BJP. It seemed to have a lurking suspicion about me and the manner in which I discharged my duties, notwithstanding that it proposed my name for election as Speaker. Over the years, as a member of the House and as the leader of the CPI(M), I had been very critical of the policies and programmes of the BJP and of the NDA governments, their crass exploitation of religion and their sectarian approach to governance, which may have led to some heartburn and bitterness. I also had the feeling that some of the parties and members belonging to the NDA were unable to reconcile themselves to the loss of power and were so upset that they expressed their disappointment by taking recourse to disruptions in the House. I once enquired of Atal Bihari Vajpayee whether he had ever thought of losing the election in

2004 and he categorically stated, 'Never, not at any point of time.' When L.K. Advani attended a breakfast meeting at my residence I asked him why his party had brought forward the Lok Sabha elections in 2004 by nearly a year when the NDA had a comfortable majority. He told me that his party had calculated it was the most favourable time as it had done well in the state assembly elections held only a few months before the general election. The future might be uncertain. These views of the two top leaders of the BJP clearly showed that the results of the fourteenth Lok Sabha election had been totally unexpected for them. And probably this shock had rendered them incapable of performing their duties as a responsible Opposition. They perhaps felt that disrupting the House was the most efficacious way of making their presence felt. It pains me to disclose that Vijay Kumar Malhotra, deputy leader of the BJP, would give a peremptory call on many mornings to 'inform' me that the House would not function on that day or that there would be no Question Hour. I was expected to take note and simply fall in line, which I found not only unacceptable but thoroughly distasteful. I must, however, record that many BJP members treated me with great respect. They expressed their regret individually for indulging in disruptions in the House, as directed by the party leaders.

There was media speculation of a no-trust motion being brought against me by the BJP in 2006 before the monsoon session. The session which commenced on 24 July 2006 could not function for three days because of continued disturbances. On 7 August 2006 the NDA decided to boycott the proceedings on the ground of leakage of the report of the Justice R.S. Pathak Enquiry Committee on the Volcker disclosures and also to protest against the forcible transaction of government business through din and noise. When I came to know of this, on 8 August 2006 I addressed a letter to Atal Bihari Vajpayee in his capacity as chairman of the NDA.

Dear Vajpayeeji,

I am extremely sorry to learn that my friends in the NDA have decided not to attend the House tomorrow and the meeting of the leaders, which I hold every day at 10.30 a.m.

I am firmly of the view that for parliamentary democracy to function, it is essential to have full participation by the Opposition in the proceedings of the House.

As the respected chairman of the National Democratic Alliance, may I earnestly request you for reconsideration of the decision taken by my friends and to join the proceedings of the House as before?

On 8 August 2006 when the opposition members had not attended the House, I made an appeal to them from the Chair to come and participate in the proceedings of the House, to which they were entitled and I observed that 'I consider that without the participation of the Opposition, parliamentary democracy cannot function adequately'. Again later in the course of the proceedings I made the following observations from the Chair, requesting the Opposition to reconsider their decision. In my observations, I said, 'If I had committed any mistake we can resolve the matter by discussion amongst friends.'

Yours sincerely,
Somnath Chatterjee

At the luncheon recess, I received a letter bearing the signature of Atal Bihari Vajpayee, containing very serious allegations. I was shocked. I have never experienced such an affront made with the intention of deliberately hurting the image and the sentiments of the Speaker and me personally. The letter stated:

Hon'ble Speaker,

Thanks for your letter dated 8 August 2006. I fully agree with you that for parliamentary democracy to function, it is essential to have full participation by the Opposition in the proceedings of the House.

During Parliament sessions, the BJP parliamentary party meets regularly on Tuesday. This morning I read out to my colleagues your letter. And what a flood of reactions it evoked! Everyone who spoke agreed that the Opposition's contribution to Parliament's proceedings was crucial. But there was unanimity also that a legislature's proceedings can be smooth and constructive only if the presiding officer is able to inspire as much confidence in the Opposition as he is able to do in the ruling parties. A stark reality is that this situation is totally absent in our House.

All sections of the National Democratic Alliance feel deeply disappointed at the manner in which the House is being presently run. I may add that confidence in one's fairness and objectivity has to be commanded; it cannot be demanded.

I regret, therefore, the decision taken by the NDA last evening stands.

With warm personal regards,
Yours sincerely
A.B. Vajpayee

The contents of the letter had been disclosed to the media even before it reached me, which was a grotesque act of unparliamentary behaviour.

When the House sat after the luncheon recess, Priya Ranjan Dasmunsi, the minister of parliamentary affairs, observed: 'It is the saddest day in the history of Indian parliamentary democracy when a leader of the stature of Mr Vajpayee makes unprecedented and highly objectionable comments on the institution of the

Speaker. Mr Vajpayee's insinuations and language were surprising and not expected of one of the seniormost parliamentarians otherwise known for his politeness and understanding of the parliamentary system.'

Former Prime Minister H.D. Deve Gowda said, 'Disrespect shown to the Speaker was not a healthy sign.' Many leaders of the UPA communicated their great resentment against the obnoxious charges made against me.

I felt that since the main opposition party did not have confidence in me, I should tender my resignation. However, my colleagues in the House strongly opposed my proposal and emphasized that I had not been elected only by the Opposition. Just because the BJP had indulged in a misdemeanour, I should not resign. It would amount to submitting to their most improper and illegal stand. I reconsidered the matter deeply and in deference to the views of the leaders, including those belonging to the smaller parties in the NDA, I withheld my resignation.

On 11 August 2006, Pranab Mukherjee raised the matter in the House and observed, 'The letter is more painful because it emanates from the pen of a person who has himself struggled to uphold the dignity of the House over several decades and is known for his commitment to parliamentary values. The Speaker is more of an institution rather than a person and any aspersion on the keystone of parliamentary democracy is an indictment upon all its constituents, who have faithfully served the people of India for five decades and more.'

Not surprisingly, L.K. Advani stated that the entire NDA strongly endorsed every word of Vajpayee's letter. He wondered how it could be construed as showing disrespect to the Chair.

Something very interesting happened after this. I had gone to my constituency over the weekend when I received a request from Vajpayee's office stating that he wanted to meet me at the earliest opportunity. I had expected to hear from him because there was a rumour that he had signed the letter with great reluctance and under pressure from some of the leaders of the BJP. I conveyed that I would be happy to meet Vajpayee at his place. However, he insisted on coming to my residence.

When Vajpayee met me at my residence, he was obviously under great mental strain. He told me that he had great respect for me: '*Aap ke liye hamare dil mein bahut izzat hai.*' He had not done anything of his own volition: '*Hamare mann se hamne kuch kiya nahi.*' What he said reinforced my great admiration for him. I was extremely grateful for his clarification. I urged him not to dwell on it any more as he had more than vindicated my position. When the media asked me about my reaction to the letter, I said I would not make any comment because of my regard for him. Needless to say, I have not absolved the leaders of the BJP, except the signatory to the letter Atal Bihari Vajpayee, for the entire episode.

It was highly regretful that a section of the BJP, which had once been in power and which was supposedly committed to parliamentary democracy, stooped down to the level of forcing a respected and senior member of their party to subscribe to something he did not believe in, with the sole object of denigrating the highest legislative office in the country, only to suit its partisan interests.

I recall the great solace I derived from the President's sentiments conveyed at the time that I had handled these developments with great sagacity. Quite a few comments were made in the media about how a senior leader like Vajpayee could denigrate the office of the Speaker of the Lok Sabha.

Dr L.M. Singhvi, the well-known jurist, a former member of the Lok Sabha and Rajya Sabha and high commissioner for India in the UK, in an article published in the *Tribune* on 11 August 2006, described the letter as unfortunate. He observed:

... [It was] so uncharacteristic of him. If the letter is genuine as it appears to be, it can only be explained by the personal compulsion of a leader who appears to have yielded to the strident voices in the NDA, in a moment of weakness ... Atalji's letter hurts not only the Speaker but all those who admire Atalji and regard him as a liberal democrat and Parliamentarian par excellence ... One wishes Atalji had introspected more impartially as a witness and an umpire. He should have guided the NDA courageously, candidly and persuasively as he alone could and still can.

His letter to the Speaker was a tragic departure from the standards of objectivity the country has come to expect of him as a statesman of exceptional stature. It was the unkindest cut of all for the Speaker, coming as it did from Atalji who allowed himself to lend his support to the parliamentary pandemonium and pressure, which appeared to be a partisan aberration. All that the Speaker was trying to do was to canalize the ire of the Opposition into informed debate. ... We expected the Bhishma Pitamah of our parliamentary Mahabharata to step forward and halt it all and give the House a clear sense of balance and direction ... Had he done so, the country's love and respect for him would have been greatly reinforced. ... What the whole nation saw was the angry flood of party-political anger and invective spelling a cacophony of conflicting voices with far too many Members of Parliament on their feet at the same time, and far too many members in the pits or the wells of the Houses, when it was the duty of one and all to give aid, support and comfort to the Chair in the thick of the unruly conduct of the deliberations of the Houses.

The House had elected the Speaker unanimously and should now ask the Speaker unanimously to stay in office, lest his resignation should raise an unprecedented and disastrous debate against our parliamentary system ...

The parliamentary system of India cannot afford to fall from its democratic grace at this critical juncture. Atalji owes it to parliamentary democracy in India and to his own distinguished

> parliamentary career, which has been a saga of a glorious innings, to take a new initiative to create a climate of mutual respect, reciprocity and reconciliation. Equally, the Speaker owes it to the system to desist from departing from the office in dismay, by means of a resignation, which would signify a tragic collapse of parliamentary culture and institutional ethos, and our sense of pride in the system.

Dr Singhvi was also very kind to write to me on 20 June 2006. He was gracious enough to state that 'I am strongly of the view that as Speaker of Lok Sabha, you have been an exceptional success despite systemic and functional failures attributable to real and substantive political pulls and pressure and the prevailing culture of our national, political and parliamentary discourse or shall I say, a certain lack of culture!'

Earlier, in an article published in the *Tribune* of 12 June 2006, Dr Singhvi had commented on the problems faced by the presiding officers of both the Houses and observed:

> Mr Chatterjee has done more than any other Speaker and in much worse circumstances. His successes are personal: the failures are systemic, cultural, psychological and partly political. No doubt the Speaker is not infallible but a tribute is due to his judicious objectivity, flexibility and sensitivity in his office. His advantage is that he is open, and he knows the rule book and the political barometer like the palm of his hand … No one should be surprised that the Speaker is an unhappy man in a high position because of declining standards in the Lok Sabha. Who in the country does not share the Speaker's unhappiness? Mr Somnath Chatterjee is, however, too much of a gentleman to blame the others, but it is ultimately for us, the people in civil society, to judge our representative institutions. The verdict of civil society is unreserved praise and encomium for the Speaker and the chairman of the Rajya Sabha … Civil society freely and sincerely recognizes

> and acclaims the magnificent role the two esteemed umpires in the two Houses, the Speaker and the chairman, has performed.

These observations gave me great comfort and I conveyed my sincere thanks to Dr Singhvi for giving his views so candidly and for upholding the true principles of parliamentary democracy in a forthright manner. And I treated the matter as closed.

I was also comforted by what the respected journalist and former member of the Rajya Sabha, Kuldip Nayar, wrote in the *Sunday Times* of 2 November 2008:

> When he steps down, an era of independent and sensitive people would have come to an end. There are not many left. But Chatterjee can go with the satisfaction that what he did to raise the standard of Parliament debates and its decisions changed the house from being the talking shop to a reflective and thinking institution.
>
> In the rumble and tumble of politics and in the atmosphere where the violation of rule of law is paraded as victory, Chatterjee's effort to raise the stature of parliamentary democracy has not been given its due. But the day will come when Parliament attains the respect and pre-eminence it should have in a system where people elect the representatives without fear and favour.
>
> The services of Speaker Somnath Chatterjee will then be recalled endlessly. At that time, even the CPI(M) may come around to take the credit that after all Chatterjee was its member.

Sadly, the House proceedings continued without any positive change. Adjournments within a few minutes of the House sitting, witnessed by visiting foreign delegations, embarrassed me acutely. The admonitions I handed down from the Chair at regular intervals are eloquent. They earned me the sobriquet of 'headmaster', which I did not mind as the position of a headmaster is an honourable one. A Norwegian delegation put a charitable gloss on the disruptions by terming it as an example of our democratic vibrancy! The Swedish Speaker, who was on a visit, expressed his hope that his members would not learn from my members! Since the admonitions were quoted extensively in the media and became part of public debate, I mention some of them here.

8 March 2007

- 'I can only say that more and more we are showing that we are not fit for democracy.'
- 'I know the Chair has no respect in this House. We have sufficiently decimated its authority.'

14 May 2007

- 'There seems to be no rule, no law and no procedure.'

15 May 2007

- 'People are looking at us. We are fighting for more money for ourselves.'
- 'I thought that people will say "No work No pay".'
- 'People will make their own assessments.'

13 August 2007

- 'Are you not ashamed of yourselves?'
- 'What are you doing? Is this the way Members of Parliament should behave?'
- 'You have no right to be here.'
- 'You are not listening even to the Prime Minister of the country.'

14 August 2007

- 'There is no glory in unruly behaviour.'
- 'This is not a place of tamasha!'
- 'The people are closely watching us and they will, no doubt, give their verdict at the appropriate time.'
- 'Now if any member wants to do whatever he or she likes, then there is neither the necessity of the Chair nor the list of business nor the rules.'

28 February 2008

- 'I am sorry I have to say that you are all working overtime to finish democracy in this country. It is a matter of great sorrow for me.'

11 March 2008

- 'Why do you make yourselves a subject of mockery by people?'

22 July 2008

- 'I think the Parliament of India is reaching its lowest position – Nadir!'

22 October 2008

- 'I can only say that you are behaving in the most despicable manner.'
- 'The whole country is ashamed of the parliamentarians.'

23 October 2008

- 'If I do not take strong action, then I am criticized. If I take one very mild action, that is also criticized.'
- 'I can tell you that this is the worst period of my life, if it has any relevance for this House.'

24 October 2008

- 'A new culture has developed to go on questioning the Speaker's ruling.'

19 February 2009

- 'I hope that all of you are defeated in the election.'
- 'You have to be taught a lesson.'
- 'This House of People should be adjourned sine die. People's money will be saved. Useless allowances should not be given to all of you. I think that is the best thing to do. You do not deserve one paisa out of public money.'
- 'You are insulting the people of this country.'
- 'I do not know how your voters are tolerating you for five years'.

I felt let down that important matters were not taken up for serious deliberation by the members purely for extraneous considerations. What suffered was Parliament's standing as an institution and the country's governance. This has had a long-term negative effect on our polity. While there was some outcry in the media about it, it was clearly not enough to get the members to mend their unacceptable ways. The 'right to recall', which I had been ceaselessly advocating for citizens, may have been a deterrent but it did not find adequate support. I also felt that disruptions were tantamount to a contempt of parliamentary democracy but who bothered to take it to heart?

Union budgets, involving huge sums, directly impacting the lives of citizens, were passed without discussion, including the general and railway budget for 2004–05 and the railway budgets for 2006–07 and 2007–08. This evoked an adverse reaction in the public and the media, but did not seem to affect the members. There were dark days like 13 August 2007, when even the Prime Minister was not allowed to speak – on the Indo-US nuclear deal – and he had to lay his speech on the table of the House. I considered it a matter of the greatest shame. Regrettably, this happened again on 22 July 2008, when the trust motion was debated. Many important bills met the same fate, and were simply rushed through, making a mockery of the House. However, I found that bills relating to salaries of members, judges and high constitutional offices were always dealt with promptly. A chart indicating the occasions when important business could not be conducted properly due to the deliberate disorders created in the House during the fourteenth Lok Sabha is set out in Appendix III.

Important initiatives like the National Rural Employment Guarantee Programme (NREGP) were not monitored by members, though the rural development minister made many requests in the House. The 'silence' of some members also irked me, as I felt that by not taking up issues they were not behaving responsibly towards the people they represented. I was also unhappy that young members were not as active as I had expected them to be, in spite of my encouragement to them to put across their views.

Members were not able to rise above their narrow political and partisan considerations to evolve a broad consensus on major issues of national importance. This would have gone a long way in tackling the problems that beset our country. The women's reservation bill seeking to provide reservation for women in the House of the People and the legislative assemblies of the states was introduced in the Rajya Sabha on 6 May 2008, amid the usual pandemonium, I believe, to ensure that it did not lapse. It is my abiding sorrow that the bill was not passed during my tenure. I had stated in many speeches outside the House that such a landmark bill, which had been on the anvil for almost a decade, should have been passed with unanimity, but that was not done.

If there was a calamity or disaster somewhere, parties would rather make political capital of it than cooperate with their opponents to control it. Factionalism, pettiness, identity politics and regionalism led us to a situation where a fractured polity teetered precariously on the brink and the loser was undoubtedly the citizen or the 'aam aadmi'. I say with a heavy heart that unless there is a sea change in the way members perceive their role and functioning, we will have to wait till eternity to fulfil the Mahatma's laudable dream of wiping the last tear from the eyes of all our countrymen.

I acknowledge that electoral reforms and deeper socio-political changes are also called for but I could not understand why members did not want to be the change leaders that the Constitution mandated them to be. Apparently, members were not concerned with the seriously detrimental effect of their disruptive and irresponsible behaviour on the functioning of our democratic structure, which had given rise to acute cynicism and feeling of abhorrence toward politics in the minds of the people, especially the youth.

I had a distinct feeling sometimes that perhaps I was not suited for the job of the Speaker. If some members did not allow the House to function properly, the responsibility was made to rest on the shoulders of the Speaker and he was targeted as having failed to ensure smooth running of the House. This was rather unfair and the easy option would have been to quit, which I was tempted to do more than once. But in view of my commitment to Parliament and the duty which was given to me by the entire House, and also the support from the majority of the members for my efforts, I did not turn my back on my responsibility. I was very conscious that my sense of judgement should not be affected by undesirable activities of some members or their parties and that my efforts should continue with utmost sincerity and determination.

Observance of the 'Lakshman Rekha' by Different Constitutional Bodies and the Fourth Estate

Parliamentary democracy is grounded on the clear delineation of powers and functions of the different organs of the state – the executive, legislative and judiciary. Parliament is the supreme law-making body which has exclusive powers to regulate its own proceedings and discipline its members. As the custodian of parliamentary rights and privileges, it fell on me to defend and safeguard them in the House and in legislatures across the country.

The Judiciary

The Jharkhand state assembly election held in February 2005 threw up a hung House. On 2 March 2005, the leader of the Jharkhand Mukti Morcha, Shibu Soren, was sworn in as chief minister by the governor and given time till 21 March 2005 to prove his majority in the House.

Protesting against the governor's decision, the BJP-led NDA organized a day-long bandh on 3 March 2005. They met the President, requesting him to recall the governor of Jharkhand. The president summoned the governor for a discussion on 4 March 2005. On his return to Ranchi, the governor advanced the date for the vote of confidence to 15 March 2005.

On 7 March 2005, the former chief minister of Jharkhand, Arjun Munda, challenged the governor's decision to appoint Shibu Soren as the chief minister in the Supreme Court, stating that his appointment was 'unconstitutional' and 'without authority of law'. On 9 March 2005, the Supreme Court issued an interim order bringing forward the crucial floor test in Jharkhand from 15 March 2005 to 11 March 2005. In its interim order, the Supreme Court issued these directions:

(i) That the session of the Jharkhand state assembly convened for 10 March 2005 be directed to continue on 11 March 2005 and on that day the vote of confidence be put to test and that the order of the court would constitute a notice of the meeting of the assembly for 11 March 2005 and no separate notice would be required;
(ii) That the only agenda in the assembly on 11 March 2005 would be to have a floor test between the contending political alliances;
(iii) That the proceedings of the assembly shall be conducted totally peacefully and any disturbance caused would be viewed seriously by the court;
(iv) That the result of the floor test would be announced by the pro tem Speaker, faithfully and truthfully; and
(v) That the chief secretary and the director-general of police, Jharkhand, would see that all the elected members of the legislative assembly freely, safely and securely attend the

> assembly and no interference and hindrance is caused by anyone therein.

The Supreme Court also restrained the Soren government from nominating a member of the Anglo-Indian community to the House ahead of the floor test, while ordering videography of the proceedings of the floor test to guard against foul play.

The order of the Supreme Court was contrary to the provisions of the Constitution of India. On 10 March 2005 I discussed the matter with leaders of parties of both the Houses. A majority expressed their grave concern over the order and its implications. I issued a statement for the information of the people of the country after my discussions:

> With all respect to the Hon. Supreme Court and without at all going into the political merits of the issue, to my mind, the order of the Hon. Supreme Court has created a disturbing situation. Separation of powers of the different constitutional organs is a basic feature of our Constitution, giving sustenance to parliamentary democracy. The judiciary is supreme in its own sphere and as such the conduct of the judges is not permitted to be discussed in any legislature. But bona fide views can always be expressed on any order or judgment of even the Hon. Supreme Court. So far as the legislatures are concerned, Articles 122 and 212 of the Constitution are two of the most important provisions, which symbolize the supremacy of the legislatures within their own sphere. The Articles provide that no officer or Member of Parliament, who is vested with the power of regulating the procedure or conduct of the business in the House or in the matter of maintenance of order in the House, shall be subject to the jurisdiction of any court in respect of the exercise by him of those powers.
>
> Today, unfortunately, because of the interim order of the Hon'ble Supreme Court, the contours of the area of supremacy

> of the different organs, specially of the legislature (apart from that of the executive authority under Article 361, which provides for complete immunity to the President and the Governor from being answerable to any court in the matter of discharge of their duties) have got blurred which, if not pondered over and corrective steps taken, will totally upset the fine constitutional balance and the democratic functioning of the state as a whole. The legislatures should seriously consider the consequences of, what may be termed as, encroachment upon their authority and jurisdiction. It is necessary that the legislatures' supremacy as enshrined in the Constitution should be clearly asserted. This is a matter which should be looked into transcending all political formations and topical developments. As such, I appeal to all to consider the important issue with all seriousness and concern, so that the constitutional balance can be and is restored. In my opinion, as has been suggested by many leaders, to resolve all questions, the President may be requested to seek the opinion of the Hon. Supreme Court under Article 143 of the Constitution.

The government did not agree to make a reference to the Supreme Court, probably because it did not wish to take a stand which the judiciary would not appreciate.

When I was asked by the media about the government's decision not to make the reference, I responded that I didn't 'care' for the government as I had already expressed my views clearly and stood firmly by them. Probably my strong reaction somewhat upset the Prime Minister. I received a call from him that evening and the next day he met me at my official residence along with the leader of the House and the minister for parliamentary affairs, to explain the government's stand. Of course, I did not change my opinion.

Since the principles at stake were very important, I also thought it fit to call an emergency meeting of the All-India Conference of Presiding Officers. At the conference, I stated:

Legislature is the sole guardian and judge in all matters relating to its proceedings and privileges. Subject to the provisions of the Constitution, in its procedure and conduct of business, each House of the Parliament and that of the state legislatures is empowered to regulate its own procedure and the conduct of its business under Articles 118 and 208, respectively. It is an inherent and exclusive authority and the courts have no power to interfere with such rules or their administration, unless there is a contravention of the provisions of the Constitution. It has specifically been provided under Articles 122 and 212 that the validity of any proceedings in Parliament or state legislatures shall not be called in question on the ground of any alleged irregularity of procedure. Further, it is specifically provided that no officer or Member of Parliament/state legislature in whom powers are vested by the Constitution for regulating procedure or conduct of business, or for maintaining order, shall be subject to the jurisdiction of any court in respect of the exercise of those powers. Moreover, Articles 105 and 194 of the Constitution guarantee immunity from proceedings in any court in respect of anything said or any vote given in the House of the Parliament, legislature or any committee thereof.

In the interim order of 9 March 2005 of the Supreme Court, the contours of the area of the supremacy of the legislature have been blurred. The points of reservations are, in fact, in regard to some basic thrust of the Supreme Court order which has resulted in the judiciary entering into the well-defined areas of jurisdiction within the purview of the legislature. The major issues before us now that are of grave concern and need serious consideration and resolution are whether the court has any right to issue directions, as has been done in the present case, for advancing the session of the legislature for a vote of confidence, fixing its one-point agenda to have a floor test, directing the pro tem Speaker to announce the results faithfully and truthfully, making out that the court's order was to be construed as constituting a notice to the members regarding the meeting of the assembly, directing the chief secretary and the director-general of police to see that all the elected members of the assembly freely, safely and securely attend the session and no interference or hindrance is caused by anyone therein, and ordering the video-recording of the proceedings with a direction to send a copy of the same to the court etc.

One may raise the question about what could be the possible implementation of the interim order of the Hon. Supreme Court passed on 9 March 2005. One would like to know if the Court had considered that if there was a violation of the order, would the Speaker or the members of the legislature be held guilty of the contempt of the Supreme Court? Would the judiciary have been able to deal with such a situation? Whether the Speaker could be summoned before the Supreme Court for having exercised his authority under the Constitution of India? Would the Speaker be liable to submit to the jurisdiction of the Supreme Court? How would the members of legislature be treated for alleged contempt of the court? Would the Supreme Court have directed the arrest and detention of the Speaker and members of the Jharkhand legislature? As clearly there was disturbance, was it the violation of the order of the Supreme Court on the part of the members of the legislature against whom no order was issued? Can a Speaker of any legislature be held answerable for not being able to transact the proceedings of the House, if members of the legislature indulge in indiscipline only with a view to disturb the proceedings? The presiding officers of the legislatures have their problems in controlling the proceedings and then to be directed by the court of law to discharge its functions in a given manner would create wholly unworkable and unacceptable situations. How could the executive authorities like the chief secretary of the state government or police officials be able to maintain the order, arrange for the presence of the legislators and for their coming inside the House? In effect, if allowed, they would substitute the presiding officers in the matter of maintenance of discipline.

My appeal to all is to consider this matter dispassionately only

> on the basis of the country's constitutional set-up, without any reference whatsoever to any political controversy, so that one of the most important basic features of our Constitution, namely, separation of powers is not disturbed, seriously affecting the balance of powers as enshrined in the Constitution.

The conference accordingly passed this resolution:

That there must exist mutual trust and respect between the legislature and the judiciary and also an understanding that they are not acting at cross-purposes but striving together to achieve the same goal, that is to serve the common man of this country and to make this country strong;

That the judiciary commands and justly deserves all the respect and dignity it enjoys;

That the legislatures also, as the supreme legislative and representative bodies which give voice to the hopes and aspirations of the teeming millions of this country, deserve the same degree of respect and dignity;

That the success of democratic governance would be greatly facilitated if these two important institutions respect each other's role in the national endeavour and do not transgress into areas not assigned to them by the Constitution; and

That it is imperative to maintain harmonious relations between the legislatures and the judiciary.

The Speaker of the Jharkhand Legislative Assembly, Inder Singh Namdhari, said that I was true to my name, the 'Nilkantha', because I had swallowed all the poison and saved the prestige and dignity of the Speakers of the assemblies and upheld the highest principles of parliamentary democracy.

Unfortunately, some leaders of the BJP thought it fit to question my bona fides in raising the issue of the Supreme Court's jurisdiction in intervening in the matter relating to Jharkhand, alleging that I was only seeking to prevent the NDA from coming to power in the state. In their anxiety to install their government, some political leaders did not mind compromising the position of the legislatures, which the Constitution had assigned to them, without realizing that their government in some states could later become victims because of this inappropriate stand.

I had raised the issue only because of its great constitutional importance. There was no question of any reference to a political controversy, but the BJP with its narrow political considerations deliberately brought the office of the Speaker into the vortex of a political controversy and confrontation. The emergency meeting of the presiding officers was boycotted by Speakers who belonged to one or the other parties in the NDA. As a matter of fact, one Speaker had already started for the meeting when he was called back by his chief minister! When the media referred to 'NDA Speakers' not attending, my comment was that I did not know any 'NDA Speaker', I only knew Speakers!

Here was a glaring example of Speakers of assemblies being directed by the parties to which they belonged, regarding the discharge of their duties and functions as Speakers. Such an attitude must change and parties must behave with a sense of responsibility, conceding full freedom to the presiding officers. Otherwise, the spirit of the Constitution and the glory of the Speaker's office will be greatly undermined.

Little did I know in 2005 that I myself would be called upon to take a principled stand against the 'diktat' of my party in 2008. More on that later.

I will move to another instance where I took a principled position vis-à-vis the judiciary. Writ petitions were filed in the Delhi High Court and the Supreme Court by ten MPs who had been expelled in January 2006 by a unanimous resolution of the House following their involvement in the 'cash for query' scam. Advance copies of writ petitions filed in the High Court of Delhi, challenging the expulsion, were served upon the standing counsel of the Lok Sabha secretariat.

In my view, the expulsion had been decided upon by the House and could not be a matter of judicial scrutiny or intervention. I, therefore, directed the secretary general of the Lok Sabha to return the copies of the writ petitions to the standing counsel of the Lok Sabha secretariat and not to appear in the court. When the matter came up before the Delhi High Court on 9 January 2006, the court directed that notices be issued to the parties, including the Speaker and secretary general. I again advised the Lok Sabha secretariat not to accept any notice of the High Court.

In the writ petition filed in the Supreme Court by Raja Ram Pal on 16 January 2006, a three-judge bench referred the issue of whether the Parliament had the power to expel its members to a five-judge Constitution bench and directed that notices be issued to the Speaker, the Union Government of India and the Election Commission of India for their views.

I convened a meeting of the leaders of political parties on 20 January 2006. Two eminent lawyers, Fali S. Nariman and T.R. Andhyarujina, attended the meeting at my invitation. The leaders and senior lawyers unanimously endorsed the position I had taken not to accept or respond to the notices issued by the High Court and the Supreme Court or to enter appearance in the court. Prof. Vijay Kumar Malhotra, however, was of the view that this position should be communicated to the court through a lawyer, which was not agreed to by the leaders of other parties.

On 4 February 2006 I called an emergency conference of the presiding officers of legislative bodies in India, as in the Jharkhand case of 2005. I reaffirmed that the legislatures were supreme in the matters of their privileges and procedures. As the custodian of the powers, privileges and immunities of the Lok Sabha, its Speaker, I could not be a party to make its members a subject matter of judicial scrutiny, contrary to constitutional provisions.

I had the privilege of discussing the matter of the issue of notice by the courts to the Speaker and the Lok Sabha secretariat with some of the most eminent lawyers of the country, including Fali S. Nariman, T.R. Andhyarujina, Shanti Bhushan, Justice Rajinder Sachar, Rajeev Dhawan and Kapil Sibal. Their considered opinion has been that I should not appear before any court of law even if any notice is issued. Dr L.M. Singhvi, another distinguished lawyer, has also stated that the Speaker was well within his right not to reply to the Supreme Court notice and that the courts could not intervene directly or indirectly in Parliament matters. Another eminent constitutional lawyer, P.P. Rao, has stated that each House has exclusive jurisdiction over its own internal proceedings and has the right to commit and punish members for contempt and that courts do not interfere with the decision of the House concerning its recognized privileges, which include the right to expel members.

In my considered view, as the holder of the highest legislative office of the country, there can be no authority, other than the Parliament itself to look into the conduct of the members in the discharge of their duties and in the conduct of the business of the House. Therefore, no court can go into this question. Order of expulsion is one of the powers which the Parliament can surely exercise on any erring member.

The following resolution, moved by Inder Singh Namdhari, Speaker, Jharkhand Vidhan Sabha, and seconded by Mata Prasad Pandey, Speaker, Uttar Pradesh Vidhan Sabha, was unanimously adopted:

The presiding officers of legislative bodies in India, having assembled in their emergency conference in New Delhi on 4 February 2006 and having deliberated on the issues arising out of and related to proceedings initiated in courts of law challenging the expulsion of members of Parliament, unanimously endorse

> the decision taken by the chairman, Rajya Sabha, and the Speaker, Lok Sabha, not to accept or respond to the notices issued by courts of law in the matter of expulsion of the members of the two Houses.

The matters pending before the Delhi High Court were later transferred to the Supreme Court and after hearing them, the court rejected the writ petitions, holding that the Parliament had the authority to decide on the matter and there was no infirmity in the decision taken to expel the members.

This resolved an issue that had attracted great public attention and much uninformed comment about a confrontation, which I, as the Speaker, had supposedly created between the two important constitutional organs. I must highlight, however, that there are certain observations in the judgment which might, in future, if not properly explained by the court, result in conflict between the judiciary and the Parliament. I sincerely hope that no such occasion will ever arise.

On several other occasions I underscored the importance of not upsetting the delicate constitutional balance between the Parliament and the judiciary. A debate was also held in the House on the matter though the related, complex issues were not flagged as sharply as they deserved to be. To my satisfaction, however, the perils of excessive and misconceived 'judicial activism', which had so far been spoken of only in hushed tones, and which to my mind contravened the spirit of the Constitution, came to be critically analysed in the media, by academics and by civil society, following up on my assertions. I received many congratulatory messages for taking the lead, as somehow the erroneous impression had gained ground that the judiciary was the only 'saviour' of the country and that the other organs had proved to be dismal failures. Even the judiciary started introspecting and I must compliment it for this. In the second Nani Palkhivala Memorial Lecture, organized by the Bar Association of India on 12 May 2005, on the 'Scheme of Separation of Powers and Checks and Balances in the Constitution', the ninth G.V. Mavalankar Memorial Lecture, organized by the Institute of Constitutional and Parliamentary Studies on 24 August 2006, on 'Judiciary and Legislature under the Constitution' and the Dr K.N. Katju Memorial Lecture, organized by the Dr K.N. Katju Memorial Trust on 26 April 2007, on 'Separation of Powers and Judicial Activism in India', among many others, I elaborated the reasons for my position on this sensitive subject. Copies of the lectures, I reckon, are available and their contents may advance the current public debate further.

The Election Commission

The Election Commission too tended to overstep its jurisdiction more than once. In 2005, it externed some members from their constituencies during the Bihar assembly elections on the ground that their presence might lead to law and order problems. I denounced this from the Chair when members from the state protested against it.

What happened in 2006 was unprecedented.

While pretending to express their commitment to parliamentary democracy, some political parties appeared intent on destroying the image of the Parliament and the office of the Speaker, as they believed it would benefit them politically to destabilize the polity.

One such contemptible effort was made through a petition faxed on 8 March 2006 to the President by Mukul Roy, general secretary of the Trinamool Congress (TMC), and now a minister of state at the Centre. It was alleged that ten MPs were holding offices of profit, and sought immediate action to check this violation of constitutional provisions. The first name in the list was mine, describing me as chairman of the Sriniketan Santiniketan Development Authority (SSDA), and president of the Asiatic Society, Kolkata.

Article 102(1) of the Constitution of India provides that a person shall be disqualified from being elected and from being a member of either House of Parliament if he holds any office of profit under the Government of India or the government of any state, other than an office declared by Parliament by law not to disqualify its holder. According to Article 103(1), if any question arises as to whether a member of either House of Parliament has become subject to any of the disqualifications mentioned in Article 102(1), the question shall be referred for the decision of the President, which shall be final. Before giving any decision on any such question, the President shall obtain the opinion of the Election Commission and shall act according to such opinion.

From the copy of that letter which was obtained from the Election Commission through a Right to Information (RTI) petition, it appeared that not a single relevant piece of information had been given in support of the contentions against me. It was neither signed, nor was the original available, nor was it verified for correctness, as required by law. According to me, it could not be treated as a 'petition' as accepted in legal circles. Incidentally, no copy was sent to me or served on me either by the President's office or by the Election Commission.

The Asiatic Society, Kolkata, is one of the most eminent institutions of research in India and enjoys a high standing among scholars. I would have been extremely proud had I been its president. I have been only an ordinary member since my student days. Yet, it was incorrectly mentioned in the petition that I was the president of the society.

Unfortunately, on 22 March 2006, the secretary to the President sent the petition to the chief election commissioner for advice, without checking its veracity and without having received the original 'petition'. I was greatly dismayed that the President's office, before making the reference, did not consider whether any bona fide question arose within the meaning of Article 103. I believe this was like functioning in the mode of a mere post office. I do not accept that every 'petition' to the President calls for his/her intervention.

The real objective with which the proceeding was initiated by the TMC was thus unwittingly fulfilled by the action taken by the office of the President. The media gave wide publicity to the matter and made imputations against me even before an opinion was tendered by the Election Commission. Significantly, although the Election Commission did not give me any notice, it put my name on its website, without there being any justification, giving an impression that my continuance as Speaker had been challenged. The Election Commission displayed a grave sense of irresponsibility and arrogated to itself power and authority which it did not possess and totally mishandled the case. It was extraordinary that the Election Commission assumed the role of the investigator, prosecutor as well as the judge. It probably did not realize the great disservice it had done to the institution of Parliament by bringing the presiding officer under a cloud when there was not an iota of evidence against him.

On 24 March 2006, the Election Commission sent a notice to Mukul Roy giving him three weeks to furnish documentary evidence or materials to substantiate his allegations, as he had not done so while filing the petition. On 15 April 2006, Mukul Roy forwarded my bio-data, which did not disclose any details about facilities or monetary benefits allegedly received by me. Curiously, the Election Commission, instead of rejecting the complaint suo motu, gave Mukul Roy time till 24 May 2006 to provide evidence, on the ground that the complainant had been unable to make out a case for conducting any enquiry. Its overzealousness was again in evidence when on 16 June 2006 it asked the chief secretary, Government of West Bengal, to furnish information about my appointment to the SSDA, details of the organization, the terms and conditions of appointment, etc. within 3 July 2006. The state government submitted the opinion of its advocate general that it was not bound to do so. This was rejected by the Election Commission.

Due to the persistent uninformed comments and insinuations emanating from different quarters, I felt it necessary to state my position before the people. I called a press conference to state that I was not the president of the Asiatic Society, Kolkata. I also categorically asserted that the office of the chairman of the SSDA, which I had been holding since 1989, was not an office of profit and that, in any event, it was not an office *under* the government and the law in this regard was well settled by the Supreme Court. On mere baseless insinuations and reckless tantrums of disgruntled persons, I would not resign from Parliament.

When the matter was raised in the House, I did not preside over the proceedings as a matter of propriety. The Government of India brought amendments to the Removal of Disqualification Act under Article 102(1)(a) of the Constitution of India to exempt, inter alia, the holder of the office of the chairman of the SSDA from disqualification. I was most reluctant to consent to the inclusion of this office within the ambit of the amending law but I received counsel from leaders of different parties, senior media persons and lawyers that the game plan to force me to resign would be pre-empted only by the proposed amendment.

More controversy arose as the President returned the bill passed by Parliament for reconsideration under Article 111 of the Constitution. Parliament insisted that the bill should be approved as passed. The validity of the amending act has been upheld by the Supreme Court by a judgment delivered on 24 August 2009.

I hope a similar undignified drama will not be enacted in future. In this connection, I formed a joint parliamentary committee to look into all aspects of the matter. Towards the end of the fourteenth Lok Sabha, a report was submitted. Political parties, however, scarcely took notice of the report as it did not suit their objectives any longer.

The Fourth Estate

I have the highest respect for the media and its important role in upholding parliamentary democracy. I have had many close interactions, formal and informal, with the media. The press advisory committee of Parliament has advised me on several issues of national importance. For the first time during the fourteenth Lok Sabha, the Bureau of Parliamentary Studies and Training organized orientation programmes and seminars for media persons accredited to cover Parliament. Many media personalities were on a panel of experts which I had constituted. They participated in programmes of the Lok Sabha Television (LSTV) regularly. I always made it a point to be open with the media as I know that without its support the future of democracy can only be bleak. My constant refrain from different platforms was that the media should not focus only on the negative aspects of Parliament's functioning. It should work constructively to create a healthy respect in the citizens' minds for democratic Institutions. However, I am sorry that the media did not always live up to my expectations. Disturbances and disruptions of parliamentary proceedings almost always received front-page coverage and continued to be flashed as 'Breaking News' by TV channels, which only encouraged the mischief mongers among the MPs. Vijay Kumar Malhotra admitted as much to me. I believe this was primarily because of compulsions of competitive journalism.

When it came to serious debates that were of national importance, like global warming, the Indo-US nuclear deal, farmers' suicides, price rise, internal security or landmark legislations like NREGA, RTI, child rights commission, affirmative action for backward and tribal communities, hardly any media space was provided. This was a far cry from the situation immediately after Independence, when they were given pride of place. I had a study conducted by the Lok Sabha secretariat and was shocked to find that newspapers with more accredited correspondents in Parliament devoted proportionately less space to the proceedings of the House.

My ruling of 18 August 2005 in the privilege notice by Ramji Lal Suman against Swapan Dasgupta of the *Pioneer* for his article, 'Speaker asks for Trouble', under Rule 222 of the rules of procedure and conduct of business amplifies my views and should provide food for thought to the media, not only about what it highlights, but the manner in which it does so. I observed:

> In the impugned article, it has been alleged, amongst others, that the present Speaker of the Lok Sabha has extra-territorial loyalty, that he is a committed Speaker, that he is partisan and that he has no sense of prestige, that he is high-handed in his behaviour and has no sense of fair play.
>
> According to me, the position in law is beyond any doubt and to anyone concerned with the parliamentary system, it is clear that the impugned article not only reeks of malice but is highly contumacious in its conception and in its contents as it deliberately accuses the Speaker of partiality and reflects on his character and actions as Speaker, which amounts to gross breach of privilege of the Speaker and also of the House.
>
> It has been contended by some members on the floor of this House that journalists enjoy the freedom of press and that one is entitled to criticize the Speaker. The present Speaker has not claimed any immunity from any bona fide criticism, which

no doubt has also to take note of the privileges of this great institution.

Freedom of the press, a cherished fundamental right in our country, is subject to reasonable restrictions, as contemplated by the Constitution itself, and cannot and does not comprise deliberately tendentious and motivated attacks on the great institutions of this republic and their officers and functionaries. Freedom of the press does not also contemplate making of reckless allegations, devoid of truth and lacking in bona fides. In the name of exercising freedom of the press, there cannot be trial by the press in which it plays the role of both the accuser and the judge.

Freedom of the press also encompasses fundamental duties of the press, which call for showing respect to others and responsible behaviour and cannot permit denigration of constitutional bodies and the institutions and their important segments.

It should be noted that although the presiding officer of this House is publicly accused of improper behaviour and of partisanship, he cannot join in any public controversy. A most disquieting development is that when the matter has been raised in the House and the Speaker has reserved his ruling, there are open discussions in the electronic media as also in the same newspaper where the concerned correspondent and his editor have tried to justify the allegations and thereby, in my opinion, have aggravated the breach of privilege. Significantly, the Speaker can only be a viewer of the so-called discussion and not a participant. The Speaker has to depend on the commitment of the members of this House, who are keen to preserve the dignity and the status of this great institution. Precisely, for this reason, I had expressed my thanks to those members, who raised the matter on 12 August 2005 on the floor of this House because only by such reference, the exposure of the contumacious acts could be made. I have no manner of doubt that if such serious accusations of partisanship and libellous allegations had been made against the judiciary, they would have been glaring examples of contempt of court.

While reiterating my view of the allegations, I wish particularly to refer to some deliberately factual misstatements made in the impugned article in an attempt to make out a case, so that the members and the country may be aware of the truth.

The impugned article refers to the so-called conflict between the Chair and one hon. member over parliamentary agenda and it has alleged that the said member felt that she was being gagged and as such had staged a dramatic protest. This accusation is clearly motivated. So far as I have been informed, the hon. member attended the House only on one day in the current monsoon session. She had given a notice of adjournment motion on an issue identical to one which had been fully discussed for several hours as an adjournment motion only on 26 July and as such could not be allowed under Rule 58 (V) to be raised again in the same session. She had not participated in the discussion and no other notice and I repeat, no other notice, or any intimation was ever submitted by the hon. member either to the Lok Sabha or to the office of the Speaker of her intention to raise any other matter or issue. Thus, there was no occasion for disallowing any matter, which the member wanted to raise during the whole of the fourteenth Lok Sabha. In spite of this, baseless allegations of gagging one particular member have been made and the motive is clear.

Further, it has been alleged in the impugned article that on an occasion, charges of high-handed behaviour ('tanashahi') had been made by some members directed at the Speaker, when it was categorically stated by the deputy leader of the Bharatiya Janata Party that the slogans raised by some members of his party were directed at the government and not at the Speaker. This statement was given wide publicity and there is no reason to assume that the correspondent and others did not know of the same yet made the most scurrilous allegations against the Speaker.

Further, it has been alleged that in the monsoon session, thirty-four calling attention motions had been admitted, of which twenty-two have been raised by the Left parties and that fourteen of the twenty-one short duration debates under Rule 193 have been initiated by the Left. These are nothing but imaginary particulars and I have no doubt that this has been deliberately concocted with a view to bolster the contrived attempt of alleging partisanship against the presiding officer. Anyone believing in truth or exactitude could not have made such reckless and tendentious allegations, which have only compounded the contumacious conduct.

In this circumstance, when the contents of the impugned article, on their face, are grossly libellous and amount to contempt of the presiding officer of the House and thereby of the entire House and of the members thereof, what should be done? One wonders what is the dignity and prestige of this august House, when it has a presiding officer with such vices and negative attributes as has been depicted in the impugned article? I ask myself: 'Does the publication even enhance the prestige of the media in this country?' I yield to none in my regard for the media and its right to discharge its functions in a bone fide and constructive manner.

Since assumption of this high office, I have been regularly meeting with editors and leading correspondents of the media and have sought their cooperation and valuable suggestion. The press is rightly described as the fourth estate, because without a free and responsible press, alive to its duties and believing in truth and honesty, this democratic system would almost collapse. I only hope that the fraternity to which the correspondent belongs would consider the matter in its proper perspective.

As to the action to be taken, I have already made my observations on 12 August 2005, which I reiterate with all the emphasis at my command. I believe that the disapprobation by large sections of this House of the contents of the impugned article clearly indicates their opinion that the publication is grossly contumacious and a deliberate affront to this House, whereby gross breach of privilege has been committed. Submission has been made with considerable force and justification for reference of the matter to the committee of privileges.

> However, to my mind, in view of the condemnation on the floor of the House, and as it would be beneath the dignity of this great institution to take further note of the motivated imputations in the impugned article, I do not give my consent as requested and I treat this matter as closed, of course, with the observation that in future reckless and contumacious conduct indulged in by whosoever would be dealt with in the appropriate manner so as to preserve and enhance the dignity of the highest public forum in our country.

On 4 August 2005, a member wanted to raise a matter by giving a notice of adjournment motion, on a subject on which there was a full-fledged debate in the House only a few days earlier. The member was, however, not present in the House during the discussion. Under the rules, discussion on an identical subject matter cannot be permitted in the same session. Therefore, I disallowed the adjournment motion. In spite of that, when the deputy speaker was in the Chair, the member insisted that the matter be allowed to be raised. She came to the well of the House and in a show of defiance and anger threw some papers towards the Chair, which fortunately did not hit the deputy speaker. On another occasion, the same member had thrown a shawl at the then Speaker P.A. Sangma.

A news item was published in the *Statesman* on 24 August 2005 on this incident, criticizing my decision as Speaker and imputing personal motives for it. On the same date, Dr Subhash C. Kashyap, former secretary general of the Lok Sabha, cast aspersions on me as a Speaker in an interview telecast on Star News.

On the basis of notices given by members alleging breach of privileges of the House on the part of the newspaper and the former secretary general, I referred both matters to the privileges committee of the Lok Sabha chaired by V. Kishore Chandra S. Deo.

In its report dated 17 May 2006, the privileges committee strongly deprecated the reckless and irresponsible behaviour of the author of the article published in the *Statesman* and also of the editor and managing director of the newspaper and cautioned them to be careful in future. The committee, after considering the unqualified apology tendered by the author of the article as well as the editor of the newspaper, recommended that 'no penal action needs to be taken against them'.

In the case of Dr Subhash C. Kashyap, the privileges committee, in its report dated 17 May 2006, held that he had committed gross breach of privilege and contempt of the House for having cast aspersions on the impartiality of the Speaker. The committee was of the view that 'the gravity of the offence has increased since the derogatory references were made by a person well versed in parliamentary procedure and practices and who once served as the secretary general of the Lok Sabha'. The committee, however, noted that Dr Kashyap, in his written comments furnished to the committee, as also in his evidence before the committee, said that he had 'highest regards for the Speaker' and that there was no 'question of any insinuation or imputation from me with reference to the Hon'ble Speaker'. He also said that the Speaker's decision 'cannot be questioned either in the House or outside'. The committee felt that had Dr Kashyap shown a little more circumspection while giving the interview, this situation would not have arisen. He was admonished for his conduct and irresponsible behaviour.

These are some examples where persons in position of responsibility get swayed by personal preferences and prejudices against the highest legislative forum and its presiding officer.

While regretting the negative aspects in the media, I must alongside record my appreciation for its positive role in exposing the rot that has set into the parliamentary system. I was told that approximately forty of the 545 members in the fourteenth Lok Sabha had criminal records. However, in public perception, all members were painted with the same brush. The onus of proving otherwise seemed to have fallen on the members themselves. They did this commendably.

On 12 December 2005, Aaj Tak, a Hindi news channel, carried footage of ten members of the Lok Sabha and one from the Rajya Sabha accepting money for tabling questions and raising other matters in the House based on a sting operation carried out by Aniruddha Bahal. Because of the seriousness of the matter, after consultation with various leaders, I constituted a committee under the chairmanship of V. Kishore Chandra Deo, a senior and respected member, to enquire into the allegations of improper conduct of these members. The committee in its report presented on 21 December 2005 recommended their expulsion from the House. On 23 December 2005, the House adopted a motion moved by Pranab Mukherjee, leader of the House, agreeing to the recommendation of the committee.

The image of Parliament received a tremendous boost because of the salutary cleansing, which was historic. While it pained me to see my colleagues expelled, the drastic steps were needed because of proven wrongdoings and were in the larger interest of probity and setting high benchmarks of integrity in our public life.

The report was discussed in the House. The leader of the Opposition, though in agreement with the findings, objected to the expulsion, contending that what the members had done was 'stupid' but did not merit the extreme punishment. It was truly unfortunate that when the House of the People was setting an example for the members and the country, a discordant note was raised. I could understand his agony because the majority of the members expelled belonged to his party, the BJP.

In the wake of another news bulletin telecast on Star News on 19 December 2005, I constituted, in consultation with various leaders, a seven-member enquiry committee with V. Kishore Chandra S. Deo as chairman, to probe the alleged improper conduct of four MPs in the matter of implementation of the Member of Parliament Local Area Development Scheme (MPLADS). I requested the members against whom allegations were made not to attend the session of the House until the matter was looked into and a decision taken. The committee recommended in its report of 13 March 2006 that the members remain suspended from the House till 22 March 2006, the end of the budget session, and be reprimanded for their behaviour which was not above board. Certain amendments in the implementation of the MPLADS were proposed. The report was accepted by the House. Personally, I thought that this was a light penalty, more so in the context of the expulsion of members only a few months ago for similar acts, which had won large public approbation. But it was a decision of the House and had to be respected. As Speaker, I had not voted either for this or the previous motion. The committee also suggested that the government initiate steps for laying down guidelines and norms for sting operators, which was supported by all members. I am not aware of the government's response to this suggestion.

It was important for members to be conscious of their responsibilities and not act in any manner that may bring them under a cloud. This is precisely what happened again in the matter of the alleged human-trafficking and misuse of parliamentary privileges by Babubhai Katara of the BJP, which was tracked by the media. I referred the matter to an enquiry committee. The report presented on 20 October 2008 recommended his expulsion from the House. This was unanimously accepted the next day. I had also asked the committee to go into aspects of codification of members' privileges and the feasibility of drawing up a code of conduct for them. Some useful suggestions were made but the consensus was that there was no requirement to go in for a codification exercise at this stage.

In this connection, I wish to record my deepest appreciation for V. Kishore Chandra S. Deo for the great service he has rendered to the Lok Sabha in his capacity as the chairman of the privileges committee and also as the chairman of the several enquiry committees that I formed consisting of leaders of different parties and groups to enquire into matters referred to above. I am convinced that his inspiring leadership and stewardship greatly helped the committees in successfully carrying out their duties and arriving at reports, which were by and large unanimous. I can well imagine the great patience he exercised and the efforts he made particularly in completing the task of the enquiry committees in a tight time schedule. I wish we had a few more members like him.

The Trust Motion of 22 July 2008

During the trust motion debate on 22 July 2008, held under the direction of the President to prove the government's majority after the Left withdrew support on the Indo-US nuclear deal, something extremely reprehensible and extraordinary happened, which affected the image and prestige of our Parliament. It was by far the worst incident ever in the history of the Lok Sabha. While the debate was on, three members of the BJP – Ashok Argal, Faggan Singh Kulaste and Mahabir Bhagora – suddenly entered into the well of the House around 4 p.m., waving several bundles of currency notes, and slapped them on the table in front of the Speaker. They shouted loudly and repeatedly that they had been bribed to vote in favour of the motion. As the proceedings of the House were being telecast live, this shameful incident was seen the world over. Understandably, it created a sensation and grave consternation. The deputy Speaker, who was in the chair, adjourned the House for a while and, as suggested by me, later, till 6 p.m. I immediately issued instructions to the secretary general that the currency notes be sealed and kept in his safe custody. After the initial adjournment of the House, I called a meeting of the leaders of various parties, along with the three members who had done the unthinkable. I asked them why they had not brought the matter to my notice. They should have raised the matter in the House only if I had not taken any action on their complaint. L.K. Advani agreed with me. Whatever be the provocations, as the presiding officer I could not countenance such performances on the floor of the House. Efforts needed to be made to ensure that this was the first and last incident of its kind. I expressed strong disapproval and dissatisfaction at what was most reckless and derogatory behaviour. Leaders opposing the motion of confidence protested the alleged attempt made by the ruling party to bribe members to vote in its favour. Some leaders sought an instant enquiry and adjournment of the proceedings till the results of the enquiry were known. Obviously, I could not have conducted an enquiry from the Lok Sabha Television footage that was available, as they demanded. It was an extremely serious matter and would have to be probed in depth. An enquiry committee, consisting of leaders cutting across party lines, would have to be appointed before considering imposition of penalties, which clearly seemed to be in order. In spite of the gravity of the situation I was not going to be hustled into any hasty decision. A broad agreement finally emerged on these lines. Mohammad Salim, the deputy leader of the CPI(M), appeared to be most agitated among the leaders. I had to ask him not to raise his voice. My admonition cooled him down, as also some of the NDA leaders, who appeared to be greatly exercised.

The proceedings resumed at 6 p.m. and I made this announcement in the House:

> Some time back, when my distinguished colleague, Hon'ble Deputy Speaker was presiding over the proceedings of the House, certain incidents have taken place, which, according to me, are most unfortunate. It is a very sad day in the history of Parliament that such a situation has happened. Thereafter, I called a meeting of the hon'ble leaders. I am grateful to the hon'ble leader of Opposition. He was very kindly present also.
>
> We have heard the three hon'ble members of the House. They had some complaints to make. I requested them to put their complaints in writing to me. I assured them, I assured the leaders and I assure the House that all possible steps that are required in that connection will be taken by me as a custodian of this House. It is my duty to do that, and I seek the cooperation of all sections of the House.
>
> Please allow me to apply my judgement, look into the matter, and I can assure you nobody will be spared if found guilty.

After an extended debate, the House approved the motion of confidence with 275 votes in favour and 256 against. The enquiry committee submitted its report to the House on 15 December 2008. Unfortunately, it was not a unanimous one. It recommended that the matter may be probed further by an appropriate investigating agency. On 16 December 2008, I observed in the House that on the basis of recommendations made by the committee the matter was being referred to the ministry of home affairs for further action. I also directed the secretary general to hand over the sealed currency to Delhi Police, as the investigative agency might require it for the purpose of the investigation. I further reiterated that this should be the first and last incident of its kind.

Some members gave a privilege notice against Argal, Kulaste and Bhagora for disturbing the House and bringing it to disrepute by their abhorrent misconduct. I referred it to the privileges committee. In its report submitted to me on 30 April 2009, the privileges committee recommended that the members be reprimanded for their aberrant behaviour. I accepted the report. However, there was no scope to place it in the House and have a debate on it as the term of the fourteenth Lok Sabha had come to an end by then.

Following the trust vote of 22 July 2008, petitions were filed for disqualifying members who had voted against their respective party whips. I heard twenty-seven cases between September 2008 and January 2009 and disqualified nine members. This is yet another record in terms of the numbers and time taken for disposal, not only in Parliament, but in all the state assemblies in the country. I personally wrote all the orders, without any assistance from the secretariat! It is another matter that I believe the relevant law must be amended to take away the power of disqualification from the Speaker's jurisdiction as it opens his decisions to judicial review, which is not desirable.

Initiatives during My Tenure as Speaker

I would not like to leave the impression that not much was achieved during the fourteenth Lok Sabha. Indeed, I look back with considerable satisfaction on what was achieved, though the going was not always easy. And I hope that my successors will build on what I initiated.

Drawing on my long experience of parliamentary affairs, I zeroed in on a few initiatives, which I believed would contribute to improving the functioning of the House, its image and outreach to citizens.

Zero Hour

This is a unique Indian contribution to parliamentary affairs that enables members to raise matters of urgent public importance after the Question Hour. There are, however, no rules to regulate it. I have often referred to it as 'torture hour' because it tended to be chaotic and unruly. During the winter session of 2004, I initiated steps to bring some order to the conduct of Zero Hour. On 8 December 2004, I observed in the House that,

> There has been a considerable increase in the number of notices for raising matters during the so-called Zero Hour. Seventy-five notices have been received and it was practically impossible for the chair to accommodate all the members. Many notices raise matters relating to constituencies and do not involve matters of recent occurrence or of national or international importance. The business advisory committee concurred that the number of Zero Hour matters may be restricted to fifteen per day, and unless matters of emergent national or international importance are involved, each member would be allowed to raise not more than one matter per week.

Not surprisingly, this was rather difficult to enforce in the subsequent sessions. Every morning my office would receive scores of notices on a plethora of issues. The first lot was received till 9.30 a.m. The moment I would set foot into my chamber, members would literally besiege me, insisting that I allow them an opportunity to raise their matters. There was barely time even to go through the notices. In the House, the clamour would get even louder, with each member demanding priority. There were occasions when members would use their lungpower to make their point even though they had not bothered to give notices!

On 24 July 2005, it was agreed that these matters would be taken up in a phased manner. In the first phase, five matters of extremely urgent national and international importance would be taken up. The remaining, including constituency-related ones, would be taken up only after 6 p.m.

While the magic figure of five was not adhered to by the members, there was some satisfaction that constituency-related mattes were, by and large, raised after the conclusion of the day's business and members did sit late to make their submissions. Matters of urgent public importance that were raised during the Zero Hour in the fourteenth Lok Sabha totalled an impressive 3,444.

Question Hour

The Question Hour is a valuable tool in the hands of members to hold the executive accountable. Generally, the Question Hour is the first hour of a sitting of Lok Sabha and, as the name suggests, it is devoted to questions. During the Question Hour MPs can ask questions on every aspect of administration and governmental activity and seek information from the government. However, this was not being utilized to its full potential. On 15 March 2005, I observed that under the Speaker's inherent powers I was not bound to follow the serial numbers of the questions as the rule required. I could take up any question. Therefore, all members who put questions should be alert as also the ministers. A number of times I had to pull up members and ministers who were not present when their questions were taken up. The ministers had to apologize for their absence. These invariably made media headlines. I am not sure what they felt about my insistence on an apology to the House, but I was firm. Often, ministers were not well prepared and I had to bail them out, much to the chagrin of some members. I allowed only three or four supplementaries for every question and insisted that they should be questions, not speeches, and often had to extol the virtues of brevity! I would not permit the same or similar clarifications to be sought by many members. Unrelated points and state- or constituency-specific details were always disallowed.

Because of my strict regulation, of the twenty starred questions (one to which a member desires an oral answer in the House and which is distinguished by an asterisk mark) that can be listed for the day's business, the House could take up more than four or five, which was not possible earlier. The fourteenth Lok Sabha listed 6,218 starred questions of which 963 were answered orally (more could not be dealt with due to disruptions during the Question Hour) and replies to 60,419 unstarred questions (to which oral answers are not called for but for which a written answer is laid on the table of the House after the Question Hour by the minister to whom the question is asked) were tabled in the House, which I consider a creditable record.

Lok Sabha Television (LSTV)

To me people power is of utmost importance. I wanted people to know how their representatives were performing in the House so that they could judge them and hold them to their promises.

Some of the proceedings of the House were being telecast live since 7 December 1994. However, I wanted the visitors' gallery of Parliament to be extended to every house in the country. There were different views on the desirability of telecasting the proceedings of the House live. Some, including the Prime Minister, felt that it would encourage members to grandstand, play to the galleries and create uproarious scenes to draw attention to themselves. They may have had valid reasons for their apprehensions, because disruptions had become more pronounced in recent years and the media, unfortunately, seemed more keen to provide publicity to disturbances rather than to informed, orderly debate on subjects of public importance. But I never believed that it was due to their being shown on TV live. I was, nonetheless, prepared to make a start and a broad consensus was built around it in late 2004. The chairman of the Rajya Sabha, Bhairon Singh Shekhawat, was rather enthused and participated in several rounds of discussions with Prasar Bharati officials on how to get the Parliament channel off the ground. It was known that the general purposes committee of the Rajya Sabha did not approve the proposal and what was originally conceptualized as a 'Sansad Channel' was eventually pruned to a Lok Sabha channel. I am, however, pleased to learn that the Rajya Sabha has again evinced interest in partnering the Lok Sabha in the channel. I hope that the details are worked out soon.

Brick by brick, the channel was built up from scratch. There were the initial expected hiccups. It was, after all, the first and only one of its kind in the world, to be founded, owned and run by Parliament. Neither was there any blueprint for it, nor any infrastructure available in the Lok Sabha as the limited live telecasts earlier had been handled by Doordarshan. Prasar Bharati's projections of financial and personnel requirements appeared rather daunting and I did not want to rush in to commit Parliament's resources without a guaranteed successful future for the channel. I consulted the leaders of the parties in the Lok Sabha and some experts. My good friend Priya Ranjan Dasmunsi, the minister of information and broadcasting, and the Prime Minister extended full cooperation for the successful launch of the channel. I acknowledge the sound advice and encouragement I received from them but for which the channel would have remained a pipedream. I requested Bhaskar Ghose – who had served as director general, Doordarshan, and secretary, information and broadcasting in the Government of India – to join as the chief executive in August 2005. Without his competent leadership, progress would have been well nigh impossible. I must also record my appreciation of the support provided by P.D.T. Achary, secretary general, Lok Sabha, and Dr T. Kumar, my principal secretary, in this unique venture.

The channel was formally launched on 11 May 2006. To begin with, the channel restricted itself to live telecast of proceedings of Parliament only during sessions. On 26 July 2006, it began operating as a twenty-four-hour satellite channel, with live telecasts of House proceedings and a unique bouquet of programmes on Parliament, democracy and a vast array of subjects of national importance. A full-fledged Lok Sabha Television Service, within Parliament's administrative structure, was created in April 2009 as an institutionalization effort. To start with, most of the personnel had been taken on a contractual basis, which had its own drawbacks, but was unavoidable.

I am glad that the Lok Sabha set up the channel at a much lower cost than what had been projected by Prasar Bharati. The recurring costs of running the channel have consciously been kept low and have become a benchmark for serious channels of this kind. Ministries and public sector undertakings have found the channel a very effective means of disseminating information on the government's programmes and policies. So far, LSTV has not had to fall back on the crutch of commercial advertising to sustain its operations. Perhaps, in future, if needed, for expansion-related reasons, a selective approach may have to be adopted to bring in a few socially important advertorials from the commercial sector. But that is for my successors to decide.

It was, no doubt, an uphill task for the channel to establish a niche for itself in the crowded arena of hundreds of TV channels offering sensational entertainment and infotainment to viewers. Three years on, I am justifiably proud that the LSTV team has made its mark and has earned well-deserved plaudits for its content and reach. According to some surveys, today the viewership of the channel is much higher than many of the older, well-established channels. The citizen now has a first-hand view of the happenings within the 'sanctum sanctorum' of Indian democracy, in real time. As has been remarked by some, this qualifies as the best 'reality show' and beats sitcoms hollow, especially during moments of high drama, of which there are quite a few. The issues, themes and persons appearing on LSTV are undoubtedly unique. I have no hesitation in crowning it the only 'people's channel' in the world. I was not seen much on the channel because it was one of my very few 'commandments' to it. I did not visualize the LSTV as a platform for building a positive profile of the Speaker.

Because of its very distinctive qualities, I always flagged the achievements of the channel to visiting overseas dignitaries. Most of them were interviewed by the channel, allowing viewers a rare glimpse of world leaders. I received many requests for assistance from them in setting up similar facilities in their parliaments. During my official trips overseas, I also proudly talked of the quality, reach and impact of the channel. I am confident that no country has been able, as yet, to match us on this score.

If I have one regret it is that I could not obtain an agreement, or even a broad consensus, on telecasting proceedings of parliamentary committees. There has been a long-standing demand for access to committees from the media and the public. The fears expressed by members on this demand were largely groundless, but I did not want to ride roughshod over their sentiments. Maybe my successor will convince them. I did, however, facilitate discussions of important committee reports on the channel which, though very important, were largely unknown to citizens so far.

I would like the channel to grow from strength to strength and become a vital mechanism to enhance the esteem of parliamentary institutions. I hope it continues to function with a high degree of professionalism and autonomy and does not ever fall prey to the machinations of self-seekers in the establishment or become a political tool of some politicians or parties, which fear, sadly, cannot be wished away altogether.

A number of other initiatives were launched and these have been detailed in Appendix II.

Before long it was time to say goodbye to five years of an exhilarating roller-coaster ride as Speaker of the Lok Sabha. The fourteenth Lok Sabha was coming to a close and it would soon be time for a new Parliament. I was extremely sorry that the Prime Minister, Dr Manmohan Singh, and Atal Bihari Vajpayee, the former Prime Minister, were not present in the House due to their illness when I made my valedictory speech on 26 February 2009, the last session of the fourteenth Lok Sabha. Pranab Mukherjee read out the speech of the Prime Minister, in which he made some kind references to my humble discharge of duties, and he was followed by L.K. Advani.

Pranab Mukherjee began by saying that he was speaking on behalf of the Prime Minister. The Prime Minister expressed regret at not being able to attend the session, and went on to say vis-à-vis me:

> In transacting business in this Parliament, you set yourself as a role model. We strained your patience and at times even your conscience. There were unusual times in which you had to take a call between defending parliamentary propriety and heeding the demands of the organization that you had spent a lifetime building. On all such occasions your sagacity prevailed. I have no words to express the gratitude of this House for upholding the dignity of both your high office and the dignity of this institution in times of personal trial. I express the sentiments of all the members of this

> House when I say: 'In Shri Somnath Chatterjee, the office of the Speaker of the Lok Sabha has been truly elevated and dignified.' History would be the best judge of your unique contribution. You stood like a rock to defend our best parliamentary traditions, and in doing so have raised the bar for those to follow …'

On the occasion, L.K. Advani said, 'I also express my gratitude to you for upholding the dignity of the institution…'

My valedictory speech – in which I tried to make a dispassionate assessment of the Parliament's performance over the last five years and my own humble contribution to the office of the Speaker – has been reproduced in Appendix I.

Thus, the curtain finally came down on my tenure as the Speaker of the fourteenth Lok Sabha to which I was fortunate to render my humble services. It also brought to an end my parliamentary career which started in 1971. Though Parliament had been an integral part of my life for nearly four decades, I stuck to my decision and did not contest the election to the fifteenth Lok Sabha.

I hope that the fifteenth Lok Sabha, with a large number of new faces under the distinguished stewardship of the most illustrious Speaker, Meira Kumar, will be able to function in consonance not only with the spirit of the Constitution but in a manner that will enhance its image before the people and will indeed become an institution to which people look towards for guidance and redressal of their grievances. I hope it will be able to lay down a new path for the progress of the nation as a whole. I had a dream when I got the unexpected opportunity to preside over the proceedings of the greatest representative institution of our country but I am sad to say that my dream has remained unfulfilled to a large extent. Maybe future generations will bring about the fruition of the dream.

7

THE EXPULSION

A GREAT SHOCK

The UPA government's decision to sign the nuclear deal with the US precipitated a crisis in Parliament. The CPI(M), which supported the Congress-led United Progressive Alliance (UPA) from outside, had a sizeable number of MPs which bolstered the government's strength in Parliament. The party was, however, vociferous in its opposition to the deal, and when Prime Minister Manmohan Singh decided to go ahead with the deal, the dominant section of the CPI(M) leadership decided to withdraw support to the government. They reasoned that the government would be rendered a minority one and would be forced to resign, which would effectively scuttle the deal. As per convention, a trust motion was called for. Amid uncertainties, the government survived the motion on 22 July 2008 rather comfortably as the Samajwadi Party threw a lifeline in the form of its support to the UPA. The

CPI(M)'s effort to dislodge the government failed though it voted along with the BJP on the motion against the government.

The motion also precipitated a personal crisis vis-à-vis my relationship with the CPI(M). On 20 July 2008, the party directed me, for the first time, to resign from my office of Speaker and vote against the motion. As things turned out, the result of the motion would not have been affected even if I had cast my vote against the motion. When I refused to bow to the party's diktat, primarily on the ground that as Speaker I could not be dictated to by the party and that I was expected to be neutral, Prakash Karat, the general secretary of the party, gave vent to his ire by summarily expelling me from the party on 23 July 2008. I responded that if the party emerged stronger by expelling me, it would be a consolation for me. But 23 July 2008 was undoubtedly the saddest day in my life since the passing away of my parents.

The party's decision to oppose the Indo-US nuclear deal at any cost – even toppling the government – was taken presumably because it felt that the deal was against national interest and would make our country dependent on the US, which the party wanted to prevent at any cost.

Prakash Karat met me at my residence a few days after the party had decided to withdraw its support to the UPA government but before it had announced it to the public. He said that he felt insulted and betrayed by what he called the failure of the Prime Minister and the chairperson, UPA, to keep the promise stated to have been made to him that he would be consulted before the government made any progress on the Indo-US nuclear deal. Because of what he called breach of promise, the party, according to him, had no option but to break with the UPA.

Significantly, in 2004, the CPI(M) had decided to support the UPA government from outside, so that the perceived greatest evil, a BJP-led NDA government, did not come to power. The party did not join the UPA government as it did not want to be held responsible for the government's acts of omission and commission. When the matter of joining the government came before the party's central committee, I had expressed my reservations about remaining outside the government. I was apprehensive that doing so would not help the party, the interest of workers, peasants and the common people, or the Left Front governments in West Bengal, Kerala and Tripura. It was a matter of concern that the party's base was limited only to West Bengal, Kerala and Tripura, where, too, it was facing many problems. In my view, the refusal or reluctance of a political party, which participates in the electoral process, to utilize the opportunity of implementing its programmes and policies for the benefit of the common people by joining the government was political suicide, and showed lack of courage and self-confidence in its programmes and in its capacity and ability. However, this perspective did not find favour with Prakash Karat and his group in the central committee which represented the majority. The party decided:

(i) Not to join the government;
(ii) Not to be a signatory to the common minimum programme, which had been drawn up by the UPA government and to which all the parties of the UPA were signatories; and
(iii) Not to be a member of the UPA coordination committee.

The party only agreed to take part in the UPA–Left coordination committee meetings.

After the formation of the UPA government with Dr Manmohan Singh as the Prime Minister and Sonia Gandhi as the chairperson of the UPA, it gradually became clear to all, specially those in the government, that the Left parties – which had sixty-two members in the Lok Sabha and on whose outside support the survival of the government depended – wanted to play the role of the 'real power behind the throne' as it were. Prakash Karat and the leaders of other Left parties had to be consulted, and their consent obtained, by the Prime Minister on every legislative proposal and important executive measures. It was quite well known that the Prime Minister and other senior leaders and ministers of the UPA were regularly meeting Karat and other Left leaders to seek their support for each and every action proposed to be taken by the government.

During my years as Speaker, the party had maintained virtually no contact with me. Neither had I been in touch with the party, except for my occasional meetings with Jyoti Basu, on whom I called whenever I went to Kolkata, more to meet him and wish him early recovery since he had not been keeping well. Of course, I took the liberty of visiting his place regularly because I had the rare privilege of enjoying his affection.

As Speaker I remained completely detached from the party and all political disputes and controversies. I never made any comment on the merits or otherwise of the issues on which the Left opposed any proposal or decision of the government and whether their stand was justified or not. But the common perception, as expressed in many quarters, was that the Left leaders were wielding the real authority without being in the government and had thus arrogated to themselves de facto powers of governance without any corresponding accountability and had also become arbiters of the government's survival. Thus, Left leaders like Prakash Karat, A.B. Bardhan and others came to acquire a larger-than-life image and influence in the governance of the country. Too much proximity to the Prime Minister and the UPA chairperson and the accommodative attitude of the government towards Karat and other Left leaders gave the latter the belief, if not the conviction, that their decisions would be

The author's mother, Binapani, whom he credits with inculcating in him and his siblings the values of simple living and high thinking

Somnath Chatterjee's father, N.C. Chatterjee, an eminent lawyer and parliamentarian, whom he regards as his greatest inspiration in life

When the world was young: The author during his student days in the United Kingdom in the early 1950s

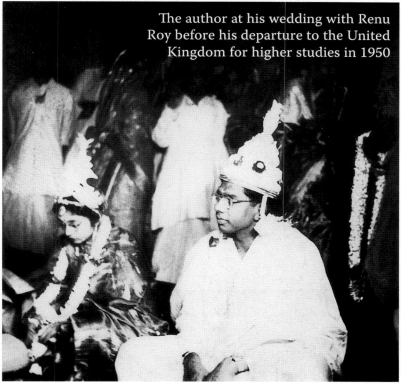

The author at his wedding with Renu Roy before his departure to the United Kingdom for higher studies in 1950

At Kedarnath, 1962, with wife and mother

On the way to Badrinath, 1962, with wife and mother

CPI(M) leader Jyotirmoy Bosu, who was a mentor to the author during his first term as MP in the Fifth Lok Sabha, 1971–77

Veteran communist leader Pramod Dasgupta, on whose suggestion Somnath Chatterjee became a member of the CPI(M) in 1973

Somnath Chatterjee with N.N. Gooptu and S.K. Acharya (centre): Acharya was instrumental in the author's entry into politics in the late 1960s

Somnath Chatterjee with Jyoti Basu, erstwhile Chief Minister of Bengal, the longest-serving Chief Minister of a state in India, and a CPI(M) stalwart, whom the author consulted on all important political matters

Sharing a light moment at dinner with Jyoti Basu and Prof. Hiren Mukherjee (seated to the right of Basu): The author considers Prof. Mukherjee of the CPI as the greatest parliamentarian he has encountered in his four decades as an MP

Celebrating 100 years of Mitra Institution in 2005, the school where the author was educated: President A.P.J. Abdul Kalam being presented with a portrait done by a student of the school, while Viren Shah (extreme left), former Governor of West Bengal, Buddhadev Bhattacharya, Chief Minister of West Bengal, and Siddhartha Shankar Ray (extreme right) look on

At an event in Santiniketan to felicitate Amartya Sen after the latter won the Nobel Prize in 1998

Felicitating K.R. Narayanan before he stepped down as President in 2002: also in the picture are former Prime Ministers I.K. Gujral and V.P. Singh; Somnath Chatterjee regards the latter highly for his principled fight against corruption in high places

Somnath Chatterjee receiving the Outstanding Parliamentarian Award in 1996 from President S.D. Sharma, while Prime Minister H.D. Deve Gowda, Vice-President K.R. Narayanan, and Speaker P.A. Sangma look on

At a parliamentary event honouring Dr B.R. Ambedkar: also in the picture are leader of the opposition L.K. Advani, President Pratibha Patil, Vice-President Hamid Ansari, Prime Minister Manmohan Singh and the Chief Minister of Delhi, Sheila Dikshit

Unveiling a portrait of the author's father, N.C. Chatterjee, in Parliament in 1995: also in the picture are the then Vice-President K.R. Narayanan, Prime Minister P.V. Narasimha Rao and Speaker Shivraj Patil

The leader of the Congress party, Sonia Gandhi, greeting the author on his eightieth birthday

With Manmohan Singh

With former Prime Minister and BJP stalwart Atal Bihari Vajpayee, with whom the author shares the distinction of being one of the longest-serving parliamentarians in India; they are also both recipients of the Outstanding Parliamentarian Award

Jyoti Basu, Sonia Gandhi, Manmohan Singh, H.S. Surjeet and Buddhadev Bhattacharya at a dinner party hosted by the author

With Sushma Swaraj at the opening ceremony of the Santiniketan Kendra of Doordarshan

In the corridors of power: with President A.P.J. Abdul Kalam, Vice-President B.S. Shekhawat, Prime Minister Manmohan Singh, and Priya Ranjan Dasmunsi

With wife Renu at their residence in Kolkata

The quintessential family man: at the wedding of grandson Shashwata; from L to R: daughter-in-law Shakuntala, elder daughter Anuradha, the author, son Pratap, wife Renu, grandsons Shashwata and Saurabh, Shashwata's wife Tarana, younger daughter Anushila, elder son-in-law Sugata Bhattacharya, granddaughters Trisha and Surya, and younger son-in-law D.P. Basu the last word for the government and that their diktats would inevitably be followed. Thus, they forgot their true strength in the House or even in the country and wanted their decisions to be treated as final and non-negotiable. The party gave the unpalatable impression that the UPA government could survive only with the blessings of the party's leaders, primarily of its general secretary, Prakash Karat. Needless to say, the common man took this to be nothing but unjustified arrogance on their part.

As the Congress remained firm in its resolve to operationalize the nuclear deal, and the CPI(M) equally determined not to give up its opposition, it seemed that a point of no return had been reached and the party might withdraw its support to the UPA government – without properly assessing the consequences of such a decision on the country and on the party itself. In such a case, the government would fall, and either the NDA would be able to muster the support of the majority of the members of the House or the country would be forced to go for fresh elections.

Talks between the Government of India and the US government on the nuclear deal had become a matter of considerable controversy, with many conflicting views and opinions expressed by academics, retired foreign service officers and also political scientists and leaders. From the nature of the contradictory views and opinions expressed, it appeared to laymen like me, who wanted to assess the matter objectively, that it was not possible to come to a definite conclusion on its merits. As far as I was concerned, I had neither feedback on its strategic or security-related aspects nor had I discussed it with political leaders or experts in the field. As such I was in no position to comment on the issue with any authority. Further, while discharging the role of the presiding officer of the House, especially when the issue was sure to come before the House for what would surely be an acrimonious discussion, it would not be proper for me to express any opinion, even if I could form one. Thus, although I felt – with my limited understanding of the intricacies of the deal – that the Left view on the merits of the deal was more valid, yet, considering the political situation in the country and the composition of the membership of the House, it would be unwise, to say the least, for the Left parties to withdraw support from the UPA government.

The Left had consistently adopted the policy of continuing to support the government while opposing many of its decisions, as was done quite stridently when the issue of price rise became a matter of great public concern. On that occasion, the Left did not think of withdrawing support to the government, or to precipitate a crisis, though a similar stand on inflation would have probably had a greater impact on the people.

As a member of the party who, until his election as Speaker, had actively participated in its affairs, I felt I should bring my views in the matter, for whatever they were worth, to the notice of the general secretary and others. On 27 June 2008, I conveyed in a note to him, through one of the comrades in the party, my views on the political situation and what would be the most appropriate stand for the party to take in the national interest.

I had suggested that the party should continue to oppose the deal since it felt so strongly about the issue. I proposed that the party take steps to rouse public opinion against the deal. No government could defy strong public opinion. I expressed my apprehension that an early election, as was likely in case the party withdrew its support, would create a difficult situation for the party. I was afraid that the electoral results might be disappointing, specially in West Bengal, where the party had only a few months back suffered major reverses in the Panchayat elections – for the first time since 1978. I felt that in the circumstances then prevailing, it would be prudent to consolidate the party's strength and activities in West Bengal and Kerala and oppose the nuclear deal as best as it could, while continuing to support the UPA from outside. I felt that the most effective way for the party to deal with the issue would be to educate the people and the political spectrum as a whole about what it felt would be the dangerous consequences that would beset the country if the deal was operationalized.

Clearly, the party leadership under Karat did not think my views even worth considering. The party's efforts, if any, met with abysmal failure. The Left found itself wholly isolated in taking its protest to the extent of withdrawal of support to the government. I wonder whether the Left parties had ever considered in-depth what the political fallout of their action would be – in terms of both the cost to the nation and to the Left movement. It seemed that Karat had decided that the Prime Minister and the UPA chairperson had to be taught a lesson for the 'insult' meted out to him.

That the controversy over the deal was hardly a matter of concern for the people was conclusively proved when, during the fifteenth general election, the deal turned out to be an issue that hardly mattered to the electorate. No party, including the Left, could make it a live election issue. Further, as I had apprehended, the election results proved conclusively that the Left had lost contact with the working and the common people, and with peasants and the deprived sections of the society. The very people the Left claimed to represent had moved away from it.

Of course, in the situation then prevailing, I had no role to play at all. The party at no time tried to find out my views on the issue, nor did I have an opportunity to discuss it with any leading comrade. I feel that the supposed 'affront' to Karat by the Prime Minister and UPA chairperson had upset him so much that he did not or could not objectively consider the consequences of his decision to withdraw support to the government. It also resulted in his taking a wholly inconsistent and rather insincere attitude towards me as the Speaker. On 9 July 2008, Karat stated in the press conference after meeting the President regarding the withdrawal of support that it was for the Speaker to decide his course of action – a stand he categorically repeated as late as on 18 July 2008. Suddenly, on 20 July 2008, he took a wholly contrary decision, clearly proving that he did not care whether his action was a principled and sincere one or not. Significantly enough, he has never explained the reasons for his volte-face. That his arrogance and intolerance had reached a peak was clearly demonstrated by the fact that he decided to expel me summarily, without even a show-cause notice. That anyone in the party could defy his diktat was inconceivable to him!

When Karat met me after deciding to withdraw support, he did not even mention my note to him on the present political situation and only stated that the party had taken the decision to withdraw support. Of course, he knew my views by then and met me probably to find out my reaction to the proposed withdrawal. During that meeting, Karat categorically told me that the party had not even discussed the matter regarding my position as Speaker.

On 8 July 2008, Pranab Mukherjee met and informed me that it was likely that after the Left parties withdrew support, the President would recommend that the government initiate a vote of confidence. For this, he informed me, the government might convene a special session on 21 and 22 July 2008. If the government survived, the monsoon session would be convened from 11 August 2008.

The Left parties met the President on 9 July 2008 to apprise her about the withdrawal of support and requested her to either dismiss the government or direct it to submit to a vote of confidence in the House. That morning, Prakash Karat rang me to convey that members of the Politburo who were in Delhi, including some comrades from West Bengal, were of the view that in the prevailing circumstances my continuance as Speaker would be 'untenable' and that I should decide my own course of action. On the same day, I sent a note to Karat with my views on some of the issues he described as 'untenable' and suggested a few alternate courses of action. But there was neither any acknowledgement nor any response to my views, thus indicating that he did not find the same worth taking note of. Apart from that, Karat never tried to contact me.

Later in the day, I came to know that in the list of CPI(M) members withdrawing support to the government, which was submitted to the President, my name was mentioned first. I was shocked! Strangely, till today I have not been shown a copy of this letter. There was intense media speculation about my possible resignation, which was neither called for nor consistent with the position of the Speaker. The general secretary himself had stated in public, at the press conference held after the formal withdrawal of support, that it was for me as the Speaker to decide the future course of action.

To quell the speculation, my office issued a statement on 10 July 2008, stating:

> The attention of Shri Somnath Chatterjee, the Hon'ble Speaker of Lok Sabha, has been drawn to the various media reports which have been published or telecast about his continuance in office.
>
> The Hon'ble Speaker does not represent any political party in the discharge of his duties and functions. It is well known that the present Speaker's election to his high office was not only uncontested but was unanimous as all political parties proposed his name. He was not elected as the nominee of any party. In the discharge of his duties and functions he does not owe allegiance to any political party. Since his election as Speaker, Shri Somnath Chatterjee has scrupulously kept himself away from all political activities.

> It is requested that the media not drag the highest legislative office of the country into controversies by speculative reports and undeserved innuendos. As and when any decision is taken by the Hon'ble Speaker, relevant to the present political context, the media will be kept informed.

Earlier, as already stated, Karat had specifically told me that the party had not taken any decision about me. Apart from what he stated clearly at the press conference on 9 July 2008, he issued the following statement on 14 July 2008:

> A lot of speculation is going on in the media regarding the position of the Speaker of the Lok Sabha, Comrade Somnath Chatterjee. I have already stated that any decision will be taken by the Speaker himself. This has been reiterated by the Speaker through a statement by his office on 10 July 2008. We do not want the office of the Speaker being dragged into any unnecessary controversy.

In response to the keen interest shown by the media and other political parties about my future course of action and about the propriety of including my name in the list of members withdrawing support, Sitaram Yechury, member of the Politburo of the CPI(M), issued the following statement on 16 July 2008:

> A disinformation campaign on the issue of the inclusion of the Lok Sabha Speaker's name in the CPI(M) MPs' list submitted to the President of India is doing the rounds. What I had said is that the Speaker's name should be included in the CPI(M) list as he was elected as a CPI(M) candidate but with an asterisk denoting that currently he is the Lok Sabha Speaker, as is the normal parliamentary practice.

Two reports appeared in the *Times of India* on 18 July 2008, based on an interview with Karat in which he said, 'On the day we withdrew support from the UPA government, I had stated in a press conference that it is for the Speaker to take a decision on the matter. I have maintained this all through. As for the role of the Speaker, I wish to make our party's views clear. By holding the post of the Speaker, a person does not cease to have political affiliations. But when someone becomes a Speaker, he/she should not indulge in party activities, or adopt partisan political positions.'

A.B. Bardhan, general secretary of the CPI, stated that 'the Left ally should not have included the name of Lok Sabha Speaker, Somnath Chatterjee, in the list of party MPs withdrawing support to the UPA government. He is a veteran leader and parliamentarian and he should decide on this matter on his own. Dragging Chatterjee into the resignation controversy was an attack on the dignity of the high post held by him. I agree the Speaker was elected on a CPM ticket. But he was elected Speaker to the Lok Sabha with the support of all parties.'

I was told by media persons that the guessing game about my resignation was due to leaks from A.K.G. Bhavan, the CPI(M) headquarters. It was a matter of great agony for me. On the one hand, the general secretary of the party had made repeated public statements that it was for me to decide my future course of action after the withdrawal of support by the CPI(M); on the other, a whisper campaign suggesting that I would soon be directed to resign appeared to have been engineered by the party itself.

Throughout my political career, I have received a lot of guidance and affection from Jyoti Basu, who had been, till his last day, my undisputed leader. In view of the controversy, I felt I should take his opinion at that critical juncture. I met him in Kolkata on 12 July 2008 and showed him my communication with the party. Of course he was fully aware of the party's stand on the deal and I had no discussion with him on the same. I also had no idea whether he agreed with the party's stand. But he advised me that I should preside over the proceedings of the House on the confidence motion. My resignation, he felt as I too believed, would suggest that I was compromising my position as the Speaker and was allowing my actions to be dictated by my political party, which would be wholly unethical and contrary to the basic tenets of parliamentary democracy, of which the Lok Sabha was and is the supreme body in our country. It would also compromise the position of the party itself, which would come across as not truly committed to the country's democratic polity based on the parliamentary system, despite taking part and benefiting from it. He further advised me that I could take a decision after the trust vote and the Annual Prof. Hiren Mukherjee Parliamentary Lecture on 11 August 2008 which, as I told him, I had as Speaker arranged to be delivered by Prof. Amartya Sen. This strengthened my resolve to carry on my duty as Speaker at least till the date of the trust vote and not to buckle under pressure.

If I remember correctly, around 15–16 July 2008, Sitaram Yechury came to my residence and talked to me about the developing political situation, without mentioning any decision that might have been taken by the party in my case. Yechury possibly wanted to ascertain what was on my mind. I informed him about what had transpired during my meeting with Jyoti Basu, who, as I was told by a reliable source, had himself sent a handwritten note to the general secretary in this regard. I do not know whether this note was formally placed at the Politburo meeting or circulated among the members or not. I presume it was done. While leaving my house, Yechury vaguely indicated that I might receive a communication from the party. This convinced me that the party had taken or would take the decision to ask me to resign.

Significantly, after 9 July 2008, Karat did not speak to me but as mentioned, he more than once publicly mentioned that the decision had been left to me. It was only on 20 July 2008 that Biman Bose, secretary of the West Bengal State Committee of the party and a member of the Politburo, contacted me. He came to my residence around 1 p.m. and informed me that both the central committee and the Politburo had decided that I should not continue as Speaker and that I should resign and vote against the government. I realized that media speculation about the party having taken a decision, contrary to its repeated public pronouncements, had a solid basis. By then I had already made up my mind, as advised by the most important leader of the CPI(M), Jyoti Basu, not to tender my resignation until the debate on the trust vote was over.

Accordingly, I told Biman Bose that I could not accept the party's directive since I did not wish to make the office of the Speaker a victim of political manoeuvrings. I told him that no Speaker could or should be at the mercy of the dictates of his party, even though he or she had been elected as an MP as its candidate and remained committed to its ideologies. I reminded him that throughout the fourteenth Lok Sabha, since my election as Speaker, I had dissociated myself from all political activity. I wondered why the general secretary had stated, as late as on 18 July 2008, that it was for me to decide my course of action. Obviously, Biman Bose was not pleased but he did not enter into any argument with me. About an hour later, I got a telephone call from him that I need not cast my vote on the confidence motion but that I must resign from the office of Speaker. I told him clearly that I could not accept his suggestion.

On 21 and 22 July 2008, the motion of confidence moved by the Prime Minister was debated and approved. The first thing the party did the following day was to hold a meeting of five local members of the Politburo which has a total membership of seventeen. I presume that no notice was given to the others of the said meeting. On 23 July 2008, the following statement was issued by the party: 'The Politburo of the Communist Party of India (Marxist) has unanimously decided to expel Somnath Chatterjee from the membership of the party with immediate effect. This action has been taken under Article XIX, Clause 13 of the party constitution for seriously compromising the position of the party.'

Later, I understood that even among those five members, the decision had been taken by a majority. Of course, I cannot vouch for it.

Obviously, leaders of the CPI(M)'s Politburo viewed my commitment to the important constitutional position of the Speaker as 'untenable', and my refusal to resign as an act of defiance. Since my election as Speaker, I had not thought it possible for the party to give me any directives. If I had any inkling of this, I would have formally given up my ordinary membership for the period I remained Speaker. Against this backdrop, I feel that a convention should evolve that during one's tenure as Speaker, a member may temporarily resign from the membership of his or her party, so as not to be faced with the unenviable situation I was confronted with.

It was most surprising and unbecoming of a principled party like the CPI(M), which I always believed never misled the people, that its general secretary and some of his close colleagues would take a totally misleading position for public consumption, while at the same time confabulating among themselves to force me as Speaker to accept a subservient role to the party, even if such a step transgressed all principles of constitutional propriety.

Although I had anticipated that the party would take some disciplinary action against me, I never thought it would be done in such haste. What happened was nothing short of arbitrary. I had believed that at least a show-cause notice would be given or an explanation would be asked for, especially since I had served the party for nearly forty years with all sincerity and devotion. Unfortunately, that was not to be.

The news of my expulsion from the party created a huge stir. I was overwhelmed with innumerable messages of support, which came from all corners of the country and from a large number of Indians residing abroad. All of them appreciated my stand of not succumbing to the party's diktats and maintaining the highest standards of parliamentary democracy. These messages gave me tremendous mental support and steeled my resolve to continue as Speaker regardless of the party's wanton decision to expel me. Some of these messages have been set out in Appendix IV.

I did not join issue with the party about the expulsion. Neither did I challenge the party's right to take the decision. The party's rules allow for filing of appeals and asking for reviews of summary expulsion but I did not avail of these. I waited for several days so that the dust raised by my expulsion settled down. I know history will judge my action with approbation. On 1 August 2008, I issued a statement, excerpts from which are set out below:

> 23 July 2008 has been one of the saddest days of my life, when I was informed through the media of my summary expulsion from membership of the CPI(M) for 'seriously compromising the position of the party'. The expulsion has meant cessation of my long association with the party for nearly forty years. I recall the day when soon after my election in 1971 to the Lok Sabha as an independent candidate with the support of the party, Pramod Dasgupta, one of the builders of the party, who was an inspiration to all the members, asked me to become a member, which I could not possibly refuse.
>
> During my nearly four decades in Parliament, I have tried my best to discharge my functions true to our parliamentary traditions. With that experience and the opportunity to serve the country as a Member of Parliament ... I could not and cannot in

> my conscience accept a position which would totally compromise the sanctity of the most important legislative office in the country. After weighing the pros and cons, I have consciously taken the principled decision to uphold the Constitution of India at the risk of being unjustifiably dubbed as anti-party.
>
> It is a canard to allege that I have done so to help any party or parties or due to some other personal considerations. I strongly and categorically deny these wholly baseless allegations.
>
> Long before the present controversy had arisen, I had declared openly my intention not to contest any further elections and to devote the remaining period of my life in the service of the people.
>
> In view of the controversies that are now being raised ... a convention should start that during his/her tenure as Speaker, a member should temporarily resign from the membership of the party and not face a situation which compromises the position of the Speaker vis-à-vis his or her party.
>
> I wish to express my sincere thanks and gratitude to the overwhelming support from the people from different parts of the country and abroad, who have sent messages supporting the stand taken by me based on my constitutional position. Such response, which I find unprecedented, emphasizes the people's desire that Parliament should function properly and discharge its role in a serious and responsible manner. Such overwhelming response and appreciation of my stand gives me strength to continue to discharge my duties and responsibilities to the best of my abilities as the Speaker during my tenure.

In the Lok Sabha elections in May 2009, the Left parties, as I had apprehended but never desired, suffered a major debacle, both in West Bengal and Kerala, which greatly reduced its strength not only in the House but in the country as a whole. Thanks to the disastrous policies and misguided actions of the current leadership, the Left parties, particularly the CPI(M), and the left and progressive forces have become extremely weak. The leftist movement in the country as a whole has become almost irrelevant and comrades who made immense sacrifices to build the party have become victims of political marauders. I thought that the leadership would accept its responsibility for bringing the party to such a pass and would make amends by voluntarily stepping down in favour of a new, active and effective leadership. Shockingly, that was not to be. I can only convey my greetings and my best wishes to the grassroots comrades that they will be able to revive the party as an effective political force sooner than later.

As late as August 2009, the CPI(M)'s weekly journal *People's Democracy* made unfortunate and misleading allegations against me regarding the matter, casting aspersions on my motives. My response to their charges has been included in Appendix VI.

Between July 2008 and the constitution of the fifteenth Lok Sabha, I continued to discharge my responsibilities as Speaker. The monsoon session was deferred till October and merged with the winter session. This created an anomalous situation but the government probably wanted to avoid another floor test, which according to the rules was permissible only once in each session. When I heard of moves to extend this till the budget session, I expressed my view that it would be contrary to the constitutional requirement. The government, rather reluctantly it seemed, prorogued the House. I also insisted that the President address the first joint sitting of the Houses in 2009, though the government did not seem to be keen, being at the end of its tenure.

I made a public declaration that I would not contest the elections and would retire from politics, but not public life, to which I will remain committed till my last breath. I hope politicians of my age will take the cue and leave the stage for younger and more dynamic leaders.

This long journey spanning nearly four decades has provided me with the great opportunity to learn about our parliamentary institutions in the company of some great leaders, political thinkers and activists of our country. As a student and as a practising lawyer, I had never dreamt that I would ever be part of such an endeavour. It has been exhilarating at times, trying at others, and also often frustrating, but never lacking in providing me with the urge to do my best in the discharge of my duties and functions.

At this important milestone, as I attempt summing-up, I must confess to a deep sense of satisfaction and an even deeper resolve to carry on with the values I cherish most. The next innings, if I may call it so, promises to be quite different, while retaining a thread of continuity. The disappointments I have encountered have their own unique lessons for me. I have always prided myself on being a perfectionist, and I hope I will continue to be one in all my endeavours. I also hope that the all-round development and well-being of my fellow citizens will become a reality in the foreseeable future. I look forward to that tomorrow with great optimism and firm hope.

8

COLLEAGUES AND COMRADES

RUBBING SHOULDERS WITH STALWARTS

After my entry into the fifth Lok Sabha in 1971, I have been fortunate to be able to serve the institution for thirty-eight years. I was a Member of Parliament till the end of the fourteenth Lok Sabha in 2009, with a short break of eleven months during the eighth Lok Sabha. My election to the House has been primarily because of my party's efforts and popularity. In the House, along with other members of my party, I have tried my humble best to serve the cause the party represented and speak for the vulnerable sections of the community who had hardly any voice in the most important institution in the country. As members of the Left, we tried to raise important issues which concerned the people in general and the working class and peasants in particular. During this long period, I came to know many important leaders and parliamentarians who contributed towards strengthening our parliamentary structure and the country as a whole.

When I first entered the Lok Sabha, two leaders of the Left with whom I became closely associated were A.K. Gopalan, leader of the CPI(M) in Parliament and a Politburo member, and Jyotirmoy Bosu, a very effective member who had by that time made a great mark in our parliamentary deliberations.

Gopalan was soft-spoken and affectionate and took great interest in seeing that young members like me had the opportunity to make a contribution to the proceedings of the House. I watched with admiration the respect he commanded from all sections of the House, including ministers who belonged to the Congress party. He had been a prominent freedom fighter and was arrested many times under British rule. He was also jailed during the Emergency, but he never showed any animosity or personal recrimination towards the government benches. He was the undisputed leader of the Kisan Movement not only in Kerala but all over India and was president of the All-India Kisan Sabha, the peasants' wing of the CPI(M). I consider myself fortunate that I could begin my parliamentary career under his leadership.

Gopalan used to stay at 4 Ashoka Road, New Delhi, which then housed our parliamentary office as well as the office of the Kisan Sabha. He used to occupy a small room there, and had the most unostentatious style of living. It was here that we used to meet him. Whenever we young members needed his help, we would visit him, even without a prior appointment, and he would always be ready to give us valuable advice and guidance.

His wife Susheela Gopalan, an important leader of the CPI(M) based in Kerala, subsequently became an MP and soon made her mark as a very effective member. Later, she went on to earn great distinction in the southern state as the minister of industry. Both of them dedicated their lives to the cause of the people and I respected them immensely.

We felt completely at ease in the presence of such important and inspiring leaders. I remember that after I delivered my first speech in the Lok Sabha a few weeks after I became an MP, I got a lot of appreciation from Gopalan himself. He called me to express his satisfaction and told me I had spoken well. That encouraged me greatly and inspired me to try and live up to the expectations of my leader and make my contribution in a manner that would receive his approbation.

Jyotirmoy Bosu represented West Bengal's Diamond Harbour constituency in the Lok Sabha for many years. I admired him for his contribution to the Parliament and he was undoubtedly one of the leading members of the Lok Sabha. People would look to him to raise issues concerning the nation's problems. He was relentless in his efforts to oppose and expose the misdeeds on the part of the administration or a minister. He fought tirelessly against the scourge of black money which seriously affected the country's economy. I was most impressed by the courage and the tenacity with which he raised important issues in spite of heavy odds and with great effect. I became very close to him soon and tried to learn from him how to become an effective member of the House.

Bosu was accessible to all. In the evenings after a Parliament session, I would invariably be present at his house along with a large number of media persons and other members. In that sense, he had an open house. I remember the meticulous care he took to instruct me on how to go about raising important issues, how to gather material, how to formulate issues and which procedure to adopt to raise the same. Dinesh Roy, his party comrade who assisted him in such matters, also helped me greatly. Bosu had a very large circle of friends, including some from the ruling party as well as from other opposition parties and groups, and that helped him earn their confidence in important matters.

My father had been a member of the first, third and fourth Lok Sabhas and Jyotirmoy Bosu was a member of the fourth to seventh Lok Sabhas. While they were colleagues in Parliament, Bosu used to come to our house in Calcutta to meet my father. He would also visit my father regularly at our Pusa Road residence in New Delhi. Although my father did not belong to the CPI(M), he was elected with its support, and had close links with many Left members. My father was very fond of Bosu because of his performance as an MP and the honest efforts he made to raise issues concerning the people. Bosu too treated him with great respect. I remember once there was some agitation in a town in Uttar Pradesh, the details of which I cannot recollect now. Bosu took my father to visit the place and meet the residents. I too came to know him well during those days. I have not seen many members over the years who could or did utilize the forum of Parliament to serve the people in such an exemplary manner. Unfortunately, he passed away on 12 January 1982, while he was a sitting member of the seventh Lok Sabha.

In my initial years in Parliament, I looked upon myself as a student, more keen to learn how to function than try to intervene, unless I was particularly asked to do so by Gopalan or Bosu, who was the whip of the party. In the fifth Lok Sabha, the CPI(M) had other effective members like Samar Mukherjee, who was then deputy leader and ultimately became leader, Saroj Mukherjee, Dinen Bhattacharya, K.C. Halder, Rabin Sen and others. They used to take part in debates regularly and fully justified the party's confidence in them. Watching them was a great learning experience for me.

Outside the party, I was greatly impressed by Madhu Limaye, Madhu Dandavate, H.V. Kamath, Chitta Basu, A.K. Roy, the trade union leader from Dhandbad, and Professor Samar Guha, among the opposition members. Of course, the most illuminating experience was to listen to Professor Hiren Mukherjee, the CPI leader, who was a member from the first to the fifth Lok Sabhas. I have already mentioned his contribution, and to me he was the most compleat Member of Parliament. With his command over the language, his choice of words, the issues on which he spoke and the respect that he showed to the Chair, his adherence to the rules and procedure of the House, I believe he set an example for all others to follow. In recognition of his unmatched and signal service to our Parliament, I as the Speaker had the great privilege and pleasure of instituting an annual parliamentary lecture named the Professor Hiren Mukherjee Annual Parliamentary Lecture, which, I hope, my illustrious successors will organize every year.

Another MP belonging to the Left who enjoyed great respect and standing in Parliament was Tridib Chowdhury of the RSP. He was a veteran member, a totally dedicated Left leader and was once an Opposition candidate of the Left for President. I have known him since my youth as he was a very close friend of my father. He used to visit us in Calcutta and Delhi very often and I have seen him and my father addressing meetings together. He also addressed election meetings for my father when the latter was an independent candidate supported by the leftists. He used to encourage me to take active part in politics after my studies. A man with frugal habits, Tridib Chowdhury epitomized simple living and was an extremely respected leader of the Left movement and of the House.

There have been several members with whom I had the good fortune of working closely in the House till the thirteenth Lok Sabha, including those belonging to our group, and who made effective contributions to our parliamentary deliberations. I would like to refer particularly to Rupchand Pal, an extremely competent member, who made a great contribution not only in the debates but as the chairman of the Estimates Committee and the Public Undertaking Committee and as a member of the Public Accounts Committee. He was also the spokesman of the party in financial matters, especially on the budget. Then there were Ahilya Rangnekar, the young and extremely competent Saifuddin Choudhury (who was expelled by the party for reasons we could not fathom), Satya Sadhan Chakraborty, Niren Ghose, Basudeb Acharia, who was the leader both before and after me, Dasarath Deb and Biren Datt of Tripura, Shopat Singh, B.N. Reddy, Suresh Kurup, Hannan Mollah, Anil Basu, Dinesh Joardar, Malini Bhattacharjee (who defeated Mamata Banerjee in 1989 from Jadavpur), Nirmal Kanti Chatterjee, who was an expert on economic issues and was always very helpful to me, Dr Biplab Dasgupta, reputed economist, Bhagat Ram, Subhasini Ali, Sunil Maitra, Mohammad Ismail, Dr Saradish Ray, Sudhir Giri, Masudal Hossain, Dr Sudhir Roy, Moinul Hasan, Sivaji Patnaik, Ajit Bag, E. Balanandan, Ajay Biswas, Subodh Roy, Ananda Pathak, Khagen Das, Bajuban Riyan, Uddhab Barman, Sunil Khan, Dr Asim Bala, Sudarshan Roychowdhury, Tarit Topdar, Amal Dutta, Mahboob Zahedi, Nikhilananda Sar, Dr Ramchandra Dome, Samik Lahiri, Ajay Mukhopadhyay, Swadesh Chakrabarti, A.K. Premajam, Minati Sen, N.N. Krishandas, Bijay Modak, Bibha Ghosh Goswami, Susanta Chakraborti, Satya Gopal Misra, Lakshman Seth among others, all belonging to the CPI(M). Both Malini Bhattacharjee and Subhasini Ali rightly came to be recognized as extremely capable parliamentarians. Members would always be present to listen to them. Both of them enriched the proceedings of the House in substantial measure and deserved to be members of the esteemed institution. I have been an ardent admirer of both of them. I also recall Dr Sebastian Paul, Francis George and my good friend, M.P. Veerendra Kumar, all from Kerala, who worked in close association with the Left parties.

Piloo Mody was a man of substance and many parts. His interjections were extremely appropriate and caused great fun and laughter in the House. Once, he came to the Lok Sabha with a label on his pocket which said 'I am a CIA agent' – a scathing criticism of the government of the day which was prone to explain away its failures on the grounds of alleged CIA activities.

Raj Narain of the Janata Party had a colourful personality whose primary claim to fame was his sensational victory over Indira Gandhi in the elections following the Emergency. He came to be known as the one who vanquished the seemingly invincible Indira Gandhi. Though he could enliven the proceedings, his antics were often not in keeping with the dignity of the House. However, nobody could ignore his presence in the chamber.

George Fernandes – in his heyday, the idol of the working class – was another prominent member I have been privileged to know. We admired his pioneering role in organizing the successful railway strike. The members of the Left extended all support to him during those days of struggle against government repression. A forceful speaker as well as a leading trade union leader, he had a large number of admirers in the House. As a minister in the Morarji Desai government, he made quite an impression in his fight against foreign multinationals including Coca-Cola. I still recall his forceful speech opposing the no-confidence motion moved against the Desai government. Inexplicably, he deserted the Prime Minister later on. His subsequent activities and decisions greatly disappointed his supporters like me. His transformation from a firebrand socialist to a supporter of the BJP and other communal parties, ultimately becoming the convener of the NDA and a minister in the NDA government, negated all that he once stood for. For a man who once fought injustice and corruption with such dedication, it marked the nadir of his career when serious allegations were made against him in connection with the *Tehelka* episode. Though he initially resigned as defence minister citing moral grounds, his re-induction into the Cabinet when an enquiry was pending not only affected the reputation of Prime Minister Vajpayee but also convinced the people that his resignation was a sham. In protest, the Opposition decided to boycott him whenever he stood up to intervene as defence minister. I felt that he had brought it on himself because of the embarrassing somersault in his political ideology and his unprincipled attachment to office. But he did make a great contribution in organizing the working class in his younger days.

The fourteenth Lok Sabha had a number of young members who made impressive contributions. I have always encouraged young members to participate in the proceedings and I wish to mention in this connection Ranjit Ranjan of the Lok Janshakti Party (LJP) and Daggubati Purandeswari of the Congress, both of whom were articulate speakers. Purandeswari also proved to be a very effective minister. Sachin Pilot, Jyotiraditya Scindia, Naveen Jindal, Milind Deora, Sandeep Dikshit, Jitin Prasada, Ajay Maken, Tejaswini Gowda and Deependra Singh Hooda were some prominent young members. Over the years, Giridhar Gamang, Manorajan Bhakta, Madhusudhan Mistry, Lal Singh and Adhir Chowdhury of the Congress; Dr L.N. Pandey, Sumitra Mahajan, Santosh Gangwar, Satyanarayan Jatiya, Maneka Gandhi, Shah Nawaz Hossain and Kiren Rijuju of the BJP; Devendra Prasad Yadav and Ram Kripal Yadav of the RJD; Braja Kishore Tripathy, Arjun Charan Sethi and Bhartruhari Mahtab of the BJD; Sukhdev Singh Dhinsda of the SAD; Mehbooba Mufti of the PDP; Suresh Prabhu and Mohan Rawale of the Shiv Sena;

and Krishna Bose and Nitish Singupta of the AITC also made significant contributions.

Dr Sujan Chakraborti, Jyotirmoyee Sikdar (on matters of youth and sports), C.S. Sujatha, Dr K.S. Manoj Santasree Chatterjee, Bansagopal Chowdhuri, Basudeb Burman, Alakesh Das, P. Karunakaran, Amitabha Nandy and Sudhansu Seal of the CPI(M) regularly took part in the proceedings. But the most alert and effective CPI(M) member was V. Radhakrishnan, who was formerly the Speaker of the Kerala assembly and was elected to the twelfth Lok Sabha for the first time. As a member of the panel of chairmen in the fourteenth Lok Sabha, he also discharged his function very effectively. Unfortunately, he died recently under tragic circumstances.

Gurudas Dasgupta of the CPI, who ultimately became its leader, was one of the most active members the fourteenth Lok Sabha had. He had already attained a name as a member of the Rajya Sabha and as a well-known trade unionist and leader of the CPI. Dasgupta was indeed a vocal and articulate member who always advocated that the House sit for at least 100 days in a year. To this, I would usually interject saying that it was more important to ensure that no sitting was disrupted.

One young member of the CPI(M) who impressed me very much was Mohammad Salim, who became a member of the fourteenth Lok Sabha. Earlier, he had made his mark as a young and persuasive speaker in the Rajya Sabha. Thereafter, he became a minister in West Bengal and was an energetic and efficient one. He was elected to the Lok Sabha from the North East Calcutta constituency and was made deputy leader of the CPI(M) parliamentary party in the Lok Sabha. He soon made his mark as an effective speaker who attracted everybody's attention. As a matter of fact, in the fourteenth Lok Sabha, he became the main speaker who participated on behalf of the party in all the major debates, including the one on the trust vote. I have always admired his ability as a speaker and on several occasions I openly complimented him for his many illuminating interventions. I only wish he had not been overused by his party.

K.P. Unnikrishnan and Vayalar Ravi, who entered Parliament during the fifth Lok Sabha, made a mark in the early days of their career. They were junior to me but we became close friends. Vayalar Ravi is still a member and is, in fact, a minister in the government but I missed Unnikrishnan's thought-provoking interventions in the House.

P.G. Mavalankar was with us in the fifth Lok Sabha and, like H.V. Kamath, a prominent and sincere member. Both of them raised issues concerning the people. Kamath was a respected politician and an articulate member. Although he had a short tenure in the Lok Sabha, he made significant contributions to the parliamentary proceedings. For Era Sezhiyan of the DMK, I had and still have nothing but the highest admiration for the painstaking research he used to put in for the issues he raised in the House, particularly on economic matters, and the efficient way in which he presented his points of view. I wish he had continued to be in the Lok Sabha for many more terms.

I did not quite interact personally with Indira Gandhi, because as an ordinary member of the party, and a new one for that matter, I had no opportunity of meeting her or having discussions with her. But what was impressive about her was her exemplary demeanour in the Lok Sabha. One could not but admire the confidence with which she dealt with issues. I have already elaborated on her tenure as Prime Minister. One could not deny that she had become the people's choice as the leader of the country, but unfortunately she failed them, particularly during the period of Emergency.

Two ministers in her government impressed me very much – Y.B. Chavan and Jagjivan Ram. Both were soft-spoken but had a tremendous capacity to tackle the House, which was often turbulent, with the most remarkable ease and expertise. Both had a very persuasive way of speaking and, of course, both enjoyed the respect of the members. Mohan Kumaramangalam was an asset to Parliament and a most impressive speaker. Sardar Swaran Singh was quite an effective minister and a respected member. Siddhartha Shankar Ray of the Congress was elected to the fifth Lok Sabha and became the Union education minister but was soon sent to West Bengal where he became the chief minister. He has always been affectionate towards me and often lamented the fact that I had almost given up my profession for politics. As education minister during the Janata regime, Dr P.C. Chunder tried to bring about a few changes but had a brief tenure. A.B.A. Ghani Khan Chaudhury was a popular railway minister. Saugata Roy was an active member but his tenure was brief. Another Congress minister, Abdul Gafoor, was extremely affectionate towards me. As minister for works and housing, he extended his help for all good causes. We became close friends and admired each other.

Parliament and the country as a whole suffered grievously due to the untimely demise of Madhav Rao Scindia and Rajesh Pilot, in separate tragic accidents. Both were extremely polite, very good speakers and efficient ministers. Each one of them contributed greatly to maintain and enhance the prestige of Parliament. I had the good fortune of being treated by both of them with affection and respect. I still mourn their passing away in the prime of their lives.

Another parliamentarian with whom I had the great privilege of working since the fifth Lok Sabha was the celebrated Indrajit Gupta, the CPI leader. A perfect gentleman and a most articulate member, he earned the respect of everyone in the House and outside it. G.M.C. Balayogi, Speaker of the Lok Sabha between 1998 and 2002, affectionately called him the 'Father of the House'.

Indeed, he was a leader par excellence, one of the finest speakers I have heard in the House, illuminating the discussion on any subject in which he participated. I interacted closely with Indrajit Gupta when I became the leader of the CPI(M) from 1989 onwards. He lived a very simple life, spending his days as an MP and even as home minister of the country in the Western Court hostel, where I visited him. I often came across him at the Parliament library, engrossed in his work, and whenever I sought advice from him, he was most willing to offer the same.

Dr Ranen Sen, Kalyansundaram, M.N. Govindan Nair, Parvati Krishnan, Naryanan Choubey, C.K. Chandrappan, Loknath Chowdhury, D.K. Panda, Ajay Chakravarti, Bhogendra Jha, Ramavatar Shastri and P.K. Vasudevan Nair were some of the other prominent members of the CPI. Amar Ray Pradhan and Chitta Basu of the Forward Bloc were other eminent members I have been privileged to know and interact with closely.

Another important and respected member of the House, who was indeed an asset, was our didi, Geeta Mukherjee of the CPI. I have seen very few members as sincere, dedicated and effective as she was. Universally respected for her commitment to the cause of the underprivileged, specially women, she fought relentlessly for the passage of the women's reservation bill. I hope that her wishes are fulfilled soon. Other members who took up women's and children's issues and tried to further the cause of the underprivileged included Meira Kumar, who as a minister dealt with the problems of her ministry efficiently and compassionately, and Renuka Chowdhury and Kumari Selja who made a significant impact on the proceedings in the House by their merit and commitment.

Jaipal Reddy made a mark in Parliament from the early days of his membership as an orator with his command over English. I admired him immensely, and I remember that once he was extremely kind to refer to me as the best parliamentarian of the time. During the Congress and NDA regimes, when we made efforts towards floor coordination, he would be the generous host and hold the first meeting before each session at his house, where we would have a sumptuous breakfast on every occasion. I remember that during the NDA regime, once when he used the word 'humongous' in his speech, there was a great uproar in the NDA benches because, I feel, they did not understand its meaning. Of course, it is an uncommon word, and I could see him relishing, with an almost contemptuous smile, the hullabaloo created by some members because of their ignorance of the language. An articulate speaker with a perfect choice of words and sense of occasion, he has been an asset to the Parliament. I have always valued his friendship and good wishes. The near extinction of the Janata Party, I believe, left him with no option but to join the Congress. However, his merit was recognized and he is now an important minister.

Morarji Desai was the first non-Congress Prime Minister of the country. Earlier he had held important positions in the Congress. Though he seemed to be aloof and was not easily accessible, everyone respected him for his commitment to what he felt was right. I was then in my second term and had no occasion to interact with him directly. But he left a mark in Parliament with his disciplinarian approach.

V.P. Singh became extremely popular in the mid-1980s because of his principled fight against the Congress leadership on various issues, particularly corruption. As the leader of the CPI(M) in the Lok Sabha, I interacted with him on many occasions even before he became Prime Minister. There used to be meetings between the Janata Dal and Left parties at which I was present. I always found V.P. Singh a perfect gentleman, highly principled in his attitude towards people's issues and a relentless fighter against corruption and impropriety in public life. One thing that always struck me was his willingness to listen to other people's views during our meetings, which leaders of other Left parties and different opposition groups would also attend.

When he became Prime Minister in the ninth Lok Sabha, heading the Janata Dal coalition government, V.P. Singh conducted himself in an outstanding manner and raised high expectations among the people. The Left parties and the BJP supported his government from outside as he did not have a majority in the House. Four of us – Atal Bihari Vajpayee, L.K. Advani, Indrajit Gupta and I – used to meet every Tuesday for dinner at his residence to discuss important issues concerning the country and the government, and we had frank and full exchange of views with him. Although the policies and programmes of the Left parties and the BJP were poles apart, we wanted the government to continue. Unfortunately, the uproar created over the Mandal issue led him to tender his resignation. But I believe he sincerely tried to serve the country to the best of his ability and led a principled fight against corruption in our body politic and the denial of human rights to very large sections of our people.

During the days of non-Congress coalition governments, H.M. Patel and Santi Bhushan proved to be effective ministers and earned the respect of the members. As the law minister, Santi Bhushan played a very important role in undoing the anti-people 42nd constitutional amendment introduced during the Emergency.

Rajiv Gandhi became Prime Minister after the tragic assassination of his mother, and soon became the darling of the masses. No Prime Minister before him and ever since has had the kind of majority that Rajiv had in the eighth Lok Sabha. I found him to be very respectful to seniors. In the few interactions I had with him, he came across as extremely polite and courteous. I believe he was full of good ideas and wanted to achieve results.

Our young colleague Saifuddin Choudhury became close to him as Rajiv Gandhi used to invite him often for discussions.

During Rajiv Gandhi's prime ministership, my friend Shiv Sankar, who was then law minister, approached me with a surprising offer of judgeship of the Supreme Court. I did not pay much attention to the offer as I felt he was not serious and, of course, I had no intention of joining the judiciary. But I found he was insistent, and he explained that Rajiv Gandhi was very keen that I become a Supreme Court judge. I still do not know why Rajiv was so keen, because I never had a direct discussion with him. It could be either because of his understanding of my apparent knowledge of law or because he wanted to get rid of me from Parliament as I had always been a strong critic of the Congress governments! I politely refused the generous offer and have never regretted it.

Rajiv Gandhi's interventions in Parliament were quite impressive, though I was often scathing in my criticism of what I believe were his government's anti-people policies and his inability to deal with the Bofors issue adequately. As a matter of fact, during his government, many of the opposition members including leftists resigned from the Lok Sabha in protest against his policies and programmes. I thought he was quite competent as the leader of the Opposition too, during the prime ministerships of V.P. Singh and Chandra Shekhar.

Chandra Shekhar enjoyed the respect of the members of the House as a very principled politician, particularly in his early days as a parliamentarian. I have always been one of his admirers, and as such his conduct towards the end of his parliamentary career came as a rude shock. In my view, he behaved in an inexplicable manner by agreeing to become Prime Minister with the support of the Congress party, which he had stridently opposed after his expulsion from the Congress. This brought to an end the government headed by V.P. Singh. He went on to found the Samajwadi Janata Party, which hardly made a mark on Indian politics. But he always enjoyed popular support and his interventions were generally directed towards upholding India's democratic parliamentary life.

Mohan Dharia, known as one of the young Turks in the Congress, was a principled politician and an impressive speaker. In one memorable parliamentary intervention, he strongly criticized Indira Gandhi for the imposition of the Emergency. Krishan Kant, another young Turk, was also an important member and ultimately became the vice-president.

H.D. Deve Gowda had a short tenure as Prime Minister. He hardly had any opportunity to show his mettle, much like I.K. Gujral. But the last speech Deve Gowda delivered as Prime Minister in the House still rings in my ears as a very effective intervention by an outgoing Prime Minister, who was utterly wronged by his erstwhile supporters in the Congress party.

I enjoyed the company and affection of Biju Patnaik, a leader in his own right and someone who was respected by all. I used to sit next to him during the eleventh Lok Sabha and he was always extremely kind to me. We would often exchange views about the various problems plaguing the nation.

I have always respected Vajpayee as an orator, a sincere politician who believes in maintaining good personal relations with the members of other political parties and who always seemed to be less dogmatic compared to many of his colleagues in the BJP or in the government he headed. I have already mentioned his meeting with me at the official residence of the Speaker. He made it a point to attend the meetings held at the Speaker's residence before the commencement of each session. I have always been and still am full of admiration for him as an MP and as a politician though I disagree with his politics based on communal divide.

L.K. Advani has been one of the top leaders of the BJP for decades. I first came to know Vajpayee and Advani when I entered the fifth Lok Sabha. Advani was in the Rajya Sabha for a long time and Vajpayee was in the Lok Sabha. But the three of us were members of a committee that the Speaker of the fifth Lok Sabha, G.S. Dhillon, had appointed. The committee on electoral reforms was headed by Jagannath Rao, a senior member of the Congress representing Orissa. We found that on many issues on electoral policy, there was a commonality between Advani's views and mine. I must confess that I was quite impressed by his knowledge of the electoral laws of the country. Obviously, he had read extensively and knew about electoral laws of different countries, and made valuable contributions to our deliberations.

Advani has always been reserved in his dealings with people, not given to effusive displays of affection or opposition, and we have maintained good relations. We were never very close, but we have worked together and been in the Opposition together. Both of us strongly opposed the Emergency. We were poles apart, and still are. I think his politics overshadows other aspects of his personality. It probably made him seem a little removed from the mainstream secular politics of united India. Clearly, the very idea behind the rath yatra that he embarked upon was to divide the country on communal lines so that the BJP could benefit from the communal feelings aroused. In fact, as I have already mentioned I asked Advani in the House if he had taken the yatra only to come to power by dividing the nation. He admitted on the floor of the House that but for the rath yatra he would not have become deputy prime minister and the BJP would not have come to power. It was a clear admission of the objective. Advani has probably served his cause and his party well. His party, however, did not benefit even after a term of almost six years in the government, because the tenure was marked by divisive policies and programmes. But

Advani has made significant contributions to our parliamentary polity and is undoubtedly one of the top leaders of our country.

Among other leaders from the BJP, I would like to mention Jaswant Singh, whom I count as one of my good friends. I have always admired him for his diction and his way with words in the House and as a friendly colleague and competent MP. He had to toe the party line both as foreign minister and as finance minister during the NDA regime, and I think he has served his party well. I had a lot of critical comments to make on his overt friendliness with Strobe Talbot, the deputy secretary of state in the Clinton government. Jaswant Singh has also suffered for holding his own views. I wish him well, though I hope he will not continue with his programme of dividing West Bengal by the creation of Gorkhaland. It is quite beyond my understanding why someone of his stature would go to such an extent to create trouble for other states, making the journey from Rajasthan to Darjeeling just to get elected by relying on divisive politics and fomenting regional sentiments.

Vijay Kumar Malhotra was the deputy leader of the BJP during the fourteenth Lok Sabha and one of its able and front-ranking leaders. He represented the BJP at the Business Advisory Committee meetings and acted as the de-facto leader in the absence of L.K. Advani. On several occasions during the course of the fourteenth Lok Sabha, he seemed to be the one spearheading the disruptions created by NDA members. He is a veteran politician and I have always considered him a friend despite the fact that we are, politically speaking, poles apart.

Sushma Swaraj is no doubt a talented and articulate MP. I believe I enjoyed her affection. As the information and broadcasting minister she performed well, and was undoubtedly one of the competent members of the BJP. But her over-the-top reaction to the possibility of Sonia Gandhi becoming Prime

Minister was quite unbecoming. She had threatened to wear a white sari and shave her head, both symbols of mourning. That did not fit in well with the impression people had of Sushma as one of the forward-looking members of her party. Still, she has a lot to offer as a parliamentarian now that she is the leader of the Opposition in Lok Sabha.

Two BJP members I have always admired are Giridharilal Bhargava (alas, he is no more) and Hansraj Ahir. Their role as members has been exemplary. I never saw them disrupting parliamentary proceedings though the BJP would often indulge in disruptions. They would raise important issues in the House after giving due notices, and await their chance to speak. As Speaker, I generally admitted their notices, and admired their sense of responsibility when called upon to speak.

I have already mentioned how P.V. Narasimha Rao was a surprise choice for Prime Minister in the twelfth Lok Sabha, the elections to which were held under the tragic shadow of the assassination of Rajiv Gandhi. He came to power when the Congress was bereft of a leader to lead it to the polls which were close at hand. He became the Prime Minister without being an MP, though he was subsequently elected in a bye-poll from Andhra Pradesh. Narasimha Rao's term has gone down in modern Indian history for initiating the liberalization of the Indian economy, of which my party and I were critical because we felt it would open a Pandora's box and India would be overtaken by foreign capital. This was the subject of one of my speeches in Parliament, a trenchant critique of the then government's economic policy, which has been included in Appendix I. Narasimha Rao's role during the darkest days of India's politics, namely the demolition of the Babri Masjid, has been in the news of late with the Liberhan commission report. I have written about this earlier but given the immensity of the tragedy I cannot but help repeat what I have already said. I tried my best that day, 6 December 1992, to call him up when we got information about the demolition. The vandalism had started, and I rang up the Prime Minister's office at least twice. I was told he was resting and could not be disturbed. It was atrocious. It was the biggest failure on the part of a man who was the Prime Minister of India, unless it was connivance with an act of sacrilege. I see Narasimha Rao's failure to rise to the occasion as an indicator of some sort of complicity. By that, he brought the office of the Prime Minister of India to disrepute. I rang up Home Minister S.B. Chavan the same afternoon. Chavan answered the call and said they were relying on the state government, which had assured them there would be no problems. It was a total abdication of power and responsibility on the part of the government headed by Narasimha Rao. It was unfortunate and tragic that the Government of India brought about the greatest shame to the country's polity, from which we have not recovered even today, nor will we ever in future.

Narasimha Rao's name also came to be associated with what was known as the JMM bribery case. His government was facing a no-confidence motion because the opposition felt it did not have sufficient numbers to prove a majority. It was alleged that Narasimha Rao, through a representative, offered money to members of the Jharkhand Mukti Morcha to vote in favour of his government. These were the low points of his career. But as a person he was quite nice. He was a scholar who, as was known, was well conversant with a number of languages. I had friendly relations with him. He was well behaved and polite, and treated me well. Whenever I went to him regarding a public matter, he generally responded.

Lalu Prasad Yadav and Ram Vilas Paswan have been two important members of the Lok Sabha from Bihar. Lalu's career has been a colourful one and he was not only a darling of the masses, but also a favourite with members of the Lok Sabha. With his earthy sense of humour and his almost rustic candour, he endeared himself to all. Although many allegations have been made against him, on which I do not want to comment, his tenure as railway minister has been outstanding. This has been widely recognized, to the extent that he was invited to address students at Harvard University and many other institutions of eminence. Following the poor performance of his party in the election held in 2009, Lalu has not been his usual self in the fifteenth Lok Sabha, but I am sure he has his finger on the pulse of the people and will continue to have considerable relevance in our political life, especially in Bihar.

Ram Vilas Paswan has the distinction of winning an election with the largest majority. I have worked with him for a long time and found him to be one of the able speakers in the Lok Sabha. He assiduously nurtured a pro-poor, secular and pro-development image but did an inexplicable somersault by joining the NDA government. He suffered a crushing defeat in the elections to the fifteenth Lok Sabha. But he is still comparatively young and I am sure he will have the opportunity in future to serve the people through Parliament.

Raghuvansh Prasad Singh, who belongs to Lalu's party, has been a most dedicated and efficient member of the Lok Sabha. I was full of admiration for him for the expertise and commitment with which he presided over the important ministry of rural development. He assiduously tried to involve the members to monitor the execution and progress of the different rural development projects in their respective constituencies, but given the general apathy of the members, he seemed to be ploughing a lonely furrow.

Nitish Kumar, the present chief minister of Bihar, was an important member from Bihar, whose interventions were always impressive and constructive. He was also a successful minister and it is a matter of great regret that he switched over to the NDA and thus strengthened a communal front.

Ramdas Athawale of the Republican Party of India was a very popular member. Everyone enjoyed his interventions and whenever he spoke, sometimes reciting poems, the atmosphere in the House became less grave. During the fourteenth Lok Sabha, he seemed to have taken it badly when he was not made a minister. Everybody believed that he would make a popular minister.

I have already mentioned V. Kishore Chandra Deo, a Congress member from Andhra Pradesh. A quiet and soft-spoken individual, his services to Parliament have been exemplary, especially during the fourteenth Lok Sabha as the chairman of the privileges committee and of several inquiry committees. He showed remarkable leadership, devotion to duty and capacity for hard work. I have never heard him raising his voice and he was unfailingly courteous. He has many years of active service left to enrich our parliamentary polity.

Mulayam Singh Yadav rose from the ranks to become a very popular leader of Uttar Pradesh and the leader of the Samajwadi Party, which he founded. He was the chief minister of Uttar Pradesh during a difficult time. I believe he has served the people of his state, especially dalits, backward communities and minorities, well. Never one to compromise with communal forces, he was an important member of the non-BJP government at the Centre, though his allying with Kalyan Singh – the BJP chief minister of UP at the time the Babri Masjid was demolished – in the 2009 elections surprised and dismayed many. We used to sit next to each other in the thirteenth Lok Sabha. I must say he always encouraged me to speak in Hindi, but I am afraid I could never fulfil his request. I tried to speak in Hindi once, but made a mess of it and asked for his forgiveness. He used to say, 'Somnathji, your speech in English is good, but how many people can understand you? If you speak in Hindi, vast sections of our people can hear your speech and benefit from it, and your message can be put across much better.' I have always regretted that I could not live up to his expectation. I consider him as one of my very good friends. He has always treated me with great respect and affection. Mohan Singh, Ramjilal Suman, Ram Gopal Yadav, Jaya Prada, Sailendra Kumar and Kunwar Rewati Raman Singh were other very active members belonging to the Samajwadi Party. Mohan Singh and Ram Gopal Yadav were always listened to with attention in the House. Ramjilal was extremely alert in the House. He and Jaya Prada raised some important issue or the other every day. Sailendra Kumar and Rewati Raman were active members and became good friends of mine, and my family enjoyed their kind hospitality at regular intervals.

I had the great fortune of coming in contact with Dr Manmohan Singh even before he became Prime Minister. On occasions when I met him, he told me about his great privilege of receiving his degree from my father, who had gone to his university to deliver the convocation address. He is an innate gentleman with impeccable credentials for whichever office he held. He is a leader who exemplifies the best attributes of a principled and committed politician. With his sincerity, probity and concern for the people, he inspires confidence as the leader of the government. As Speaker of the fourteenth Lok Sabha, I used to meet leaders of different parties before each session of the House. Manmohan Singh and his party leaders used to meet me too, and we would have discussions about the possible subjects that could be raised in the House and how best to conduct the proceedings. I must record my deep appreciation of the constant help he gave me in the discharge of my onerous duties as Speaker.

Pranab Mukherjee is undoubtedly one of the ablest parliamentarians today. He was a member of the Rajya Sabha for a long time and entered the fourteenth Lok Sabha with the 2004 election. A man of great experience and ability, I believe he has very few enemies in the political field because of the courtesy he shows to others. As a minister, he has made significant contributions, and his party has recognized his services in good measure. He is one of the most efficient ministers of the Congress government. I cannot but express my gratitude for the help and cooperation I received from him during my tenure as Speaker. Pranab Mukherjee was then leader of the House. He is known for his prolific memory and his ability to deal with several subjects, including finance, with as much competence as anyone else. He is an asset not only to his party but to Parliament as a whole.

Sonia Gandhi has shown remarkable dignity and an exemplary attitude as leader of the Congress party, leader of the Opposition and as chairperson of the UPA. She made a tremendous mark on the Indian psyche by refusing the prime ministership of the country in 2004. She also resigned from the Lok Sabha after allegations that, as chairperson of the Advisory Council of the UPA, she had been holding an office of profit – and sought re-election successfully. I had the opportunity of interacting with her mainly during the thirteenth Lok Sabha when she was the leader of the Opposition and I was the leader of the CPI(M) legislature party, and opposition parties were trying to coordinate their activities inside the House, as also during my tenure as Speaker because she used to attend the meetings at my residence along with other leaders of the Congress party before each session of the House. She participated in the discussions without being domineering, and expressed her views very persuasively and articulately. So far as I am concerned, she has shown me great respect and that has been mutual.

Her son Rahul Gandhi has also made a mark in political life. In a short period, he has showed that office is not the only thing a politician should seek. That is why I think he has earned the admiration of a large number of people in this country. I remember he came to me once and told me he wanted to learn how to become a better MP. He did not come to seek any privilege or favour as a Member of Parliament. It demonstrated that he is a good student of politics. I believe he has a tremendous future ahead of him.

Priya Ranjan Dasmunsi, who has been seriously ill for quite some time now, was a very articulate member of the Lok Sabha. He was one of the most successful ministers for parliamentary affairs and, during my tenure as Speaker, rendered great help in the proper running of the House, which I openly recognized. I wish him early and complete recovery.

I would also like to mention that since the fifth Lok Sabha, I have had the opportunity of interacting with a long line of other successful ministers for parliamentary affairs, namely Raghuramaiah, Bhisma Narain Singh, Ravindra Varma (during the Janata rule), Sheila Dikshit, Pramod Mahajan of the BJP, Ghulam Nabi Azad, P.R. Kumarmangalam (he shifted from Congress to the BJP), Suresh Pachauri (member of the Rajya Sabha) and Pawan Kumar Bansal, among others. For the house to run properly, the role of the minister for parliamentary affairs is extremely crucial.

Apart from Arjun Singh, I would like to mention two ministers who are still part of the government and who have been extremely efficient. They have always made effective contributions as ministers and fully justify their reputation and standing. They are Sharad Pawar and P. Chidambaram. I believe Chidambaram has been most impressive as the home minister. I have always admired his sense of the occasion, his articulation and his very pertinent response to the issues involved.

My very good friend Murli Deora is a very kind-hearted person. He came across as someone keen to help any member who had any health problem. Once he forced me to take admission at Breach Candy Hospital in Bombay for treatment under the famous physician Dr Woodwadia. Needless to say, he made all the arrangements and bore all the expenses of the medical check-up. A most sincere friend, indeed. He is known to be competently discharging his duties as the minister of petroleum. I believe I helped him in getting over the initial uneasiness that he clearly exhibited as the minister during Question Hour. I shall always remember his affection towards me.

Among others, Mani Shankar Aiyar, A.R. Antulay, Sunil Dutt (unfortunately, he is no more with us), Kamal Nath, Anand Sharma, Kapil Sibal, Sushil Kumar Shinde, Santosh Mohan Dev, Subodh Kant Sahay, Praful Patel, Prithviraj Chauhan, Vilas Muttemwar, Oscar Fernandes, Dasari Narayan Rao, Jairam Ramesh, Dr Ramadass, R. Velu, Ambika Soni, Saifuddin Soz, T.R. Baalu, Dayanidhi Maran and E. Ahmad have been impressive and have efficiently dealt with their subjects in the House.

P.M. Sayeed was one of the most popular members of the Lok Sabha. He discharged the functions of deputy speaker with great dexterity and success, specially after the untimely demise of Balayogi. He represented Lakshadweep continuously for, I believe, eleven terms, and everybody was surprised when he was not elected to the fourteenth Lok Sabha. One of the most competent members and presiding officers, he was an extremely courteous person and we became very close friends. He spoilt me with his regular supplies of tuna fish. His sudden demise came as a great shock to me. I hope his son, who has been elected to the fifteenth Lok Sabha, will emulate him.

Satyendra Narayan Sinha, who was earlier the chief minister of Bihar, was a respected member of the House. He was extremely affectionate towards me and I have had the privilege of enjoying his hospitality at his residence both in Delhi and Patna on quite a few occasions. His wife, Kishori Sinha, a very gracious hostess, subsequently became a Member of Parliament and took part in the proceedings, regularly and ably. I continued to enjoy their affection, and the news of the demise of Satyendra Babu, also known as Chhotesaab, came as a great shock to me. Their son, Nikhil Kumar, was an active and articulate Congress member during the fourteenth Lok Sabha. Earlier, he was the commissioner of police in Delhi; he is now the governor of Nagaland.

I shall be failing in my duty if I do not refer to Sharad Yadav and P.A. Sangma, and their role as MPs. My recollection of Sharad Yadav is that of a lanky young man who came to the House after a bye-election victory, full of energy and enthusiasm. Soon, he made his mark as a rousing speaker, though he seemed to be a little restless. I became his admirer. Now he has matured to become a national-level leader, though his open and active support to the NDA still remains a mystery to me.

I have always treated Purno Sangma as my younger brother. He made a lasting contribution as a young member, as a minister and as our presiding officer. He was a very popular Speaker though on occasions he expressed his exasperation from the Chair because of the behaviour of some members. His decision to hold a special session of Lok Sabha during the golden jubilee year of our Parliament was extremely praiseworthy and we had excellent discussions. The members adopted an 'agenda for action', as proposed by Sangma. I hope that in the coming years he will take more interest in national politics and in Parliament. I wish him and my niece Agatha Sangma all the best for the future.

Omar Abdullah was elected to the twelfth Lok Sabha in 1998 and re-elected to the thirteenth and fourteenth Lok Sabhas. I remember him as a young and impressive speaker. He was a minister in the NDA government, but dissociated himself subsequently from the BJP and the NDA. He made a memorable speech during the debate on the trust vote in July 2008, for which he received well-deserved plaudits from large sections of the House and the media. Asaduddin Owasi representing Majlis-e-Ittehadul Muslimeen (MIM) of Andhra Pradesh also made a good contribution to the proceedings of the House.

Here, I must mention the great role played by my most illustrious predecessors in the office of the Speaker of the Lok Sabha. Beginning with the most respected G.V. Mavalankar and up to my immediate predecessor, Manohar Joshi, all of them have contributed substantially, commensurate to the important role which our Constitution makers have provided for the most important representative institution of our country, namely, the House of the People. To Shivraj Patil goes the great distinction of introducing the system of standing committees, which has now become an important part of the Parliament's functioning. The Lok Sabha has played an important role as the supreme body of the people of our country. I have humbly and to the best of my ability, maybe inadequately, tried to uphold the tradition laid down by the earlier Speakers. I have learnt a lot from the rulings and decisions of my predecessors. It has been my great privilege as an ordinary member of the House to witness how Speakers since the fifth Lok Sabha very ably discharged their function. It is for posterity to judge whether the tradition has been maintained or not during the fourteenth Lok Sabha.

I take this opportunity to convey my respectful regards and very best wishes to the present Speaker, Meira Kumar, who has already created a great impact. Charanjit Singh Atwal of the Shiromani Akali Dal was unanimously elected the deputy speaker of the fourteenth Lok Sabha. He is soft-spoken and a person of cool temperament and controlled the House effectively. He was a source of great strength to me and I feel we formed a good team that sincerely tried to discharge its duties during the turbulent periods in the House.

I also wish to record my highest appreciation of the very important and difficult role played by G.C. Malhotra, who was secretary general when I became speaker, P.D.T. Achary, the secretary general who was appointed during my tenure, and the officers and staff of the Lok Sabha secretariat. As an ordinary member, as chairman of different parliamentary and standing committees over the years and lastly as the presiding officer, I have had nearly four decades' experience of the functioning of our secretariat. I consider it a most efficient one and I have openly acknowledged so in the House. I do not wish to name any particular officer or staff but I have nothing but admiration for the way they have been discharging their duties and functions. As Speaker, I enjoyed the respect and affection of the staff and I was touched when the Lok Sabha Employees Association at their function to bid me farewell described me as the 'People's Speaker'. I do not know whether I have done justice to the description but I have always considered all of them as my brothers and sisters and tried my best to look into their genuine concerns and solve them. I wish all of them the very best for the future. I have nothing but admiration for the officers and staff in the speaker's office, led by Dr T. Kumar, without whose active and constructive help I could not have even tried to discharge my duties in adequate measure. Indeed, I owe a debt of gratitude to all of them for their sincerity, devotion to duty and undoubted capabilities.

It has been a long journey during which I have had the great privilege of serving the most important institution of our country, and I recall with some satisfaction that I have had the opportunity of knowing many important leaders, interacting with them, listening to them in the House and humbly trying to contribute to strengthening our nation and the unity and well-being of our people. I have mentioned only a few of my colleagues in the Lok Sabha because of constraints of space, and I do not wish to give an impression that others have not made a substantial contribution towards strengthening our parliamentary polity. In 1996, I had the great fortune of receiving from my peers, recognition as an outstanding parliamentarian. Only three parliamentarians before me had received such recognition – Atal Bihari Vajpayee, Indrajit Gupta and Chandra Shekhar.

I have always felt that every leader and every political party owes a lot to strengthening our democratic polity which is based on electoral politics. Democracy gives centrality to the people of the country. People are the deciding factor. Members of Parliament come to the House as the people's representative. They come to discuss people's issues, and there is no dearth of issues in our country. Large sections of the people are still illiterate, suffer from acute poverty, and have no proper health care. Many children are out of school and working in tea shops and roadside dhabas. I feel there are some national issues on which all parties should work together to bring about a solution. But that has not been the case, except when opposition parties united to fight against the Emergency. Nowadays we have coalition politics, so parties have to adjust their policies and programmes according to the coalition dharma. But unfortunately, we are yet to reach a stage where national interest is given top priority by all parties. On many occasions party interests overshadow or overtake national interest. This is an area where Members of Parliament can work together and demonstrate greater maturity and selflessness in the interests of the sanctity of both the Parliament and the nation. Only then will Members of Parliament do justice to the faith the people of the country have reposed in them.

APPENDIX I

Motion of Thanks on the President's Address, Fifth Lok Sabha, Indira Gandhi as Prime Minister, 7 January 1976

Mr Chairman, Sir, starting from the address of the President to the speech which we have heard just now, an attempt has been made to justify the Emergency on the basis of vague generalizations and mere abuses and vilification of opposition parties without specifying the supposed treasonable activities on the part of the opposition parties. I am very sorry that having been swayed by emotions and probably encouraged by the presence of the Prime Minister, a sober and responsible minister as we thought him to be, Mr Chandrajeet Yadav himself chose to use this occasion to vilify the CPI(M) on a wrong and misleading basis because, realizing that they cannot justify the Emergency on any positive ground, the best thing is to go on beating the Opposition with whatever stick comes handy. That is why it was said that there has been a sort of ganging up between the right reactionaries and the CPI(M). Sir, it is known that this is wrong and that this is an absolute calumny. Only on a very important issue like civil liberty, there had been cooperation and we, Sir, certainly support anybody who raises a voice of protest against the deliberate denuding of personal and civil liberties in this country by a repressive government. Whoever will come and support us, we shall certainly seek their support and give mutual support.

Now, Sir, as Miss Patel rightly said when BLD people join Congress, they become progressives overnight. When ex-rulers and ex-zamindars joined you, joined the ruling party, they certainly become progressives. When Swatantries and when Jana Sanghis join the Congress they became progressive. Do not apply such double standards everywhere. This is my request.

You have declared Emergency. The people of the country know why. You declare Emergency on the plea of internal disturbances, when there was already an Emergency. Because of the powers under the Constitution of India, which you wanted to exercise or which you did not want to take the trouble of having obligations under, you could do it under the existing Emergency of 1971. All the powers, the Defence of India Rules and so on, have not been promulgated now. They were actually promulgated in 1971 and this is now being used under the new Emergency. Not a single extra constitutional power was obtained by proclaiming this new Emergency. Then, what was the Emergency for? Was it for economic reasons? Then, there is a specific provision under the Constitution, Article 360, for declaring a financial emergency. You did not take recourse to that. When there was rampant inflation, when the whole economy was out of gear, as Dr Rao has said, as he has reminded us, when the Government of India was not functioning so far as the finances of the country were concerned, you did not take recourse to financial emergency. And what emergency powers for internal disturbance are necessary to meet an economic situation? Sir, 'internal disturbance' has been used as a plea because the position of a particular individual became at stake. This is the reality.

It should be understood. I am sure members opposite realize it in their own heart of hearts. But they cannot say so. The press in this country has been gagged. The Opposition has been mercilessly gagged. Their own people have been gagged. Today the whole intention has been to create a fear psychosis in the country to bring about a feeling of terror in the minds of the people. People are not allowed to open their lips. This is a stark reality in this country. No good denying it. If you deny it, you are denying it for the purpose of record only, not in your own heart of hearts.

What I was asking the government, the Prime Minister and others was this: What extraordinary powers did you need for which a second proclamation was made? Now, if there was internal disturbance alone, why have you brought out so many other justifications for this Emergency? How can you take the pretext of late running of trains for internal disturbance? This party has been in power since independence in this country. If the trains had not been run in time, it is very easy to go on blaming the workers. Why have you not been able to inculcate a sense of discipline among the workers? Why have you not been able to make them feel part and parcel of this country, make them feel that they are one with the administration? Why are they alienated from you? Why are the common people alienated from you? You have no answer. You never ask yourselves those questions. For everything that is not happening properly in this country, an emasculated Opposition is supposed to be responsible. You ridicule the opposition and say 'the people are not with you', but you hold that very emasculated and miniscule Opposition supposedly responsible for the ruination of this country. You have been in uninterrupted charge of the government of the country. You have not delivered the goods to the people. Poverty has been accentuated. People's miseries have increased a hundredfold, and you say you are not responsible for that.

That is why I say that your right to govern this country now is based on repressive power. You cannot function without draconian laws. You cannot function under ordinary laws of the country. The Constitution of India which twenty-five years ago had been commended to the country by no less a person than Jawaharlal Nehru, the Constitution does not suit you, because it gives some powers even now to the people of the country. You do not like the people of this country to have any power. You do not want that the people of this country can raise a voice of protest. That is why you have come up with proposals, those obnoxious proposals, the source of which has not been denied.

As I was saying, if discipline was the reason, then a false reason has been given in the proclamation of Emergency that internal disturbances were there which threatened the security of the country. If Mr Jayaprakash Narayan had been guilty of treason, try him for treason. Give him exemplary punishment under the laws of the land. If Morarji Desai, or for that matter any person, has been guilty of sedition try him. Give him an opportunity. Let the people of the country know. Mr Jayaprakash Narayan has been arrested. He is a right reactionary. In the name of fighting fascism and right reaction, you have arrested MPs like Mr Jyotirmoy Bosu and Mr Noorul Huda. Do they belong to right reactionary parties? You have arrested trade union workers. You have dismissed trade unionists, government servants, under MISA. You have detained them. You have dismissed them under article 311 (2) without even letting them know what is their wrong. Even the present Constitution, as it stands today, gives enormous powers to the government. A government servant can lose his job in a minute. A person can be kept in detention indefinitely. Even his right to move the court is extremely limited. What have you done? You are afraid to face the people. The Supreme Court of India has given clearance to the Prime Minister's election. One of the judges who upheld her election had made an observation. I do not know whether she has had the time to go through the judgment which has been delivered in her own case. Mr Justice Chandrachud has observed that law should not be what the king emperor thinks is law; it should be decided in the anvil of constitutionality; it should be tested on the principle whether it is for public good. ... Today an attempt is being made to stifle popular and democratic movements and stifle the ventilation of the people's grievances. If I say something here which is not to your liking, the people outside will not know; they do not know that there is another version possible on a particular issue. People may think: we have sent him to Parliament; we want to know whether our representative toes the line of the government or he has some alternative proposals to make. But now people will not know. Look at today's papers and see how Mr Samar Mukherjee's speech has been reported. It is a travesty of reporting parliamentary proceedings. Is this the way you are going to take the country along the path of progress?

Mr Chairman, I want to make this appeal to the members opposite through you: do not feel that patriotism is your monopoly; or the desire to do good to the country is only your monopoly. We are as much anxious that this country should be governed and governed properly; we want that this country should proceed on right lines; if my line is a little different does it mean that I do not have patriotism? If I do not want the zamindars, the landed gentry and the black-marketeers to control our country, does it mean that I am not patriotic? If I want to say something which the people of the country want me to say, should I not be allowed to say it? If a judge delivers a judgment which you do not like, you say that the judge is wrong and therefore you want to take away the court's powers. Why are you so arrogant? You do not want anybody to judge your action. Why should not the judges decide whether you do something rightly or wrongly? It is a system which has worked for so many years. Take the last amendment of the Constitution which this Parliament adopted. We were willing parties to it. We had been demanding that the Constitution should be so amended that no vested interests can take advantage. We have enlarged the powers under Article 31 of the Constitution; we have given enormous powers to the government. But how has this government utilized those powers? What legislation has stood in their way? How have the courts stood in their way? ... we on this side have extended our support even to a capitalist and reactionary government as this when they thought of welfare legislation. Whether they were implementing that or not, we had extended them full support. Let them give one example of one single welfare legislation which had been held up by us in Parliament? I challenge them. On the other hand, in the name of bringing about a balanced society, egalitarian society and welfare and socialism in this country, they have reduced the quantum of bonus without reducing the cost of living. They have taken away the rights of the workers even to hold meetings and demonstrations. They have not even the right to go to their managers to ventilate their grievances. There is a case in regard to Bank of India, I am not going into merits because the matter is sub judice. It is a nationalized bank and I want to tell the members what happens there. The authorities there issued a circular deducting the salaries of the employees, because their representatives had gone to a meeting with the manager for ventilating employees' grievances who even entertained them. But after the meeting the manager issues a notice to them; you did not work during the time you came to see me and therefore you are not entitled to wages for that period.

Is this the way of getting the willing cooperation of the ordinary people of this country? Is this the way you want their participation in your so-called nation building? Mr Chairman, Sir, the position is this. In the garb of Emergency, what is being sought to be done is to create and maintain a hegemony. We are opposed to that. The attempt is to create and maintain a particular attitude of government which is not in tune with the national aspirations of this country. You are utilizing this not for the betterment of the people because inflation has been contained. It is said that Emergency should remain and continue not because of inflation but because of other economic reasons and therefore elections should not be held. See how the reason is put forward by this government. Sir, what is the position in the economic field? What is the position in the small industries, small-scale industries like bulb manufacturing industries? Mr Maurya is here. He has got the statistics fully. The small-scale industries are almost closed down. The wagon-building industries in West Bengal are completely at a standstill. J.K. Aluminium is being closed. Hindustan Motors has introduced a rotational system of layoffs of employees.

Now, who is coming to their protection? Are you using Emergency powers against the management of Hindustan Motors? You have got all the powers under the sun. You don't care for the people's rights under Article 19 and under Article 14 you have suspended them. But you have not suspended Article 31 which guarantees property rights. You have forbidden my right to free speech. You have taken away my right of equality to be treated equally amongst equals. But you have not taken away the right of propertied class. That is why Article 31 has not been touched. This is the true position of the government.

Sir, in the jute industry, what is happening? Concession after concession has been made but layoffs and closure are continuing. More layoffs and more closure and more retrenchments are continuing. In the jute mills, even the jute growers are not getting concessions. Concessions have been given to the jute mills but jute growers are not getting even the support price. Same is the thing with regard to the textile mills. In those mills which have been taken over the Textile Corporation, the workers are extending all support, not a single complaint has been made against workers. They are doing extra work. But they are in doldrums because the management is still as bad as it was. No attempt has been made to have the stocks cleared. The retailers cannot even taken them, far less the consumers because of high cost of textile goods.

Sir, this is the position in this country and we are only told that something was being done for which Emergency must be imposed. Therefore, I request my friends, through you Sir, do not take the people of this country for a ride. Try to do something good for them. If the people are with you, why are you afraid of them?

Speech in Response to the House of People (Extension of Duration) Bill, Fifth Lok Sabha, Indira Gandhi as prime Minister, 4 February 1976

Sir, this is another glaring instance of misuse of constitutional provisions and is nothing but an outrage on the Constitution and also on the people of the country. The statement of objects and reasons is nothing but a joke. The real purpose of the statement of objects and reasons is to indicate the scope and necessity of a bill. But what has happened here is that the necessity itself is given as the reason for the necessity of the bill. In his speech, the minister has relied upon the so-called proclamations of Emergency, which we say are nothing but hoax and trumped up. The Constitution no doubt provides for extension of the term of the Lok Sabha, but this should be treated as an exceptional provision, like the emergency provisions of the Constitution. But this government has made the emergency provisions in the Constitution the normal provision for the governance of the country. This government cannot function under the ordinary laws of the land. The Constitution which is the organic law of the people, which the people of this country have given unto themselves, is now being treated as a mere plaything by the ruling party. I am sure the framers of the Constitution had never dreamt that there could be such abuses of the Constitution itself. The emergency provisions which should be taken recourse to only in exceptional circumstances are now being used for their political ends.

When this clause in the draft Constitution was being discussed in the Constituent Assembly, Dr Ambedkar moved an amendment to Clause 68 (2), which corresponds to the present Article 83 (2). In the draft Constitution, it was left to the President to extend the term of the House. It was substituted by 'Parliament by law'. But even then Dr Ambedkar said, this was nothing but an invasion of the ordinary constitutional provision, which means this should be taken recourse to only in exceptional and extraordinary circumstances. By this bill, what Dr Ambedkar had apprehended has actually happened, namely, there is an invasion of the Constitution of this country. At the same time, the rights of the common people of the country are being invaded by a power-hungry executive and a power-hungry ruling party. Their hunger for power is insatiable and its latest manifestations are this bill and what was done recently in Tamil Nadu, with the consequences which you have just now reported to the House.

It is clear to the people that the whole object of this bill is nothing but to perpetuate the status quo because it suits their political interests. Having muffled the voice of the people, having taken away their right of personal liberty, having banned all meetings and processions, having gagged the press, freedom of expression and speech, having kept Members of Parliament in detention for an indefinite duration without telling them the charges they are supposedly guilty of, having taken away, with the active support, I shudder to think of Mr Gokhale also, all the people's fundamental rights, what the ruling party wants is to continue with a rubber-stamp Parliament to suit its own political ends. It is the tragedy of this country, I say, that this is all sought to be done in the name of the people of this country, when the people are the real targets of this attack. I submit that this bill is an obnoxious attempt and a crude attempt to justify a non-fact, I call it a non-fact because it is the so-called Emergency. Just now the minister said that everything is peaceful in the country, there is no trouble, law and order is restored, production has increased and the sense of despondency has gone away from the minds of the people. But you do not want to face the people. This is the situation in this country.

The people have been made ineffective in the name of maintaining democracy, and this government has shown complete antipathy towards all sections of the people which do not belong to their hue, or is not their ally, who do not listen to their voice. They do not want to listen to either constructive criticism or practical suggestions and they do not wish to enter into a dialogue with the people of this country. That is why I say that this bill is not a bona fide measure and is not in the public interest. Will this government continue to deny and deprive a large number of people of their fundamental and basic rights?

They say that the people are with them, they say that the people are not with the opposition parties; they say that the vast multitude of people in this country are behind one individual who is the leader of the political party which is in power. By mere propaganda they want to create an impression that they alone represent the public views and public sentiments. But how do they ascertain the views of the people in this country? What is the mandate of the people? The mandate given to this House is going to expire shortly. How do the people express their views? The other day I told this House how meetings in West Bengal called by the leftist parties have been banned one after another since the proclamation of the Emergency. Even a condolence meeting called in the memory of Mr Chou En-lai, the Chinese Prime Minister, was stopped by issuing an order under the Defence of India rules. We wanted to take out a procession, a silent procession, in memory of those persons who have been killed in Chasnala. That was not permitted and that was stopped. Then how do the people express their views? You have banned all meetings, you have banned all the discussions, you have banned all processions and you have banned all publications. You have imposed ruthlessly censorship regulations and yet you say the people are supposedly with you.

There is no method of ascertaining what the people really think about you and what the people really want. Now they want to seek to project that the people are with them by officially sponsored demonstrations. Official agencies, like the DTC buses in Delhi, are shamelessly used, you organize the people, you create a hullabaloo and then you say that the people are with you. The mass media are shamelessly used for your own purposes. But you do not want to find out what the people think about you. The public or the people have not been given the right to express their views freely and fairly by means of an election, through the ballot paper.

Have the people of this country been given the right of recall? They have no right to recall their representatives, even if they have proved unworthy of their trust. How do the electorate control their representatives for a term of five years and we are now trying to extend it without consulting them. Suppose the 20-point programme requires the continuation of this House, why do you not approach the people and ascertain their views?

I say that though this is being done in the name of exercising constitutional power, this is committing rape on the Constitution by flagrant and motivated abuse, reducing the constitutional scheme of this country to a mere mockery. Abuses we have seen. Article 352 of the Constitution has become very handy for the ruling party and article 356 of the Constitution is used to achieve party ends.

The other day, Tamil Nadu was brought under President's Rule under Article 356. We feel that if the DMK ministry did not justify the faith reposed in them by the people of the state, then the people of the state should have been given an opportunity within few weeks to express their views, and if they wanted, they could have thrown out the ministry and the party into the dustbin of history. Why should the Centre intervene at this stage and get a convenient report at a convenient time from the governor and impose President's Rule under Article 356?

The DMK was the party with which the ruling party cooperated openly only five years ago, in 1971. You gave up the right to contest even a single Assembly seat. You were so much enamoured of them because that suited your political purpose and you wanted some candidates to be returned to Parliament from Tamil Nadu. Now you do not want them because you have got the Emergency and the Constitution is being abused and misused for your party purposes. Under the garb of Emergency you can do anything in this country. This is what is happening.

I am not holding any brief for the DMK ministry as such, but see the way this government behaves and misuses constitutional provisions. You engineered the charges to be made against the ministry and then you assume the role of prosecutor and then judge. On these charges framed by yourself, you issue the order of President's Rule. This is the way the people's verdict is being respected by this government.

The Tamil Nadu people have voted them to power for five years with the greatest majority. You cannot wait for another six or ten weeks for the purpose of giving them an opportunity for giving their views again.

The governors in this country, I am very sorry to say, are behaving as clerks, and they are defiling the Constitution by their abject surrender to the vested interests which are monopolizing the Centre.

Even before the so-called Emergency in June 1975 do we not know how many by-elections have been kept pending. For what reasons? Why was not the parliamentary by-election from Trivandrum held? Why was it cancelled at the last moment? Why are so many seats kept vacant in Bihar, West Bengal, throughout the country? No explanation has been given. It is because it does not suit them, because they found that the wind was not in their favour. What with Jabalpur and other places, they felt that they could not face the people.

I charge that this bill has been conceived by this government, by the ruling party, as a means to avoid facing the people because they want to run away from the people. It is a product of nervousness and cowardice, and that is why it is being given as a lollipop to their party MPs, along with the bonanza of a tax-free allowance, so that they would keep quiet. They believe that they have never had it so good in the country in the past and they want to perpetuate their hegemony by rampant abuse of the Constitution. One should have thought that it was wholly immaterial whether 'A' or 'B' remained in Parliament or not. We do not believe in, nor do we preach, the indispensability of any body of persons or individuals.

They think they are indispensable; they think their indispensability is because of their leader and that is why the want to perpetuate themselves as the only arbiters of the fate of the people of this country. But they forget thereby they are expressing lack of confidence in themselves.

Today the stark reality is that they want the people to remain enslaved with no manner of freedom whatsoever. They want a committed and ineffective judiciary and they want a majority in Parliament consisting of their yes-man with conscience mortgaged and tongue-tied.

The attitude of the ruling party is that the people are no long the masters but they are the masters of the people. It is no longer a democracy of the people, by the people or for the people. This democracy is in spite of the people. That is why they do not care to seek the verdict of the people. What justification they have to continue this Parliament without placing their balance-sheet before the people of this country and getting their sanction for their continuance?

This duplicate Emergency is being utilized as a ruse to continue in power. On 3 December 1971, an Emergency was declared when there was really some danger to the security of the country by foreign aggression. But our jawans won a great victory within thirteen days and Bangladesh was liberated. Everybody hailed that. We applauded the victory of the jawans although the credit was sought to be arrogated by one single individual for that great victory. Even after that, when the country had been threatened with foreign aggression and even the external aggression was continuing, elections were held in so many states, including the border state of West Bengal, which was of course nothing but a farce, as we saw there the fine though sickening example of rigging and manipulation. But even then you did not take recourse to the Emergency for the purpose of avoiding the people of this country.

What is the justification for not holding the elections now? They say with the implementation of the 1975 proclamation of Emergency, now it is milk and honey that is flowing in this country. Everybody is going to office in time. Trains are running on time. Everybody wants that trains should run in time. Everybody wants that people should work in the offices. Therefore, so long as trains are running in time, there should be no elections; so long as office-goers report to the office at 10 o'clock there should be no elections! According to them the Emergency must continue. If trains are to run on time Emergency must continue. If the country is peaceful, if they are achieving what they wanted by this Emergency, if there is no internal disturbance which was sought to be the justification for issuing the second proclamation of Emergency, then how can you utilize this Emergency for the purpose of not facing the people of this country?

During the last twenty-six years of our Republic, we have had to live with Emergency for more than ten years. Like poverty, Emergency is supposed to remain forever with the people of this country. Under the Congress rule, Emergency provisions have come to be regarded as part of normal state of affairs in this country, giving rise to what Mr Setalvad described as 'constitutional dictatorship'.

Mr Gajendragadkar has said: 'The continuous use of such unfettered power (it happened in 1965–66) may ultimately pose a serious threat to the basic values on which the democratic way of life in this country is founded.'

What he had said has proved to be true with a decade from when he said that. Thirty-four eminent persons in this country like Chief Justice Mahajan, Chief Justice S.R. Das, Chief Justice Sinha – they are not belonging to any political party or the opposition party for that matter – said on 27 February 1966 as follows: 'A grave Emergency lasting over three years and resulting in the exercise of arbitrary powers by the executive for such a long period has not been known in a democratic country'.

But we had another ten years since then.

The situation is this. They are now trying to write a new definition of democracy under the leadership of one individual because they have equated an individual with the country and the country with an individual. Now, democracy is of 'X', for 'X' and by 'X'.

We oppose this Bill.

Speech on the President's Address to the Joint Session of Parliament, Tenth Lok Sabha, P.V. Narasimha Rao as Prime Minister, 4 March 1992

Sir, the contents of the President's address prove that we were fully justified in boycotting the joint session of Parliament because we did not wish to participate in the ritualization of a very solemn occasion which has the sanctity of Constitution behind it.

If one goes through the address, one hears the voice, not of the President of a vibrant and progressive India, but the voice of a President of a country which has lost its self-reliance and self-dignity. That is why the President of this country was made to indulge in banal platitudes and sterile homilies without any indication of any independent and pro-people thinking or of any basic policy formulation in the whole address.

Sir, I am very sorry to say that the address is the product of a government which is in bondage, a government which is on leash led by the nose by the combine of Bush, Camdessus and Preston who have become the arbiters of our nation. That is why we find that the address does not enthuse the nation but condemns the people, compromises their dignity and ridicules their commitment to self-reliance. This Narasimha Rao government, now headed by a sober-gentleman-turned-arrogant within a sphere of a few months, will go down in history as the one which has mortgaged our country to the imperialist financial marauders for some tainted lucre. Our economic sovereignty and national prestige have become negotiable and we are projected to the whole world as cringing supplicants to those agencies whose imperialist and capitalist design so far as the Third World countries are concerned is very well known. They are more anxious to maintain their hegemony than to come to the real rescue of the developing and the Third World countries. That is why very serious problems faced by the ordinary people, common people of the country, not the highest income brackets of this country, like the steep and unabated price rise of essential commodities, have received a tongue-in-cheek reference of about six lines in an address covering nineteen pages while sixteen lines have been devoted for the fulsome praise of Bush and company's so-called humanitarian philanthropic and democratic pretensions.

... the current year's budget has put the final nail in the coffin of the principle of self-reliance and mixed-economy which was the dream of Pandit Jawaharlal Nehru and which was adopted, by and large, as our national policy. But Pandit Jawaharlal Nehru has become an inconvenient name to the Congress party. And Nehruvian economic policy is being projected as dirty words. ... And the Nehruvian economic policy is being projected as an anti-growth concept. We do not any longer hear that the public sectors occupy the commanding heights of our economy ... Those who still believe in the same, in the primacy of the public sector, are being dubbed as anti-nationals. Now to the Congress party and to the Congress government, market economy of the US variety has become the mantra and Pandit Jawaharlal Nehru has been given an indecent burial. Our objection to the Centre's economic policies so far has been against the tardy implantation of the principles of self-reliance.

Our objection so far has been against the weakening of the public sector and the Congress government's continuous pampering to a handful of monopolists and speculators in the country and perpetuating the miseries of the common people. But what has happened now? This government has not only reversed the policy without any mandate from the people, without there being even a mention in the election manifesto, without having a majority support from the people of this country but they have also changed the path of our economic growth or direction and they have adopted brazen facedly the capitalist path of market economy which will only multiply the miseries and sufferings of the common people. And it has already resulted in surrendering to the stranglehold of monopolists, foreign agencies and even compromising our ability to decide our own future.

Today, the Prime Minister's intervention was very significant. Why I say this is because he has become arrogant, he has become insensitive. He is very happy. He said that the people outside were very, very happy with his budget and with his economic policy.

According to the Prime Minister, people are praising this budget sky high. But who are these people? It is *Washington Post*, a newspaper of the American imperialists, NRIs, FICCI, ASSOCHAM and the like. Dr Manmohan Singh is being projected as having saved this country. But has the budget been welcomed by the common people, by the toiling masses? No. They – the common people – consider the finance minister and the Prime Minister of our country as the messiahs of our financial doom and of economic perfidy ... We want to make it very clear that we can never be and we shall not be a party to this process of dismantling and defilement. We shall protest both here and outside ... We shall protest both inside and outside this House, on the streets, in the factories, in the fields and in every nook and corner of the country. We are giving this advance warning to them.

They are very happy also that some sarkari economists and some sarkari journalists are made to sing paeans of praise of the budget. These people always do. They always praise the government budget, whichever is the government and whichever is the budget. They praised Rajiv Gandhi's budget and now they are criticising Rajiv Gandhi's budget and applauding Narasimha Rao's budget. But nobody is able to deny the effect of the IMF and the World Bank conditionalities on the preparation of their budget. And very significantly this government deliberately kept suppressed from the people and this Parliament those documents which ultimately they were forced to disclose by pressure of public opinion and opinion in the House. It had disclosed a very sorry and serious state of affairs.

I would request my honourable friends from the treasury benches not to make it a partisan issue and to please go through the documents very carefully for the sake of their government only, if this temporary majority they wish to perpetuate. You may now ignore and you may play with the future of this country. That is why, in one of my earlier interventions, I had requested my very good friends from the treasury benches to please go through them. Please do not mortgage your conscience. This is not a matter of whip. When so many people are raising this question, please try to go through those documents and find out what commitments this government has already made.

... We charge that this government has compromised our economic sovereignty and this budget is the faithful implementation of the fiats of the IMF and the World Bank. I am not today dealing with the budget in detail. That will be dealt with when we come to the budget discussions.

... In 1991–92 the total debt servicing was estimated to be Rs 11,936 crores of which the share of commercial borrowings was Rs 4,158 crores. It was 35 per cent of the total debt servicing which means a debt trap. These are not my figures. Who is responsible for this and how are you trying to solve this? The only way they have chosen is to go on bended knees to the IMF and to the World Bank.

We had even opposed the '1981 approach' to the World Bank, when the present Rashtrapatiji was the finance minister. He had gone to the IMF to take loan. I would like to know as to what agreement was entered into then. Would you please disclose the 1981 agreement with the IMF and the World Bank? We would like to know as to what were the conditionalities there. What has forced you to completely surrender your rights and completely bind your hands and feet, so far as our economic policies are concerned?

So far as the borrowings from the commercial banks are concerned, the solution was not to go to the IMF, but to restrict non-essential imports and to increase exports. But, that was not the policy that was adopted.

What is the direction of the present plan? The present deputy chairman circulated some documents containing the outline of the plan. It was said that the success of the plan depends on and it can only succeed if there is an increase in the export to the extent of 13.6 per cent every year. It is impossible to reach that. They are no longer making that forecast. Then, the Planning Commission itself says that the planning process will come to a halt. Who is responsible for this and what are the ways out? Is it only to go to the IMF and the World Bank? Is there no other way in this country? Is it for this that this country has been fighting, dismantling everything? What was the role of the public sector when this country became independent and after that? Who came to the core sector?

Not a single monopolist came to the core sector in this country. In the steel sector, in the oil sector, who were the people, who were the industrialist-friends of yours who made investments? It was the public sector which came there and Jawaharlal Nehru realized that the public sector was the only panacea, the only way out. On the basis of his experience, he presented the Industrial Policy in the House in 1956, which the Congress party adopted. But, that Congress, of course, is dead and gone.

Public sector undertakings like ONGC, Indian Oil Corporation, Steel Authority of India, etc. have helped this country to grow. With nascent democracy which was to develop under the trauma of Partition and huge mass transfer of people from one place to another, the public sector has taken the role and now it is being ridiculed. Who is responsible for the mismanagement of the public sector? Today you are selling the shares of the public sector undertakings, of profitable concerns, to whom? To the multinationals and to the monopolists.

... What is the provision made and what is the indication given in the President's address as to how the price rise will be dealt with? Just a casual reference was made to that. Their manifesto – I hope they have not torn out page 25, because 25 is rather unfortunate for them – says on page 25, that the Congress is determined to roll back the prices to levels obtaining in July 1990 in case of diesel, kerosene, salt, edible oils, etc. Either that has been torn away or you have put ink on this. Page 26 is also the back of 25. Tearing of that page will help them. It is said, 'The Congress will create 10 million new jobs per year and 100 million jobs by the end of the century.'

... The annual rate of inflation has been 13.5 per cent for wholesale price index – the highest in the decade as the seasonal downturn in prices proved to be rather modest. Between April and December, the major portion of which this government has functioned with the blessings of IMF, the rate of increase in prices stood at 13.7 per cent compared to 9.3 per cent. Even Mr Chandra Shekhar performed better than you. An analysis of the trends in a month-wise rise in prices for 1991 shows inflation at 16.3 per cent which was the highest in September as compared to 12.2 per cent in June. The rate of rise in prices for primary articles during the calendar year on a point to point basis has been estimated at 18.9 per cent.

... Neither the budget nor the President's address makes any provision as to how to contain the price rise, far less to bring it down ...

Another very serious situation which the country is facing, specially the common people, is the problem of unemployment. Sir, in 1951, number of persons who were unemployed were 3.29 lakhs. The wonderful Congress contribution to this country at the end of 1989 was 3.27 crores. This figure refers to the registered unemployed people.

... In March 1991, with the help of the Congress, the Chandra Shekhar government's performance resulted in having 34,890,000 as registered educated unemployed persons. And what was the average number of vacancies notified during that period? It was 38,000. For one year, the figure comes to 33.48 lakhs against unemployed persons in the exchanges and only a maximum of 4.56 lakhs could be employed. What will happen to these unemployed people? What is the source of livelihood for these people? Where will they go? Can the agricultural sector or the industrial sector bear any further employment? From where will they earn their livelihood? Please tell us. I would like to know about it. And now, over and above, what is happening? We are told of employees being redundant. Four lakhs of railway employees are going to lose their jobs. Government offices are being closed and you are encouraging exit policy. You have not adopted a policy for reviving a single sick industry. The new modern hi-tech industries will provide very little employment to the ordinary people because they are highly mechanized and automatic machines are used, so far as we know. Then, where will these people go for jobs? What are you doing to help them to earn their livelihood through small-scale industries? What entrepreneurial assistance are you giving them? Sir, over two lakhs of sick companies are in private sector about which they are so enamoured. Why so many private sector industries are closed or sick?

What are you going to do to help these people and now, you are getting rid of employees of the public sector. You are sending the units to the BIFR for closure and winding up. But what will happen to the employees? What is the hoax about the National Renewal Fund? It is said that it will be for retraining and redeployment. With all sincerity and seriousness, I am asking as to where will you redeploy them. What alternative training will you give them? How many people will you train with the amount in your renewal fund? For heaven's sake, please tell us about this. What is the fate of those people who are unemployed who are not criminals or antisocial elements? They want to live a decent life with an ordinary amount and not crores of rupees. They want to look after their families and lead a decent life. Where will they get deployed? Please tell us so that we can inform them not to worry and that this benign government will give them jobs.

Sir, the exit policy has been thrust upon this country by the IMF. If you go through the history of Latin American countries which had gone to the IMF and the World Bank, you will find that exactly similar and identical words were used. We hear the very same words 'macro-economic policy', 'structural adjustments' and so on. This is the jargon that Dr Manmohan Singh is using now and we have heard every word before. Brazil, Peru and many other countries had to swallow these words. Have you become completely blind and insensitive just for some foreign exchange? Have you given up your right to think and to decide for yourself? What will happen now? Even the Rashtrapatiji is being made to utter words, if I may say so, which are against the interests of the common people of this country. He says that there should not be any strike and there should not be any industrial action. People may lose their jobs and die of starvation. But they should not protest. Is this country a country of slaves or sheep or goats? That they silently starve and die and shall not protest against all this? This country will never accept an attempt by the government to prohibit industrial action. It is not a charity from the government. It has been earned by the working class through their struggle over a long period of time and they will never give up their right of industrial action to fight for their own rights.

Today we find that there is a very grave economic situation. Is it reflected in the President's address? What is the policy statement that has been made in the address as to how to solve this grave economic situation? Nobody is denying it. Even the government is saying that there is a grave economic situation. But where is the reflection of that in the President's address? Earlier, we were at least told that the address was prepared in a great hurry and they could not even think about it properly. But now, they had seven months of informed assistance from IMF also to prepare the President's address. But this is the position. This address is nothing but a parchment in which every thing that this country needs has been consciously omitted to be mentioned. Without meaning any disrespect to Rashtrapatiji, personally, I may say that it has become a useless document and it should be thrown into the wastepaper basket.

There has to be an alternate approach. We have suggested it many times. But who is listening? This government is under the bondage of the IMF and the World Bank. Were they listening? We have circulated an alternate proposal. They did not even have the courtesy to come and discuss with us or even to call us and discuss this alternate approach.

Now, what about land reform? Have you ever thought of bringing about land reforms in this country? We have suggested that without land reforms and without wider dispersal of ownership in industrial capital, without the use of a technology which is both modern and labour-intensive, a technology which will use labour and not replace it, we can never improve our economy. When we bring about this type of reforms, then and then alone we can increase the purchasing power of the common people and then and then alone agricultural and industrial growth can follow on the basis of expansion of domestic market and not otherwise. But that is never an area to which they pay any attention.

Instead, we find that in the economic sector, this government has launched an outright attack, a comprehensive attack on the public sector. Even the Parliament has not been taken into confidence when they took the decision with regard to 49 per cent disinvestment in the public sector. And this is one of the most dangerous policies. Then they have adopted the exit policy. With a sleight of hand, they dismantled the provisions of FERA and MRTP ... and the FERA has become a useless document. Now they are supposedly thinking on the Dunkel proposals, which will bring ruin to the agriculturists of this country and drug industry in the country. But this government is thinking on those lines. Today we find it in the newspaper. It has been discussed in the other House also. The minister has said that there are some positive features in the Dunkel proposal so far as the agriculture sector is concerned. But, Shri Chidambaram has said that without discussing the matter in Parliament, the government will not take any decision. But, Sir, we are hearing not a word about any action taken against any of these big industrial houses. Rs 50,000 crores of black money are circulating in this country. Is this not a pressure on our economy? Is there any step taken to unearth this black money? On the other hand, we know what this government has done.

The top ten industrial houses in this country have taken loans up to 31st March, 1991 from the following financial institutions:

IDBI Rs 1486 crores

IFCI Rs 553 crores

ICICIRs 626 crores

The total comes to Rs 2665 crores which is outstanding from these ten business or industrial houses to these important governmental agencies. When the small-scale sector or the medium-scale sector go to these banks for the purpose of loans and advances, no money is made available for them. They are working overtime for the purpose of giving loans to these big industrial houses which have been allowed to remain unrealized for years and years.

Even the interest is not paid. What is the credibility of this government or of this party which has ruined this country by their misrule of over forty years?

What is the performance of the present government—Shri Narasimha Rao's government? Overnight, they have taken a somersault. Nobody is saying anything these days about Shri Rajiv Gandhi.

The overall rate of growth is minus 2.3 per cent. The GDP growth instead of 8 per cent is 2.5 per cent. The overall rate of growth was minus 8 per cent from April to October. Food grains output has dropped by 1.5 per cent during this government's regime. Agricultural production is stagnant. Population is increasing but agricultural production is not increasing. The balance of payments position was a little difficult. I do not know whether they would have agreed to give us the copy of the World Bank report but we have somehow managed to get a copy of the report. There, you will find that the only reason for going to the World Bank was to get some foreign exchange for imports. Then, why this performance of our economy? Why industrial production is going down? Why agricultural production is going down? Why GDP is going down? What have you done for the last seven or eight months? This is the performance of this government? We are told today by the Prime Minister that they have nothing to say ... Now, the Prime Minister is only reading FICCI's circulars, not even the ordinary papers of this country. He has lost touch with the common people of this country. That is my fear. That is our misfortune. Probably, our Prime Minister is not allowed to think on his own until IMF and World Bank permits him to think.

Speech on the Motion of Confidence in the Council of Ministers headed by Atal Bihari Vajpayee, Eleventh Lok Sabha, 27 May 1996

For five hours now we are discussing this motion and not for once has either the Prime Minister or his present supporter Mr Fernandes claimed that this government has the majority support of the House. Then, what is this exercise going on! That is why we had made a request to put this motion to vote without any discussion. We felt that this constitutional aberration called the Vajpayee government should be ended immediately without any ritual. I am very sorry to say that a person of the eminence of Atal Bihari Vajpayee has spoken in this debate not as a Prime Minister really but more as a devout Shiv Sainik and RSS functionary. The manner in which he has spoken clearly shows that he has no heart as he has not bothered to refer to the relevant issue, namely trying to prove his majority support in the House. We can understand his agony. He will go down in the history as a Prime Minister of this great country for the briefest period. But we cannot help him. It is not our obligation to keep him in power. Mr George Fernandes was arguing as if it is our duty to keep BJP in power. ... But whether the United Front comes to power or not does not mean that BJP should remain in power without any mandate either of the country or of the majority support of this House.

Today we have heard a unique speech in this House. I had an apprehension, which I expressed in the meeting also, that this debate will be utilized for something else, that is to make election propaganda and not for the purpose of adverting on the real subject because it is a question of numbers, the question of head counting.

How long they could have taken? Hon. Rashtrapatiji's mandate was to prove the majority and not indulge in gimmicks or propaganda. Sir, even now I would like to know, as Shri Chandra Shekhar pointed out, do they claim majority support in the House. If not, then why should the debate continue? That is why I felt that this opportunity will be misutilized for purposes which they think will suit them. I was listening to the Prime Minister very closely. He was not really addressing the members of the House to persuade them to vote in his favour but he was addressing the people outside this House hoping that he will somehow convince them. Towards the end of his speech he tried to spread the germs of mistrust and a feeling of separation. He tried to divide people on the basis of religion and, Sir, we cannot but protest and protest till the last and we shall not rest until this government which has no mandate goes out of power from this country.

Mr Speaker, Sir, an attitude of injured innocence has been taken as if we are doing great injustice today. Why does Shri Vajpayee not think as to why nobody is coming to his support? ...

Well, this United Front is formed after the election. They have been talking about it as if we have committed a crime. The Prime Minister was saying that theirs has become the largest party in Parliament. I did not expect that Mr Vajpayee will stake his claim only because of an electoral fortuity. Does their getting 194 seats with their allies with 20–25 per cent votes mean that they have the majority support in the House? It is very clear. Of course, I personally have great respect for Shri Vajpayee. I have the great opportunity of being in this House together with him for so many years. I have personal respect for him. But when things like this come from a person of his eminence, one cannot but question, 'Is he a free man or a prisoner of his party, the Saffron Brigade?'

Sir, the invitation of the President obviously meant that the acceptor would have the minimum basis of support for running the government. If Shri Vajpayee knew that he had no majority in the House, on what basis could he accept the invitation of Hon. Rashtrapatiji? Sir, I am not going into the decision of the President. Mr Fernandes has tried to provoke us to go into it but I am not doing so. Sir, the only basis for this could be that they wanted to get into power by hook or crook, to remain there even for a few days – and I will try to humbly show how they have misused these few days that have elapsed when they have remained in power without any authority. Sir, they talk of constitutional propriety and they talk of political morality, but what sort of political morality can we see when they have no support in Parliament? Shri Sharad Pawar has rightly reminded of what Shri Vajpayee has said in his election campaign. The leader who had been projected as the future Prime Minister said, 'I give my word that I shall not stake my claim unless I get at least 225 seats.' He said that. But there is a deficit of 75 seats. He knows that he is in splendid isolation in this House. Nobody is with them. That is why, Sir, we have been waiting for so many days to know how this minority could be transformed into a majority. What was the magic, what was the game-plan, if the intention was not to manoeuvre, if the intention was not to win some members with lollipops, or if the intention was not to make crude attempts at what is known as horse-trading? Could there be any other method of getting a majority in this situation without indulging in manoeuvres or secret deals? Obviously that was being done for all these days that have elapsed.

Sir, many of the hon. members have rightly said here that once they got into power, threats started coming. The so-called responsible leaders are hurling threats, threats of civil war, threats of balkanization, threats of disintegration, threat of collapse of internal security, threat of dissolution etc. Is it not blackmailing the country and blackmailing the Members of Parliament? What are the real objects of saying all these things? I heard the other day on television one of the big functionaries of the BJP saying, 'We are trying others. Left are too principled. Therefore, we are trying with the regional parties.' By that what was meant? The regional parties had all fought against the BJP; they had fought against the communal parties; and they had fought on a secular plank. On what basis are they being asked for their support? I was waiting to hear from Mr Fernandes as to why he decided to give his support.

Sir, his concern was that why should the UF be formed. Why should the UF be called to form a government when you have criticized each other? I would like to know did Mr Fernandes support the demolition of Babri Mosque. Do you support what has been said in the BJP's manifesto? May I read, Sir, with you permission? Page 15, last paragraph: 'On coming to power the BJP government will facilitate the construction of a magnificent Sri Ram Mandir at Janmasthan in Ayodhya which will be a tribute to Bharat Mata. This moved some of the people in our land. The concept of Ram lies at the core of their conscience.' Then, I shall take it that Mr Fernandes now supports; Mr Fernandes now supports the economic policy of the BJP; Mr Fernandes now supports their pledge to disband the Minorities Commission; their pledge to repeal Article 370 of the Constitution. Does Mr Fernandes support all these? Then, if he is not supporting that – is he on a principled alliance with the BJP? While he did not answer this, he did not refer to this, he only gave us – if I may not be misunderstood – a lecture as to how we should behave; as to how we shall look after ourselves. We have also come with the mandate of the people. I do not know what is Samata Party's mandate. Today we find that there is also a fracture in the Samata Party. Even with eight members they cannot remain together.

Mr Speaker, Sir, as I said not only have they utilized this period to hold our threats, take up sort of a blackmailing attitude but how have they misused it for the sake of their party, not for the governance of the country. Within one day or two days we saw television shows going on where every minister was making promises without even having the right to continue; without being aware whether they could be able to be on this side of the House on the first of June. Everybody was making promises, everybody was announcing policies. Which minister was not doing it? Of course, our very very good friend Mr Sikander Bakht lost five to six days. He at least did not go on making pronouncements either on urban affairs or on employment or on external affairs. Except your picture with the Haj pilgrims, we did not see any activity. So what did you propose to do? What did you really think so as to propose all this? Was it not your political morality which demanded that you should first get the mandate of this House which the President wanted you to get? If the President had come to a decision that you had the majority, you had the mandate, you would not have put this condition that you should get the support of the House by 31st of May. Therefore, when the President was himself in doubt and you have not proved your majority in the House – of course, you have no majority in the country – you had gone on a spree of making promises, policy announcements and what not.

My very good friend, Mr Jaswant Singh – I do not know whether he is originally getting into the North Block because the finance ministry was earlier decided to be given to somebody who wanted it and did not get it. He also made announcements for the next three or four or five years. First of all please see whether you will remain minister for seven days. What else is this than misleading the people and the country? Sir, I believe that political propriety demanded that such announcements should have been made only after they proved the majority on the floor of this House.

Sir, even for ten days they cannot show a united Cabinet. A very distinguished member was absent even from the first Cabinet meeting, the second Cabinet meeting and what do you know further, they cannot even put up a united stand on very important issues.

Sir, there is one very important matter. They came to be sworn in on the 16th and today is the 27th. I do not know whether my information is correct or not and I shall stand corrected, if I am wrong. I am told that there was a special Cabinet meeting today at 1.15 p.m. to approve the revised counter-guarantees of the Enron power project. Was it politically proper? Was it administratively just? If my information is incorrect, please tell us! You are on the threshold of losing your position today. In the absence of any claim of majority even now – obviously you have not majority; the hon. Prime Minister said, 'You may be greater in number…', he said that at one time of his speech, during his speech – such an important decision is being taken on the day this confidence motion is being discussed. The Cabinet of this country which is on trial, yet to prove its mandate, is taking a very important decision of approving this counter-guarantee. There is no objection! Then I take it that it has been done.

Sir, I do not think, there can be anything more politically and administratively incorrect. This is nothing but an affront to Rashtrapatiji because he has desired that the majority must be proved; it means, he obviously meant before any serious or important decisions are taken.

Sir, the people of this country have decisively voted for secularism and against communalism. We feel it is our solemn obligation as members of this hon. House not only to accept the verdict of the people but to see that the politics of this country is not polluted by communal and fundamental forces which are out to destroy the unity and integrity of this country. I feel that the continuation of this government in power for every second means not only showing disrespect to the people's mandate but also amounts to weakening of the secular fabric of this country.

Sir, we are very sorry that our respected Rashtrapatiji because of some constitutional obligation had to indulge, a few days back, in an irrelevant exercise of addressing both the Houses assembled together because the government which is yet to prove its right to govern could have nothing to tell the people until its right was established. But Sir, I must take very serious exception to the very conscious attempt that was made to create a simulated situation. Consciously they omitted any reference to the abrogation of Article 370, adoption of a Uniform Civil Code, of Hindutva, of the construction of Ram Mandir at Ayodhya, of disbandment of the Minorities Commission and they consciously did not mention even anything about what was going to happen after the demolition of the Babri Masjid. During the campaign they had relied on this and that very evening, one of the distinguished members of this House in the BJP benches, who has just now claimed, rightly though, that he has won by the highest majority in Maharashtra, went on television claiming, 'This is only our first year's quota of work, we have not given up any of our demands.'

Therefore, it was openly said, 'Yes, we shall continue to do this. We shall support the repeal of Article 370.' They were not giving up their plan to construct a temple at Ayodhya. They have mentioned other things in their agenda, which were given so much prominence. They deliberately omitted that to project, what I call, a simulated secular credential for it. Sir, I say that this attitude is nothing but insincere and ephemeral.

You have deliberately tried to give an impression to the people of this country that you have changed your priorities and that you have changed your policies and programmes. The President did not mention anything in his address, which shows that those parts of their election manifesto have no longer been insisted upon by this party. Sir, that was not so. Therefore, I am very sorry to say that even the office of the President was misutilised to mislead the nation.

Sir, the Prime Minister gave a broadcast to the nation on television. He did not, rightly according to him in keeping with the President's address, make any references either to the demolition of the Babri Mosque or the construction of the temple but he made one observation and I quote: 'If the problems related with religion are not resolved for a long period of time then the result is what happened in Ayodhya.'

What is the significance of this statement except to give threats? Sir, I cannot think of a more shocking approbation of one of the most heinous happenings in the history of our country.

Sir, our Prime Minister has given another interview in one of the newspapers, which is close to them. He said: 'If the minorities continue to think in the language of minorityism, then the majority will start thinking in the language of majoritism and this will increase the gulf between the two communities.'

His speech today was, of course, different. Only a few days back, this was stated by him when he was probably expecting that there would be deserters from this side or he would be able to procure some defection. Sir, he made it very clear because he has his own constituency to serve. Sir, lest it was thought that he was softened in his stance on the temple issue, I quote what he said on the temple issue: 'Our goals are the same. It is a part of our strategy, which party will adopt at which point of time, strategy has to always be flexible.'

Sir, what else is it but doublespeak? You project something in the President's address. You say something in your address to the nation and then outside you go on reiterating what your election manifesto is in all its width and amplitude. The leading personalities of the BJP say, 'Yes, this is our first year's programme of action. We are not giving up any of these things.' They are not having the political courage to mention it in the President's address.

Sir, one thing is very clear. Yesterday, I found that in another moment of agony our Prime Minister has given an advice to the Maharashtra government to revive the Srikrishna Commission and also the Minorities Commission in Maharashtra. Neither their election manifesto nor the President's address had advocated for its reconstitution until yesterday's contrived message to the Maharashtra government.

Sir, I am sure, not a tear will be shed in the country as this government is being voted out of power. Sir, this country deserves deliverance from communal operators. Sir, as I said, the accidental emergence of BJP as the single largest party is nothing but electoral arithmetic. It does not give the right to anybody, to any party, either to claim the right to governance or the right to shape the future of this country. Sir, no doubt, we have many problems to solve. The people of this country deserve a government which will fight against communal divide of the people and the country. We cannot play with our unity and integrity. The secular parties have formed the United Front – however, Mr George Fernandes may try to ridicule it – to provide a secular, humane and pro-people government and that should take charge soon.

Sir, I repeat Mr Chandra Shekhar's suggestion. I say to the government that enough is enough. For the sake of the country and the people, I request the usurpers of the powers to please go. You have no right to remain a minute longer. The people of this country, at least, are entitled to be governed by those who command majority inside the House. So, those who got 20 per cent vote cannot have any claim to be the majority, any right to majority. Sir, as such I oppose this Motion and I am sure this nation opposes this Motion.

Motion of Thanks on the President's Address, Eleventh Lok Sabha, H.D. Deve Gowda as Prime Minister, 25 February 1997

Mr Chairman, Sir, I support the motion moved by Shri Sharad Yadav.

Sir, last year's President's address was a product of what I call a constitutional absurdity, lacking in political and moral authority. We are happy that this year hon. Rashtrapatiji has been able to read out a speech prepared by a legitimate government. That is why the speech reflects the urges and aspirations of the people of this country and addresses some of the basic problems facing the country and the people.

Mr Chairman, the United Front is not just a combination of political parties born out of political expediency. It is the result of a clearest mandate of the people of this country who have, in no uncertain manner, given their mandate against the forces of communalism and sectarianism. I believe that the people of this country did not vote for a single party. But they have made their choice and expressed it in no uncertain manner, in unmistakable form, that they have opted for a secular and democratic administration in this country and they want a government to be guided by transparency, probity and accountability.

Sir, coalition governments have come to rule the country. I believe that the people of this country realized that one-party rule has not been able to solve the problem of this country when most of the fifty years since our political independence we have had one-party rule. But, Sir, what we find and what is matter of great importance is that 75 per cent of the voters, three out of four voters in this country, in the last election gave their verdict against communalization of politics. Sir, their mandate is clear and loud. The people's choice for secular, democratic and liberal administration has to be respected and that is why some of the political parties, thirteen or fourteen, have come together to carry out the mandate of the people. It is not a matter to be scoffed at. We have to have a government in the Centre. We have to provide an administration which will look into the problems of the people, and try to solve them. Therefore, this United Front, which has been born out of the people's choice and the people's mandate, has a very important duty to perform.

Mr Chairman, Sir, we are told by the major opposition party (BJP) in this country that the government lacks legitimacy because on its own it is not the majority party, that it is supported from outside by the Congress party which has been ousted from power, and it is supported by the United Front parties not all of whom have joined the government. Sir, as I said, the clearest decision of people of this country is that the communal forces have to be halted. This country cannot be allowed to be overrun by those who want to divide the country once again, by those who divide the people on the basis of religion, those who have desecrated a place of worship, those who have violated the Supreme Court order and those who have brought in seeds of discord in the body politic. Sir, as we have to get rid of the economic corruption from our body polity, from our political life, we have also to get rid of this virus of communalism and separatism from our national life and that is the great obligation which has been imposed on this United Front and it would have been letting the people down, ignoring the people's mandate, if these political parties who are now in the United Front had not come together to provide an administration which will cater to the needs of the people.

Everybody will realize that it cannot be a bed of roses for the government, it cannot be a smooth sailing affair, but they have risen to the occasion and the common minimum programme has been constituted and framed. I believe that even the Congress party has accepted it, which is nothing but, according to me, a testament of hopes, urges and aspirations of the people of this country. It is a charter of comprehensive development of this country and which all parties together, as a post-electoral alliance, framed. Considering the future of this country, considering the duty of us who are in Parliament, in political life, in public life to try sincerely to remove tears from every eye in this country, they have joined and formulated the United Front, its charter, its programmes and its formulation. I feel that it is the bounden duty of all of us in the Parliament, or even outside, to see that the government is allowed to do its duty to fulfil the expectations of the people, as indicated in the United Front's common minimum programme.

We have always said and I am happy that the Prime Minister has emphasized on that from time to time, namely, our primary objective is towards the common people, the poor people, how to remove poverty from this country, how to take recourse to the poverty alleviation programmes, how to see that not a single person in this country remains unfed or not fully fed, how to try to provide a shelter on their heads, how to provide that they should have treatment when they are ill or sick. These are the basic minimum rights of any civilized society and it is our bounden duty to fulfil them, specially when a long time has elapsed. Five decades is not a small period. As a nation, we cannot absolve ourselves of the shame that still in our country there are people below the poverty line, without decent standard of living, there are people who are unable to go to schools or places of learning, there are people in this country who do not get pure drinking water and there are people who die without medical treatment. Therefore, are we not here in this House obliged to see that these minimum facilities are made available?

Sometimes, probably, we are more concerned in finding out what divides us than what unite us. But there are certain areas and objectives which, according to me and my party also, should be the bounden duty of everybody in this country to see to. There should not be disparity from people to people.

Let them enjoy the minimum rights which the Constitution makers have provided for the citizens of this country. Let not the Directive Principles of State Policy be mere narration of such rights and goals only in papers. Let Fundamental Rights of citizens of this country be not paper rights only. Therefore, how will we achieve it unless we are able to concentrate on this, able to put our heads together, able to put our energies together?

It is a developing country. We have tremendous resources. Our biggest resource is human resource. But unfortunately, we are not able to fully utilize these resources. We find that our young boys and girls and brilliant academicians are waiting for opportunities to serve the country, and they are going out of this country because here, they are not respected, they do not have job opportunities. They are contributing to other countries' development and progress and we are not able to retain them here, in our own country.

This is the position. But we cannot lose hope. We cannot throw up our hands. We cannot say: 'Thus far, no further and we cannot do it.' History will not pardon us. Those who have decided to participate in political and public activity cannot but redeem our pledge. Otherwise, future generations will never exonerate us.

Sir, I know the limitations of the United Front. I know the problems which will be there when so many parties are working together. I know that this country has complex problems, problems of unbalanced development, problems of lack of development, problems of infrastructure and problems of inherent weakness of our economic set-up also. We have to depend on other countries. We have to borrow money from other countries. We cannot provide the wherewithal with our own resources. We are not even able to provide water to our farmers who are toiling every day and producing our biggest asset, namely food.

These are the problem and we have to tackle them. But in the present context, how do we do it? Merely nibbling at each other and merely criticizing will not do, and there again I appeal to all sections of the House that there are some basic aspects, some basic issues which should not be allowed to be compromised. There cannot be a let-up in that.

Sir, nobody, I believe, wants an election now. The Bharatiya Janata Party may be having its dreams. But with their performance in Gujarat and Rajasthan and with some negative votes here and there, they may think that they would be able to come on top of the world. But what have we seen Delhi? Even the other day, the ballot boxes were seen on the streets under their administration. What is happening in the state of Maharashtra? In Maharashtra, people like Dr Datta Samant are killed on the streets. How are the elections being held there and what is the percentage of voting there? I found that not more than 50 per cent of the people had voted. How are they dealing with their political opponents in Maharashtra? These issues are there. But at the moment, I do not wish to have a confrontation.

Sir, the duties towards the common people and the poor people will have to be discharged and in this context, I must congratulate the Prime Minister and the government. I know that they would be facing the problem of providing subsidy of over Rs 8,000 crore. But you cannot play with the future of the people below the poverty line. We have been insisting, rather pressing hard for it, because that is one of the commitments made in the United Front's common minimum programme that we must provide, at a cheaper rate, at half the rate to the people below the poverty line, at least rice and wheat. I must congratulate the government on this issue that the Prime Minster has made that announcement yesterday and this would provide great relief to them. Let us have this satisfaction at least that those who need the most have been provided with this opportunity of survival.

Sir, I shall request the government, particularly the Prime Minister who is here, that it has to be seen that there is a proper implementation of this programme. All risks should be avoided. It is the duty of every citizen to see that this is properly implemented and those who indulge in black marketing with these food grains – let us follow Jawaharlal Nehru's wishes – should be hanged from the nearest lamp post. I do not mind that, because you cannot play with the lives of the people. The people of the country will be paying for the subsidy, but this is a subsidy which has to be borne by this country. It cannot be helped.

Therefore, I hope there will be the proper implementation. The West Bengal government is hoping to introduce it comprehensively within a month. It has already done the process. Similarly, I am sure other governments will also sincerely try to do it. Let us not play with the lives of the poor people when the entire country is making the sacrifice very legitimately.

Sir, there are many other programmes which this government has taken up. The provisions have been made. I find a very wholesome change in the approach. I must thank the Prime Minister when he rushes to places where people have suffered because of fire, because of natural tragedy and natural calamity. This is what is expected from a pro-people government and pro-people administration. It shows the concern of the government for those who are afflicted in our country. I quite appreciate the concern that is expressed by my friends from Orissa. Yes, when you are saying this, please see that it reaches the needy. The Prime Minister has made a commitment on the floor of the House. It should reach the proper people, reach quickly and should not be wasted.

Sir, I also wish to thank this government and congratulate the government for another milestone which it has achieved, namely, entering into the Indo-Bangladesh water treaty. It has changed the entire atmosphere in the subcontinent. It has brought about a real change of attitude and feeling between the two countries. Sir, nothing can be more important than our closest and friendly relations with Bangladesh. I know the BJP will not be happy. They are not happy. They are trying to find out some loopholes with or without the support of Mr Sharad Pawar's lieutenants. I do not know how many groups you have. But, at least, some individuals seem to be not satisfied.

Sir, this has opened a new vista of relations and economic activities between the peoples of these two countries who have suffered because of the Partition and other problems between them. Our chief minister has played a role in this treaty which has been admitted.

The treaty with Nepal is also commendable. I must congratulate the government for the very firm role and attitude which they displayed during the CTBT discussions and agreements. These are very positive points. Let us go on in these matters with or without BJP and try to serve the people.

Sir, the other aspects on which I wish to make a reference is the improvement in the relations between the Centre and the states. We have been saying and we have been crying hoarse as a matter of fact that the time has come for restructuring the relations between the Centre and the states. After all, it is a federal structure for facility of administrations.

If we find that certain division of powers has not helped either in the establishment of true federal structure or providing wherewithal to the people of all areas in an ample measure as they deserve, something was basically wrong. Long before this Manmohanamics came in, the West Bengal legislature passed a resolution asking for scrapping of the licensing system so far as industry was concerned because it was felt that the licensing procedure was being misutilized in Delhi. We are not getting licences for setting up industries in different areas. Today, I do not grudge Mr Sharad Pawar's Maharashtra. I appreciate that. But are the people of North-East India, people of Orissa, Bihar, West Bengal and Assam not entitled to it? Are they not entitled to the benefits of industrial development?

Orissa, with all the mineral resources, is crying 'give us water, give us some development grant'. Kalahandi seems to be the poorest district in the country; people are dying of hunger. They are crying for a little drinking water and a little water for their cultivation. What is the per capita income of some people in some parts of this country? Why is it half in some states? This is how we have created areas of discord. We have thereby encouraged people to take up arms against others because they feel alienated from the mainstream. This has not helped the country's development. So many ethnic groups, so many pressure groups, are all trying to have their own say in the matter. Why? They ask for separate states or separate districts or separate administration because they feel that unless they shout, unless they make their presence felt and unless they create problems, nobody is going to look into it. It was not for one state or one group of people that this restructuring has been asked for.

What is happening in the National Development Council? I have come to know that in every meeting of the National Development Council, all the chief ministers, at least secretly or privately, ask for more money. All of them do not have the courage to say that in the presence of the Prime Minister. They will come and ask the Left Front chief minister: 'Why do you not talk for us also?' They are not to be blamed because they want money for the development of their states. I am sure Sardar Surjit Singh Barnala would agree with me that every chief minister has been facing this problem. I am sure that our esteemed Prime Minister also faced this problem earlier as the chief minister of Karnataka. Therefore, some restructuring was necessary. The Constitution contemplated the setting up of an inter-state council. It was in limbo; nobody bothered about it. The National Development Council hardly holds one or two meetings in a year and, sometimes, not even that. The state governments are getting more and more alienated from the planning process. There was no discussion on the approach plan; there was no discussion on the draft plan worth the name. In one day, all the state chief ministers will come and make their speeches and go away. It was supposed to be a discussion on planning.

Here, the Centre has to take the lead. On the Sarkaria commission's recommendations, there are certain things which we have supported and on certain things we have reservations. But there are certain basic issues which have been dealt with by the Sarkaria commission. I am glad that proper attention is now being paid, and a standing committee of the inter-state council has been constituted which will look into all these problems and try to sort them out.

As we said, our great advantage is that there is a basic unity amongst diversity in this country. Let us not only emphasize on what are the diversities, but we should also not forget what the basic unity of this country is. Unless this basic unity is kept in front of us, we shall lose our way and we shall be more concerned with matters of division or with matters of discord.

I also congratulate the government for the way they have conducted the elections in Jammu and Kashmir and in Punjab. Whatever government was formed, it is welcome. It is for the people of that state to decide and we respect the people's verdict. But the point is that they have been allowed and they have been able to exercise their franchise. That is the most important thing. It is for the different political parties to make themselves acceptable to the people. But the point is that the people's wishes must be respected; they must be given full opportunity. I have my good wishes to the governments of Jammu and Kashmir and Punjab.

They should prosper. Their problems should be solved. It has to be a cooperative effort not only between the Centre and those states but all over the country to solve their problems.

When I talk of problems, they are still galore. There is no doubt about that. We are concerned about the price rise. Unfortunately, it is still there. People are feeling the pressure of it.

There is the problem of, what you call, the sick undertakings in this country. Many people are still not getting employment. Even today, in the morning, the question of NTC mills came up. These mills are there in so many of the states. They are lying closed or they are almost getting closed. The wages of the employees are not being paid. Therefore, these are matters which have to be dealt with immediately.

There is the question of self-reliance in our industry. It has to be looked into. My colleague Shri Syed Masudal Hoosain will deal with the other problems. I am not getting into them.

So far as the serious problems of terrorism and ethnic struggle in Tripura are concerned, these are matters on which action has to be taken immediately. I know this government has taken some steps. The home minister has been there. On these matters, as I said just now, action has to be taken very quickly.

I would also like to request the Prime Minister that while replying to this debate, he should give us fuller information about the poverty alleviation programme and how he wishes to give a thrust to the projects for supply of drinking water to the people.

The other aspect which also took quite a long time in this House today is regarding the issue of corruption. Obviously this is a matter on which there can be no compromise at any level, at any point, whoever may be involved. We have expressed our sincere thanks to the courts also. Because of the judiciary, we have been able to pursue with the investigation of the JMM bribery case, the Hawala case, the St Kitts inquiry and so many other scams. But our duty does not end there or our obligation does not end there. It is one of the primary duties of this government to assure the people of this country that all these inquiries and investigations will be pursued most vigorously and that those who are guilty, however highly placed he or she may be, should not be allowed to go scot-free. Nobody tainted with any scam or anybody guilty of any offence, economic offence primarily, should be allowed to enjoy the benefits of any weakness or any lackadaisical attitude on the part of the government or the investigating agencies.

Sir, I need not go into the details about Bofors. So far as Bofors is concerned, we have discussed the matter. This is also one of the cases where it is high time that the people of this country are given the full details, subject to the rules, regulations and whatever provisions are there.

The people of this country, as I said, are waiting to receive just and humane treatment. They do not claim much. The ordinary common people of this country are satisfied with little. Therefore, our demand is that these very minimum demands of the people of this country are met.

There is still raging unemployment in this country. We have to solve this problem on a war footing. Young boys and girls, educated, skilled or even unskilled people want to have a decent standard of life. They want to earn their livelihood on their own and look after their families. It is our duty to see that they are able to do their job and earn their livelihood.

Sir, it is said and if I may quote: 'This is a transition period which will be guided by the need to strengthen the principles of democracy, secularism, federalism and social justice. In the building of this new India of equality, justice and fraternity, we seek the fullest participation of all citizens. The hallmark of the United Front government's approach will be the greater and greater involvement of our people in all its endeavours.'

This should be the mantra of this government. So long as you do not deviate from this commitment given to the people of this country, I am sure they will have the confidence of this House.

I support the President's address and I sincerely hope that the government will take all measures to implement the very important commitments, in a time-bound manner, made to the people of this country so that the people of this country can get what they fully deserve.

Speech on the Motion of Confidence in the Council of Ministers headed by Atal Bihari Vajpayee, Twelfth Lok Sabha, 27 March 1998

Mr. Speaker, Sir, I rise to oppose this motion as I consider this to be my patriotic duty. I have heard our Prime Minister's speech with rapt attention and I never disturbed him. I was thinking of the slogan that was used this time 'Abke Bari Atal Bihari', but what Atal Bihari, which Atal Bihari is this? Is it Atal Bihari with a guilty conscience, feeling the weight of the combination that he has formed? His speech clearly betrays the guilty conscience. He has talked of consensus, but that consensus is to surrender to this type of politics.

Sir, I do not think that the Indian political system has ever exhibited in the past a more opportunist, a more power-hungry, a more brazen-faced and a more dubious political combination than this which is today masquerading as alliance partners.

Mr. Speaker, Sir, our attachment or commitment to secularism and unity and integrity of the nation is not a mere slogan. Our Constitution provides for a secular, democratic republic. Our Supreme Court has construed that secularism is one of the basic features of our Constitution to which we all swear. But this multi-religious, multi-ethnic and multi-linguistic character of our society is under severe attack today. In regard to Hindutva, about which Shri Sharad Pawar has spoken, I will not read out the manifesto of the BJP again. It is based on the RSS slogan of 'one nation, one people and one culture' and to them, the minorities like Christians, Muslims and Parsis are acceptable if they follow the Indian tradition or Hindutva as they understand. We have seen the intolerance of the BJP and its supporters to other religions, other viewpoints and other thoughts. I know, they got upset when I refer to the demolition of Babri Masjid ...

But what is it apart from intolerance? Only a few days before the elections were held we read about the attack on a museum of modern art in Delhi. One of the leading luminaries of the BJP staged an attack because he did not like two paintings of Shri M.F. Husain, and one of the most celebrated artists of this country was beaten up. This is their spirit of tolerance for others. One of the most celebrated litterateurs of this country who is a member of the Sahitya Akademi has spoken of the fate of the Bharat Bhavan in Bhopal...

Sir, this is the intolerance. They are not even prepared to hear others and now to talk of a consensus sounds very hollow. Let it be very clear; we shall never make any compromise on the question of democracy and secularism in this country. We can never allow the unity and integrity of this country to be destroyed. We have already had one division of this country...

Sir, our country has not been strengthened. Let not a situation be created when we have another attack on the unity and integrity of our country.

Sir, we are told ad nauseam – even today the Prime Minister had referred – that the people of this country had voted for a change, for a stable government under an able Prime Minister, where different political parties entered into an alliance even before the elections. We know the figures, we have also heard the figures and I need not repeat them. But, I believe, the time has come when this myth of pre-poll alliance has to be exploded.

I am sorry, Sir, with all my respect and unbounded veneration of our Rashtrapatiji, he seems to have also fallen into this error that there was a pre-poll alliance. Sir, after that 13-day constitutional aberration ended, I had said in this House that I would like to see Shri Atal Bihari Vajpayee as the permanent ex-Prime Minister of this country. But I have been proved wrong, I have been proved wrong because I wrongly assumed that Shri Atal Bihari Vajpayee had a conscience. I assumed that he was committed to certain basic values and that grievous mistake was made by me, a very humble political worker. My mistake was, I thought that the BJP believed in political morality and we have been lectured on that from housetops.

Sir, we have heard from the BJP, from Shri Atal Bihari Vajpayee, his friends in his party and, maybe, his present cohorts also, about the danger to the country emanating from corruption. Shri Sharad Pawar has rightly reminded us how in the House we had also joined in our protest against the activities of Shri Sukh Ram. We remember how Shri Atal Bihari Vajpayee and his friends had criticized Shri Lalu Prasad Yadav. I had also, on the floor of this House, demanded his resignation. I admit that.

Sir, I remember how some of the events in Tamil Nadu had been criticized on the floor of the House. We admired the decision of Shri Lal Krishna Advani when he resigned from even the membership of this House and for his decision of not contesting the election because he was under some cloud. Happily he is free from that. ... But as Shri Atal Bihari Vajpayee is only a mask, all your commitments to fight corruption are nothing but also masks. That is why we see today another constitutional distortion. We have found that all their commitments, all their so-called moral stand, have been breached in every aspect of it, with only one object, to get power by hook or crook or on the basis of give and take as Laluji said the other day.

Sir, alliance means coming together. For what purpose? There has to be a purpose even if you go by literal meaning. So, what was the objective? What was the common basis? It has been correctly pointed out. What was the purpose? Was there any unity of purpose on economic policy or was there unity of objectives between the BJP and any of the parties? As has rightly been pointed out, if yes, then there would not have been separate manifestos. The Samata Party, the AIADMK and the Trinamool Congress are all entitled to have their own separate manifestoes. They did. What is the foreign policy of the different parties? What is their attitude towards Swadeshi? What is the attitude towards land reforms? We know nothing of it. They had no common policy at all. They had no common objective. What is the attitude of the respective parties on industry and on multinational corporations? There was no common programme, there was no common manifesto and there was no commitment to any principle or to unity of action. So, what was this alliance then? Today, I am thinking of the day, 1st of September 1997, in this House when the celebration of the golden jubilee year ended with a resolution, which was passed unanimously during the special session. The resolution was moved from the Chair by your distinguished predecessor, Shri P.A. Sangma. Sir, I quote a few lines:

'Having reflected upon the state of the nation with the preamble to the Constitution as the guide…

'That meaningful electoral reforms be carried out so that our Parliament and other legislative bodies be balanced and effective instruments of democracy; and further that political life and processes be free of the adverse impact on governance of undesirable extraneous factors including criminalization.

'That continuous and proactive efforts be launched for ensuring greater transparency, probity and accountability in public life so that the freedom, authority and dignity of the Parliament and other legislative bodies are ensured and enhanced; that more especially, all political parties shall undertake all such steps as will attain the objective of ridding our polity of criminalization or its influence.'

One of the great leaders in the House said and I quote: 'The demon of criminalization of politics is devouring the basic tenets of our democracy.'

I am reading from the synopsis of the debate issued by the Lok Sabha. 'In order to identify and declare ineligible candidates from contesting elections, we shall have to consider every aspect of this malady and judge according to the law who is a criminal. Then, the whole house has to reach a consensus on the twin issues of criminalization of politics and corruption in public life. Corruption is devastating our public life. The entire country is fed up because of this problem. People should not give bribes to get their work done. Ultimately, it is the duty of our leaders and administrations that such practices are dealt with a heavy hand and stringent steps should be taken to curb this menace.'

Sir, thus spoke Shri Atal Bihari Vajpayee. Probably every word has been breached today. That is why I know that he has a guilty conscience.

Sir, the BJP manifesto, if I read one sentence, says: 'BJP will set an example of unimpeachable accountability and impeachable probity in public life, it will expeditiously deal with unresolved cases of corruption in which no action has been taken in the last 12 years.'

Of course, they have not spoken of new cases of corruption or of their alliance partners.

Sir, shall we try to find out what is the commonality? We have to refer to this UP government episode because this is a party of so-called principles and morality. Well, I do not know all the details. But who does not know of a government consisting of deserters, those who defected from one party to several other parties? I remember the picture which came out on the TV and newspapers on the day Mayawatiji was ensconced in the centre with Shri Vajpayee on one side and Shri L.K. Advani on the other side in the main committee room of the Parliament House Annexe announcing the great alliance and sharing of the chief ministership every six months – what I had called a constitutional monstrosity. That was the first time ever when the high office of the chief ministership became a matter of *sauda* or a matter of sharing every six months. I am sure, Mayawatiji will be able to defend herself now, who is at the receiving end, because she is not supporting them.

We cannot forget Shri Sukh Ram, who was a very prominent member of this House and a minister. We remember, even in the room of the hon. Speaker, how he was trying to impress Shri Advani, Shri Jaswant Singh and others about his supposed innocence. But it was not acceptable to anybody.

Now, let us see what has happened in Tamil Nadu. What is the common basis? We cannot forget that Shri Vajpayee had to send a list of 240 members. Where were these alliance members – eighteen members of the AIADMK, four members of the PMK, three members of the MDMK and one member of the TRC? They were supposedly alliance partners, who fought together on a certain basis and it was supposedly a pre-poll alliance.

Now, the Prime Minister has not said to us as to why their names were not included in the list. He said: 'Now, the ball is in the President's court. Rashtrapatiji called me, and I never staked the claim.'

They could not stake the claim because they deserted you then for other *saudas*. How can we forget what had happened here when there were cases against the leader of that party there in Tamil Nadu?

What was their attitude towards the former Bihar chief minister? I am not going into the details. But how many cases are pending against the leader of the party there in Tamil Nadu? We see in the newspapers and in the journals the list of cases. Now what is that approach? If Shri Lalu Prasad Yadav was wrong in sticking to his chair, if a Sukh Ram was wrong then, not now, then how could this type of alliance be entered into? Today, I find a host of cases. I need not read them and I do not wish to take up the time of the House. Today one of the leading national dailies says that one of the ministers has been asked to appear in court on 6 April or the court will issue a non-bailable arrest warrant. I am not taking any name on the floor of the House ...

I have not even taken any name. I have only said that he is one of the colleagues of the hon. Prime Minister in his Cabinet now. Let us see the perfect understanding and relationship between these alliance partners. I do not know he may be somewhere, the leader of the Janata Party.

Let us see the perfect understanding and good relationship between the alliance partners ...

I am reading from *India Today* of 23 March. 'The Janata Party president described her as mentally unstable, charged her with colluding with LTTE to assassinate Rajiv Gandhi, and initiated corruption case that have dogged her since she lost power in May, 1996. On her part, she described him as a pathological liar.'

What else have we seen in Tamil Nadu but a drama? We miss, particularly I miss my very good friend Shri Jaswant Singhji in the House. He should have been here. ... But he is very handy, useful, the Prince Charming. The articulate Prince Charming was sent there. Although he could not win over the hearts of the people of Chittorgarh, yet he could win over her heart ... It was a real palace coup or a Garden coup, Poes Garden or something, I do not know. ...

Sir, Shri Vajpayee and Shri Advani were accused of taking a negative attitude. Even Shri Advani was accused of mocking her, making fun of her ... Although she did not want to indulge in a slanging match with Shri Hegde, she did retaliate. She said that she also had brought Shri Hegde's behaviour to the notice of Shri Vajpayee and Shri Advani. Perfect harmony! Perfect understanding! Great personal respect for each other ...

She complained that the AIADMK and its allies were treated as inferior partners and second-class citizens. She further said: 'If this is their attitude before forming the government, what would their attitude be after forming the government?'

She then referred to very important issues concerning Tamil Nadu. I am not minimizing the importance, issues such as Cauvery ... I agree that these are very important issues for Tamil Nadu which were raised by her ... The question of Cauvery, the 69 per cent reservation, raising the height, the level of the Periyar dam and the question of making Tamil an official language were all put as conditions for her support ... I say that these are important demands. I am telling them about this. I do not know what to do ... I am not objecting to them. I am supporting you. You please get those demands accepted by them ... As I said, Shri Jaswant Singh went there and we were told of a happy resolution ...

Mr. Speaker, Sir, I have never said that those demands are unjustified. Please listen. Do not be too touchy. I know why you are touchy. I am only saying that for three, four days, the second-biggest alliance partner of the BJP, the AIADMK and its allies with eighteen members, refused to send a letter of support. As Shri Sharad Pawar said: 'Letter is coming.' Then I said, Shri Jaswant Singh did the trick. Of course, that was all inside the room. We do not know. We are humble mortals. We do not know what happened there.

[*At 1303 hours the Lok Sabha adjourned till thirty minutes past fourteen. The Lok Sabha reassembled at thirty minutes past fourteen*]

It seems many of my hon. friends on that side felt upset about what I might have said or might have meant. I wish to make it categorically clear that I never meant any disrespect to anybody, nor have I said, had in mind even, anything derogatory about anybody either within or outside the House.

It is very painful to me that after twenty-eight years, I am being charged with some sort of an alleged impropriety. Without in any way admitting that I have committed any impropriety, since some of my hon. friends felt very upset, I regret if there was any misunderstanding about what I have said.

What I was saying was that initially the AIADMK did not agree to join the government for a few days. Thereafter they changed their mind and they expressed their intention to join the government. What I wanted to say was that there must have been some terms and conditions on the basis of which some agreement was arrived at or there was this change of mind. That was what really I wanted to mean. We would not know this until it is disclosed. We know of the demands that were made.

I remember having seen on the television Shri Jaswant Singh, my very good friend, who, again I say unfortunately is not here, said that what has been agreed to will find a place in the national agenda, if I am not mistaken. He also very categorically said, I believe I am quoting his words, 'the past is behind us, the future is beckoning us'. Therefore, we would have been very happy if the hon. Prime Minister had said what ultimately was arrived at, what was agreed to. Why I am mentioning this is because I am trying to show that this alliance is a fragile alliance and this so-called pre-poll alliance is a myth. That is my contention. They would not agree. But allow me to say what I feel.

Similarly, in my state, the BJP had a seat-sharing arrangement with the TMC and I congratulate them for having won so many seats. It is the people's verdict. We accept it.

I am very unhappy that Shri Tapan Sikdar has won, but I respect the people's verdict. I have congratulated him. My understanding is that he is out of the government because of some comments that he had made – 'Didigiri Nahi Chalega'. This came out in the papers, nobody denied it. Therefore, it has been repeated even after the formation of the government, if I am not mistaken. She is here, she will speak about it. There was only a seat-sharing arrangement. I was in my constituency, I did not know anything except what appeared in the papers.

I read that even in her meetings the leader of the Trinamool Congress did not allow BJP flags. She did not share the platform with the BJP leaders. That is what I saw. If I am wrong, please correct me. Therefore, where is that alliance? What is the commonality of the viewpoints or the approach or the attitude or the policies and programmes?

As a matter of fact, they contested each other at least in one constituency in West Bengal. I was trying to find out the basis of the claim that there was a so-called 'pre-poll alliance' and the distinction which is being sought to be made with the understanding between the UF government and the Congress understanding after the 1996 elections. It was being said that was a post-poll alliance or a post-poll understanding. Now, they take greater credit saying that this is pre-poll alliance and therefore the people have voted for them.

The people have voted for which manifesto in West Bengal, in Andhra Pradesh, in Tamil Nadu and in Orissa? We do not know what the Biju Janata Dal's economic policy is, if there is any; we do not know what their education policy is, what their policy about MNCs is and what their policy about the nuclear option is. But they say that they are allies. Can seat sharing during an election be the basis of a durable alliance? This is an issue which is staring the country in the face.

Now, of course, the AIADMK has said that it will unconditionally support this government. We saw that there was a denial that any particular ministry was asked for. I accept it if they have denied it. I am not questioning it. There are many versions coming out in the press but we do not find any denial.

What was said in the press? I am referring to very responsible journals. I will not take long. Now, I quote: 'Refusal by the AIADMK leader to forward a letter of support for the BJP has upset the party's plans to form a government at the Centre.' I remember those two or three days when television was showing Shri Atal Bihari Vajpayee not in a very happy mood, all of them sitting very glum faced, waiting for a letter to come from Tamil Nadu. That is why he was forced to go to the hon. Rashtrapatiji with 240 names.

We have been told then of a Tamil Nadu package, we have been told now of a West Bengal package and we have also been told of the Orissa package! We have been told that they will find a due place in the national agenda but where are they? We have not seen them in the national agenda. This is what I wanted to mean. There must be some hidden agendas on which they are not taking the people of the country into confidence, about which they are not telling the people. Therefore, according to me, this national agenda is nothing but a 'national tamasha'. Where are those agreements? Mr Prime Minister, where are those packages on the basis of which you have got their support?

In this national agenda, one aspect is very clear. As we had seen in the President's address of 1996, they have suddenly omitted their main issues, main demands like building of a Ram Mandir at Ayodhya, abrogation of Article 370 and bring in a Uniform Civil Code. Earlier, Shri Sharad Pawar has read it out and I need not read it out again. These issues find primacy in their manifesto. They get primacy in the BJP manifesto. But today, the national agenda does not mention about them. There is only a very fleeting reference to corruption. They have referred to it only in the case of electoral reforms. These are very difficult subjects for them now.

Although building of Ram Mandir is not national agenda, what has been said by many of our hon. friends?

Shri Vinay Katiyar was here. He had very categorically said, 'Atalji will make the mandir possible.' That was his statement on 21 March. Then, 'Hindutva hawks want Ram revived.' Under this it is said, 'The BJP high command has incurred the wrath of some MPs, chiefly sants-turned-politician – I find quite a few here – and Ayodhya-based sadhus, who resent the party's soft line on Ayodhya and the uniform civil code.' I am not reading the entire report. Therefore, there are already protests in the BJP itself on the omission of the Ram mandir issue from the national agenda. Then what is cohesiveness? The BJP itself is not cohesive. How can the government be united ... We would like to know from the Prime Minister on this point. He should tell us and take the people into confidence on this when he is asking for confidence vote. You cannot ask for confidence vote without disclosing your commitments to different so-called alliance partners.

I want to make it clear that I do not grudge any special arrangements or any benefits given to any state in India. I am glad that the Prime Minister said that for a strong India, there have to be strong states. And that is our demand all along. We had quarrelled with Congress and we still quarrel with them because they feel that a strong Centre will be sufficient which does not help the development of this country. There are areas of disparities from place to place.

I cannot but comment in view of the AIADMK and its allies in Tamil Nadu being the major partners of this alliance. I am reminded of what

Dr Shyama Prasad Mookerjee had said. He said, 'India, that is Bharat,' that is, Tamil Nadu now. This government's life depends on this. Sir, there are very disquieting reports that the hon. minister of law had already said that certain cases are falsely instituted. Within a day or two of his assumption of power, he passes judgement when the cases are pending in the courts ... Very well, did not pass any judgment but made comments ... I agree and stand corrected. The law minister cannot pass judgements but he has passed comments ... he has passed comments about the truth or the correctness or otherwise of certain cases ... Therefore, with a government of such disparate and desperate forces, I wonder what will happen to this country.

As I said earlier, Shri Atal Bihari Vajpayee is a mask. ... Sangh Parivar has utilized Shri Vajpayee's charismatic leadership and stature. I feel that if unfortunately this government continues and is saddled in power, apart from the common people and the country, the biggest victim will be Shri Atal Bihari Vajpayee. He does not know when the rug will be drawn from under this feet ... Then, it will be: 'Abki Bari Lal Bihari aur Pramod Bihari'.

Extracts of Speeches Made on the Riots in Gujarat, Thirteenth Lok Sabha, Atal Bihari Vajpayee as Prime Minister, 11 March 2002 and 23 July 2002

Should we be proud to be Indians when we have behaved in this manner? Between man and man, innocent people have been the target ... On the forenoon of 27th itself my party, the Politburo of CPI(M), issued a statement and that was published on the next day on 28th February in the newspapers. We wish to make it very clear that these serious incidents should be properly investigated and punishment should be given to whoever is guilty ... Nobody can kill people whatever may be the reason ... we are all proud of Gujarat's achievements in the fields of industry, business, trade and its contribution to India's freedom movement. One cannot but avoid the impression that we have seen what is the worst type of state-sponsored mayhem of innocent people ... I had the opportunity of being a member of the all-party delegation. We had seen very heart-rending scenes. We visited some of the relief camps which the organizations were running. Also, we had the briefing by the topmost officials of the state administration. We have seen wounds caused by injuries by swords, injuries by stone throwing, injuries by bullet, burn injuries and all types of injuries ... It was a well-organized massacre and annihilation of innocent people only on the basis that they belong to a particular religion. There is no other reason. You belong to this religion, and therefore, you have to suffer. Secularism is one of the basic features of our Constitution. Shri Advani's very favourite expression is pseudo-secularism. Whatever may be, is the government, is the major party, the BJP, committed to secularism or your brand of secularism, namely, a hegemony of the majority sections of the people? ... Fortunately, in no other state there has been any incident, except, maybe some stray incidents in UP. But no such incident was there in any other state and it is very fortunate. But it was not by accident. It was because the state governments took preventive action ... But in Gujarat, it started burning; within a few hours 26 towns had to be brought under curfew on the same day. Why did the BJP not try to resist the VHP from giving a bandh call? ... Not a single preventive arrest was made. We asked the police authorities there after our visit. Not a single preventive arrest was made. No special deployment of the police was made even in Ahmedabad city and in big towns and cities like Baroda. On the other hand the chief minister has said, quoting Newton, that every action will have a reaction. This is a most condemnable attitude on the part of the chief minister. This is direct encouragement given to the killings and murders that followed ... My charge is that there was an organized attack on minorities because of the frenzy that was created designedly as a sort of *badla* for the incident that had taken place at Godhra. This is unfortunate in the politics of Gujarat. It has become the laboratory of Hindutva of the BJP brand and VHP brand ... This blot on our country will remain for many, many more years. We will be under its shadow. Others are questioning our commitment to secularism in this country.

India's unity is dearest to us all. Therefore, we demand that the chief minister of Gujarat should not continue in the post for a day more. Also, the home minister has no moral right to continue in his post for minute longer …

We were given a figure of death … I do not remember the figure correctly. I did not note it down. We saw two camps … Why is it that about 30,000 people of Ahmedabad are in camps? This is the most important city in Gujarat. They are there either because their houses were burnt or their relatives have been killed. There is no sense of security. There is nothing to live on. They are forced to go and stay in the camps. This has been happening since the 28th February or the 1st March … Now, I would like to know what was the crime committed by these people? They have to leave their hearths and homes and stay in miserable conditions. Some children say that their parents have been killed. Some people say that they have no houses. Businesses have been destroyed. They say that if they went back, they would be butchered … These camps are occupied by thousands of people because of a lack of sense of security, because of lack of housing accommodation, because their businesses are destroyed and there is nothing to fall back upon. The very interesting thing is that none of these camps in Ahmedabad is run by the government. The biggest problem, apart from food and medicine, is total lack of sanitation. The representatives of voluntary organizations said that there is no arrangement of sanitation and the government is completely oblivious … A distinction was made so far as the quantum of compensation was concerned – Rs 2 lakh for Godhra victims and Rs 1 lakh for the rest of the areas. But we were told later on by the Relief Commissioner Shri Koshi that now the kar sevaks have agreed to reduce the amount of compensation, therefore, it has become Rs 1 lakh for all …

We are told that within such and such time police was sent; within such and such time they tried to provide relief and within such and such time they sent buses, etc. But this is all after the event. When the things were becoming hot, should the government not have taken minimum steps? If there is no intelligence report on this, then there is a total failure of the law enforcement machinery and somebody must be responsible for this ... There was an almost mechanical approach or totally bureaucratic approach by the chief secretary and the home secretary. I do not blame them because they have to operate within a particular atmosphere, under a particular dispensation. They were hardly masters of their own respective offices or duties ... The victims are the innocent people of this country. Their crime is that they belong to a particular religion. They are totally defenceless. Police cannot function, would not function. Policy officers are not taking steps. The Army is not brought in. Even the Army is not properly deployed in time. If we consider every issue in this country on the basis of religion, what remains of this country? Those people who have been massacred, butchered, those who have lost their homes, are they not Indians? ... I am quoting the words of the police authorities: 'There was a mass frenzy; there was a mass uprising...'

23 July 2002

I would like to know from the hon. minister as to what steps have been taken under Article 355 which enjoins on the Central government to take appropriate steps for the protection of the people there ... Across the board, independent organizations like the National Human Rights Commission, the Minorities Commission and other bodies have expressed their gravest concern about the things that have happened ... Compensation for the destruction and damage of the house is taken by the landlord who is nowhere there. I have been shown cheques of compensation amounting to Rs 50, Rs 100 and Rs 150. For destruction of a house, I was shown a cheque of compensation of Rs 81 and if business is lost, the compensation is Rs 250...

Nobody can say that the situation is totally normal. Trials that are going on are absolutely mockery ... The police is dancing to their tune. There is no law and order and there is no sense of security. Therefore, our demand has been that there has to be proper relief and rehabilitation for each and every surviving human being there ... There is no attempt to create a situation where everybody will get back the courage and confidence to stay on as citizens of an independent country.

A political game is being played to take advantage of the miseries of the people …

Speech on the Representation of the People (Amendment) Bill, 2003, Thirteenth Lok Sabha, Atal Bihari Vajpayee as Prime Minister, 6 August 2003

… I think it is a very sad day in the history of Parliament today. This Bill had been considered by the Standing Committee on Home Affairs headed by Shri Pranab Mukherjee. I am reading from the report of the committee. It says: 'There is, however, lack of consensus in the committee on the issue.'

There was unanimity that there was a difference. I am further quoting: 'In view of the divergent perceptions in the committee on the subject matter of the bill, it is the considered view that the Government should explore the possibility of evolving a consensus on the issues before piloting the bill in Parliament.'

I would like to know from the hon. minister what exploration was made to find out the possibility of evolving a consensus. Nobody can deny that this is an important bill. Even with all the eloquence of Shri Bansal, he did not say that it was not an important bill. There was no attempt made to evolve a consensus on this issue.

Sir, there is a total flouting, total ignoring of the unanimous recommendation of the Standing Committee. When there was a clear divergence of opinion in the committee, I feel, my party feels that this is the most brazen-faced attack on some of the basic features of our constitution. The only justification which is put forward by the two hon. members who have spoken and the hon. minister who has piloted the bill is that there are some corrupt voters in the Rajya Sabha elections.

On the basis of trying to find a solution to deal with corrupt activities of some members of the legislative assemblies, this atrocious attempt is being made to dilute two very fundamental provisions of our Constitution, which the Supreme Court has laid down repeatedly to be the basic features of the Constitution, namely, secrecy of voting as also the federal structure of the Constitution.

This bill is a direct and blatant attack on these two very essential and ennobling basic features of our Constitution. The statement of objects and reasons is so naïve and so cynical that it is nothing but an affront so far as Parliament is concerned. The way this matter is being treated is as if it is a question of just curing the corruption of the MLAs. This is an admission on behalf of the ruling party and – I am very very sorry to say – the Congress, with such a glorious tradition that they have, but they have succumbed to this. They are unable to control the presence of unscrupulous and corrupt people in the party. Some opportunists are there in different ranks.

Sir, there are some opportunists and some corrupt elements in their ranks – in the ranks of the ruling party and also some of the parties supporting this bill – and they have no faith in their party policies and programmes, if any. They have treated themselves, and allowed themselves to be treated as purchasable commodities. Now, these few corrupt people in some of the assemblies are going to decide the fate of this country's future.

Sir, the object is very clear. It is to enable some politicians to enter the Council of States from states to which they do not belong; with which they have no affinity and that money may not be collected by some corrupt MLAs. It will be an open book, and, therefore, secrecy of the voting must be done away with because some corrupt MLAs here and there fall prey to the lures of cash payment or whatever it is.

Sir, in this country, Mahatma Gandhi had led the struggle for Independence, and people had made tremendous sacrifices without hankering for any post or position of power. Now, some people in these parties feel themselves so indispensable that when they are rejected or cannot be elected by their own people they see to it that they come back to Parliament by hook or crook. There are also politicians who have no support in their own state and must come to Parliament. ... It is a matter of concern, and there is no doubt about it.

What is the remedy? Please look at the statement of objects and reasons. Have you got a copy, Mr Deputy Speaker, Sir? Section 3 of the

Representation of the People Act prescribes residential qualification for contesting elections to the Council of States. There have been numerous instances 'where the persons, who are normally not residing in a particular state, have got themselves registered as voters in that state simply to contest an election to the Council of States'. Of course, Sir, my friend, whose name is on the list as the mover of the bill answers that description, that is, to get himself elected to the Rajya Sabha, he made a foray into Gujarat and got himself registered as an ordinary resident there. Just for this purpose, that is, to enable these people to get elected, should we approve of this system or the proposal that is being brought about?

One of the members of this House, we have all respect to him, Shri Bansal says that his party is not a beneficiary. I am very sorry to say, without meaning any disrespect because people know the respect in which we hold the leader of the Opposition in the Rajya Sabha, could he not have served this country by remaining outside the House? He is a man of tremendous ability, great knowledge and expertise. He has held extremely important positions. This is not a reflection on him.

Sir, is parliamentary democracy being strengthened? We know a person who has given in a state his address, which is but a godown. There are members of Rajya Sabha who have nothing to do with the states from which they have been elected. My simple query is: is anybody so indispensable in this country that politics of this country cannot survive or the Parliament cannot survive? As I said, our freedom fighters, like Mahatma Gandhi and Jayaprakash Narayan, never hankered for any position. Have they not served the country? The tallest leaders of our country have remained outside the elected office. Unfortunately, some very good candidates may lose an election, but that is not the end of the day, end of everything or end of the road. Good persons should come to this Parliament. There is a provision for nomination also representing different facets of life in this country. But for whom are we changing this law? Are you changing for these persons? What will remain of the identity of the state?

The whole objective is, according to this statement of objects and reasons, to do away with money power. Money power is being indulged in by whom – the members of the legislative assembly. They say, well, there are big moneybags who get themselves elected. They cannot bribe anybody and everybody, and they have to bribe some MLAs. How many such instances are there? Shri Kuldip Nayyar has made some study. Earlier, it was three per cent from other states, and it has now come up to ten per cent. For ten per cent, that is, 25 people in the Rajya Sabha, you are mutilating the Constitution of India.

I will ask a simple question. Why do you allow such persons, about whose honesty you are not convinced, to remain in your party? What action is taken against them? You indulge in having opportunists as your members, corrupt people as your members, you give them tickets, they become members of legislative assemblies, and then they take bribe and elect somebody else for the sake of money. That may happen without changing the residence also. It can happen in the same state.

We are unable to understand how this can be the whole consideration. Very well, what will happen now? An MLA cannot take bribe. Who will get the money now? The party is astute enough. The party will collect money and give nomination. Now, those crooks with moneybags will purchase nominations from the party. Once they get the nomination, everything will be open. They will get themselves elected. Money will change hands; instead of unscrupulous MLAs, it will be unscrupulous parties now. Instead of some individual corrupt MLAs selling themselves, the parties will sell themselves. This is going to happen.

By these proposed changes, are you not insulting all members of legislative assemblies in all the states? This is a direct insult to them. There are many people in politics, hopefully, who believe in some principles, some policies, some objectives, who have some party loyalty, who work for the common people and not for themselves. Are you not insulting them?

All people are not purchasable commodities. All the MLAs are not purchasable commodities. Just for some crooks, I would not like MLAs in my state to be treated as purchasable commodities belonging to a party. They are not. We the Left parties stand alone today amongst all my friends here; we know that on this issue we are isolated. Even then, we shall go on objecting to this. We shall never accept the deliberate decimation of constitutional provisions in this country just for the sake of a handful of criminals who may have sneaked into some legislative assemblies.

So far as the residential status is concerned, what is the plea given here? The Election Commission, while discussing this aspect at an all-party meeting in April 2000, was of the view that a precise definition of 'ordinarily resident' was very difficult and emphasized that it was for the political parties acting through Parliament to carry out what in their judgment might be the best possible solution in the light of experience in the past fifty years. It was because of the misuse that was being made, probably, the Election Commission thought three years back that Parliament might consider it.

But as I said, there was no discussion with the parties.

Now, there is a reference to the Ethics Committee. The hon. minister also referred to the Ethics Committee of Parliament. I am reading from the statement of objects and reasons. This is the most atrocious statement I have ever seen in my humble career of 32 years.

The Ethics Committee of Parliament, in para 9 of its first report presented to Parliament on 8 December 1998 recommended that the issue relating to open ballot system of election be examined. But the issue has given rise to concern in the wake of allegations of money power.

Therefore, only one observation was made by the Election Commission that the 'parliament may consider it'. Where has the Election Commission recommended that anybody and everybody can be sent from anywhere in this country? What is meant by the federal structure of this country? Our constitution has made it very clear. Kindly see Article 1. You know it, Sir, very well. I am sure Shri Bansal knows it by heart. 'India, that is, Bharat shall be the union of states.' States' boundaries have been laid down by the Constitution of India, and the Upper House is called the Council of States and not the House of the People. The difference is so obvious. That is the whole basis of our Constitution. That is why the seventh schedule has been provided here about the separation of powers between the Centre and the states.

Every state has been given its own identity. That is why we are also so keen to preserve the rights, powers and identity of the states. We always object to encroachment by the Centre on the states' territory. Why? It is because that is the basic feature of our Constitution. Every state has its own ethos, its own culture, its own problems and its own issues which are shared by the citizens of that state. They may speak different languages, they may belong to different religions, they may belong to different castes and creeds, but they are residents of a particular state.

Sir, we feel proud to say that not only hundreds, not only thousands but lakhs and lakhs of people from all over the country are staying in my state, West Bengal. They are staying with dignity and honour. They consider themselves to be essential part and parcel of the state. They are contributing towards its development. I must admit with great happiness and pleasure that the people from outside who have made West Bengal as their state have contributed substantially and are still contributing to the development of our state. We have no grievance or quarrel with them. They are residing there. They proudly call themselves that they belong to West Bengal. Similarly, those who belong to Karnataka also proudly say that they belong to Karnataka and those who belong to Kerala proudly say that they belong to Kerala. Everybody belonging to a particular state will say so about his state.

Sir, the other day – although it was unseemly and I was very unhappy to observe – some of our hon. friends from Karnataka and Andhra Pradesh were, sort of, criticizing each other over a discussion on water. They were trying to find fault with each other. Why? It was because each one of them felt that his state's interest was getting affected. We must concede full bona fides to them. Shri K. Yerrannaidu fought for about fifty minutes trying to make out a case for Andhra Pradesh. Similarly, friends from Karnataka also spoke trying to put forward their case. This is not chauvinism as such, because the Constitution of India postulates this. States have their own rights. States have their own problems. States have their own issues. Then, who will respond to them?

I do not want it but if Shri P.C. Thomas has to be elected from Himachal Pradesh, where will his commitments be? This is not dividing the country, please. This is our unity in diversity. Therefore, if there is a dispute between Kerala and Himachal Pradesh, for whom will he respond? Whose cause will he uphold? This is the basis of it. That is why our Constitution is there.

Kindly see, Sir, the importance which has been given to the states.

Article 80, as you know, Sir, is about the composition of the Council of States. Article 80 says: 'The Council of States shall consist of twelve members to be nominated by the President … and not more than two hundred and thirty-eight representatives of the states and of the union territories.'

Now, come to Article 249. Article 249 is a very important article. It deals with the powers of Parliament. It says: 'Notwithstanding anything in the foregoing provisions of this chapter, if the Council of States has declared by resolution supported by not less than two-thirds members present and voting that it is necessary or expedient in the national interest that Parliament should make laws with respect to any matter enumerated in the State List …'

It is stated so because it will be the view of the people of the state. Similar is Article 312 that speaks of formation of all-India service. It says: 'Notwithstanding anything in (Chapter VI or Part XI), if the Council of States has declared by resolution, supported by not less than two-thirds of the members present and voting … they can constitute an all-India service.'

Sir, nowadays we do not hear the name of Dr B.R. Ambedkar. What did he say? In the constituent assembly this I what he said with regard to this: 'Ex hypothesis the upper chamber represents the states, and, therefore, their resolution would be tantamount to an authority given by the states.'

What are the considerations of the members of the Rajya Sabha, representing a particular state, if they do not belong to their states? Now, even pretence of being ordinarily resident will go. In future there will not even be a pretence of being an ordinarily resident. No false declaration would be necessary. Very well, if you can get a nomination from your party, which has got a majority in the Assembly in a particular state, he will send you there. There are some indispensable people in this country.

He becomes indispensable by his service, or indispensable because of the monetary contribution he makes.

Sir, what does Sarkaria Commission say? It says that the Rajya Sabha has been constituted to enable the states to give effective expression of their viewpoints at the parliamentary level. Take the composition of members of the Rajya Sabha who belong to different states. If there are fifteen members, two belong to Bihar, two belong to Kerala, two belong to Gujarat, two belong to Pondicherry, who will speak and for whom? How will the state give effective expression to their viewpoints at the parliamentary level? What are you doing? You are striking at the very basis of our parliamentary functioning and the basic character of our Constitution.

Sir, in Bommai case, what was done? What was said by the Supreme Court? It said: 'The states are sovereign in the field which is left to them. The states have an independent constitutional existence, and they have an important role to play in the political, social, educational and cultural life of the people. They are neither satellites nor agents of the centre.' Now we will have agents of political parties inside, not the representatives of the states. You would not have the representatives of the states any longer in the Council of States.

Sir, we have a federal structure of government – some call it quasi-federal, some call it federal. Its very basis is the existence of Centre and the states with distribution of powers, but it is ultimately for the benefit of the country as a whole. The Supreme Court has repeatedly held that federalism is a basic feature of our Constitution.

Therefore, either from the point of view of the federal character or from the point of view of dealing with corruption of some MLAs, should you change the basic structure of the Constitution? I appeal to my friend not to do permanent damage to us. They are institutionalizing corruption. They are not dealing with money power. They are giving primacy to money power today.

Is there any provision, Mr Minister, in this bill, to control persons taking money for giving nomination so far as political parties are concerned? Can he control if political parties take money for giving nomination? I would like to know this. So, they are saying that individual

MLAs should not take bribes, but the top people can take? That is the ridiculous situation that they have evolved.

Although the Election Commission said that there should be some discussion to find out the procedure, nothing was done; no meeting was held. The government did not try to find out a solution in discussion with parties. I do not know whether the Congress party was called for a separate discussion on this. Probably anticipating the support from Congress, they may not have called them or they may have called them separately.

The Constitution is being finished! Let me take a little more time, but not longer; may be 5-10 minutes more.

Another situation has been commented upon – that those members who get elected from other states do not take any interest in the affairs of the state. This is the situation, except perhaps our distinguished minister of law and justice – I wanted him to be here – who is often found in Gujarat in the company of the discredited chief minister. Probably he is trying to create more trouble for the minorities there! I do not know what his role is in the trial in the Best Bakery case.

I do not call him a discredited person. He is a very eminent person; he is a very eminent parliamentarian; he is a very eminent lawyer and an eminent minister, but may be in very bad company!

This bill strikes at the very root of the federal set-up of our Constitution. So, I strongly object to it and I protest against this attempted pollution of our Constitution ...

The other point is very important, which is the question of voting. The Supreme Court has expressed its agony.... It has said that the very basis of the parliamentary democracy is secrecy of votes. This is not the first time this has happened.

I forgot to mention one very important thing here. There is a document called the US Constitution. Mr Minister, the party under which you are working today gets its inspiration, if not sustenance, from USA. In their case, a Senator has to be the inhabitant of the state from which he is elected. This is in case of the upper house. Even for the lower house, a representative needs to be only twenty-five years old and a citizen for seven years but the residence requirement is the same, namely, he must belong to that state. This is true even for the House of Representatives. By custom, a representative must reside not only in the state but also in the district from where he is elected. President Bush will get annoyed. He will be very upset since you are not following that. You are following the World Bank, IMF or even others. Also, if President Bush wishes to send troops to Iraq, you are conceding to that. But here you are against that.

There are other two very important international documents; Article 21 of the Universal Declaration on Human Rights to which India is a party and Article 25 of the International Covenant on Civil and Political Rights, 1996, to which also we are a party and we are bound by them. There is a mandatory provision that the will of the people shall be expressed in periodic and genuine elections which shall be held by secret vote. The Supreme Court says that it is the very essence of our parliamentary democracy.

Another inspirer of yours is the American Supreme Court. Of course, any constitutional lawyer does refer to the American Supreme Court because it has pronounced outstanding decisions. The American Supreme Court has pointed out the danger of open voting in the following words: 'Absolute secrecy in voting addresses effectively a great number of evils including violence, intimidation, bribery and corrupt practices, dictation by employers or organizations, the fear of ridicule and dislike or of social and commercial injury. In fact, all coercive and improper influence of every sort depending on a knowledge of the voters' political action. Secrecy of ballot has been considered and described as a postulate of constitutional democracy as it serves a vital public interest that an elector or a voter should be absolutely free in exercise of his franchise.'

This is the basis. That principle is being given a go-by in this country for a handful of corrupt and crooks, in some legislative assemblies and for some handful of power-hungry politicians who consider themselves indispensable and who must enter parliament by any method that may be available to them, even to the extent of filing false applications. Today, for them we are not only tinkering with the Constitution, we are injuring the very heart and soul of the Constitution.

This is nothing but an outrage, a sacrilege committed so far as the Constitution is concerned. Although we may be alone here, but Sir, I have got the great happiness, privilege and great satisfaction of opposing it today even if we are isolated, this lawless law, this attack on the Constitution of India.... I oppose every sentence, every word of this bill. I hope even now some of the hon. members will reconsider their position and will see that this great Constitution of India which was framed in the next hall, of which we all are proud is not diluted, polluted in this manner because of a handful of crooks in this country.

Speech in Response to the Felicitations on Being Elected Speaker, Fourteenth Lok Sabha, 4 June 2004

I am extremely thankful to you for unanimously electing me to the high office of the Speaker of this august House. I do not have words adequately to express my feelings for the great honour bestowed on me and I accept the same with all humility and gratitude. I am overwhelmed by the generous sentiments expressed for me by all sections of the House.

Today, I cannot help remembering the day when I first entered this great chamber in the year 1971 as a new member and I must confess that I was overawed in the presence of giants and luminaries who added great lustre to the proceedings of the House. As a backbencher, I had the opportunity to listen to some of the great orations inside the House which inspired me to be worthy of the confidence reposed by the people by electing me to the House. I cannot also forget witnessing from the Visitors' Gallery on occasions the proceedings in the House when my father, late Shri N.C. Chatterjee, was one of the members. I had the great privilege of hearing some of the most inspiring interventions by, amongst others, Pandit Jawaharlal Nehru, Sardar Patel, Pandit Pant, Dr Syama Prasad Mookerjee, Shri N.C. Chatterjee, Prof. Hiren Mukherjee, Shri Nath Pai and many others. Please excuse me for the nostalgic feeling that I have on this occasion.

I am also grateful to the hon. Prime Minister for his kind reference to my father. I find his award of degree to him was well justified and he has more than proved his merit, and today I must congratulate him once again for occupying this position of high honour.

Hon. Members, the fourteenth Lok Sabha has got the people's mandate to usher in a new era. This is a unique responsibility bestowed on this august House. Our country has made progress in various fields since Independence. However, a lot more needs to be done for the benefit of the common people. We have to ensure that the creative potential and energies of our people are harnessed for fulfilling the hopes and aspirations of various sections of our society, particularly the deprived and the dispossessed, by providing a developing, pro-people and secular administration.

The Lok Sabha is the highest elected body in the largest parliamentary democracy in the world and occupies the pivotal position in our political system. Our founding fathers, after considerable deliberations, decided to adopt the parliamentary system of governance with the Lok Sabha, elected on adult franchise and the council of ministers responsible to the same. The people of India participate in the parliamentary process through their representatives in Lok Sabha. Members of Parliament who are elected on the basis of their pledge contained in their manifestoes are expected to articulate the urges and aspirations of the people, to discuss problems and issues facing the nation and to deliberate upon the formulation of national policies and programmes with a view to finding solutions to them. The very postulate of parliamentary democracy as is enshrined in our Constitution is the collective responsibility of central council of ministers to the House of People. For every action of the government it is liable to answer in this House.

This House represents all sections of our people with their very socio-cultural identities, ethos and genius, differences of ideas, interests, approaches and objectives as they are bound to arise during the deliberations in the House. As a strong integrating force in the country, this House, which is the people's institution in the true sense of the term, is called upon to resolve the various socio-political and economic problems faced by the people.

Even after more than five decades of Independence, in course of which we have celebrated the golden jubilee of our Parliament, a very substantial number of our people still face awesome problems and do not enjoy even the minimum rights which the Constitution, our organic law contemplates for them. Abysmal poverty, illiteracy, high child mortality, absence of adequate healthcare, lack of job opportunities, non-availability of pure drinking water in many areas, amongst others, are the problems which still haunt the common people and result in effective denial of the constitutional and indeed the basic human rights to our people.

The common people of our country, particularly the toiling sections, the workers, the peasants and the farmers, the Scheduled Castes and the Scheduled Tribes, the women and the minorities have not been able to fulfil their minimum needs. The condition of the working class in the country is still extremely uncertain with mounting unemployment figures. In such circumstances, I humbly feel that it is the bounden duty of us all, as Members of Parliament, to play a very active, responsible and effective role to meet the aspirations of the people.

The Parliament is constituted by the people. It has to deliberate upon and deal with the problems of the people and ultimately find their solutions for the people.

The Rules of Business and Procedure in Lok Sabha have been framed for the orderly conduct of its business and several avenues for obtaining redressal of the people's grievances have also been provided in the rules. My appeal to all the hon. members is to utilize these rules in a proper manner so that they can play an effective role as members of this august House.

Nowadays considerable criticism is being faced by the Members of Parliament about their failure to maintain decorum and dignity in the House. The behaviour and conduct of some legislators have become the subject of justified criticism and in some cases even of ridicule. Unfortunately, there is developing more and more an attitude of confrontation than cooperation in our political life which finds its reflection in the House. We should resolve to change this perception in the minds of the people by our own conduct, both inside and outside the House.

Hon. Members, I am fully conscious of the responsibility bestowed on me as the Speaker of this august House. The willing cooperation you have promised today on the floor of the House gives the strength to shoulder the great responsibility and prove myself worthy of the trust you have reposed in me. Conscious as I am of the responsibility that has been entrusted, I can assure you that I shall always endeavour to conduct the business of this House in keeping with the lofty ideals and noble goals enshrined in our great Constitution and in the rules of procedure and in tune with the highest parliamentary traditions.

I am fully aware that as the Speaker, my conduct and behaviour will always be under close scrutiny. Maintaining the high standards laid down by the distinguished predecessors starting from Shri Vithalbhai Patel, Shri G.V. Mavalankar up to Shri Manohar Joshi, I shall spare no effort to uphold and, if possible, further enhance the dignity and prestige of this high constitutional office in regulating the proceedings of this House and addressing the concerns of its members.

I shall discharge my functions entrusted to this office more as a duty rather than as an authority. The non-party character of the office of the Speaker in our parliamentary polity places on me a special obligation to be totally non-partisan and judicious while regulating the proceedings of the House. So long as I occupy this exalted Chair, I assure you that I shall always strive to protect to the best of my ability the rights and privileges of the House and of its members irrespective of their political affiliations.

Hon. Members, I can assure you that to me, all the hon. members are of the same status and are entitled to the same facilities, irrespective of the party to which one may belong, and will be entitled to the same opportunity. The only status that I recognize is that all of you are elected and hon. members of this great institution.

Pandit Jawaharlal Nehru had observed at a seminar on parliamentary democracy held on 6 December 1957 that:

> Deliberately and after long argument, we in India adopted a Constitution based on parliamentary Government. We praise the parliamentary form of Government because it is a peaceful method of dealing with problems. It is a method of agreement, discussion, decision and accepting the

> decision even though one may or may not agree with it. However, a minority in a parliamentary Government has a very important part to play. Naturally, the majority by the mere fact that it is majority must have its way.

Parliament should function through debate, discussion and consensus and it can only do so if the deliberations are marked by a sense of commitment to the cause of the people and the atmosphere in the House is kept free from bitterness and acrimony. Unless the rules, regulations and well-established parliamentary conventions are respected by each and every member and unless the members exhibit mutual accommodation and respect whenever there are differing points of view, our parliamentary democracy will remain imperfect. The treasury benches and the Opposition have equal responsibilities in ensuring good governance in the country. While discharging their parliamentary responsibilities, both sides are expected to be accommodating and forbearing to each other, particularly when contentious issues are debated on the floor of the House.

A Member of Parliament occupies a very high place in the eyes of the people. The effectiveness of the functioning of this House would depend to a great extent on how scrupulously we, the members, follow various rules and guidelines which are a prerequisite for the orderly transaction of parliamentary business. Here, I need hardly emphasize that the observance of discipline and decorum on the part of the members is an essential precondition for the smooth and efficient functioning of the House. Besides the rules of procedure and conduct of business, there exist numerous customs and conventions, rules of parliamentary etiquette and unrecorded traditions, which have to be observed by every member in the interest of parliamentary decorum. One need hardly emphasize that it is the quality of our behaviour and the substance of our deliberations that will decide whether we are able to enhance the prestige of this august House and promote faith in our parliamentary institution.

With many young faces making their debut in the Lok Sabha in the just concluded general elections, this House has the benefit of utilizing a pool of constructive energies together with experience of the senior members in responding to the issues concerning the hopes and aspirations of the common masses.

I hope every newly elected member will function with commitment and learn and follow the rules of the game and make valuable contributions to the proceedings of the House. May I suggest the newcomers may get themselves conversant with the established parliamentary traditions and conventions and learn to make full use of all their valuable procedural devices so that they may contribute effectively towards redressal of the people's grievances.

The role of the media in providing an effective interface between the people and the Parliament cannot be overemphasized. I am fully confident that a responsible and adequate coverage of the proceedings of the House by the media will go a long way in projecting the right image of the supreme national forum. I seek meaningful cooperation from the media.

I am grateful to the hon. members for their warm expressions about me and for assuring me their unstinted cooperation. I express my grateful thanks to the hon. Prime Minister, hon. leader of the house, Shrimati Sonia Gandhi, Shri Atal Bihari Vajpayee, hon. leader of the Opposition, Shri L.K. Advani, leaders of various parties and other distinguished friends for the warm sentiments they have expressed about me. To run the House successfully, I look forward to your cooperation. On my part let me assure you once again that I shall endeavour my best to justify the trust that you have reposed in me and meet your expectations.

Let us all join our hands in heralding a new era of peace, progress and prosperity for our country through the discharge of our duty as the chosen representatives of the people. I earnestly seek your kind cooperation and help in the discharge of my onerous duty.

As a leftist, as one belonging to the Left party, friends on my left may rest assured that I have a natural leaning towards the left. Let us resolve that we shall perform the task assigned to us to the best of our ability and with sincerity. We should ask ourselves when the House rises for the day every evening as to what we have done during the day for the country and for the people and whether we have justified the people's faith in sending us here. Nothing will give us more satisfaction than the feeling that we have tried and done our best.

Valedictory Speech, Fourteenth Lok Sabha, 26 February 2009

Hon'ble Members, I take this opportunity to express my profound gratitude to all sections of the House for the support and cooperation extended to me in the course of the discharge of my duties as the presiding officer of this great institution. At the end of the last session of the fourteenth Lok Sabha, I feel that now is the appropriate time to take stock of what this House has been able to achieve in the last five years and make a dispassionate introspection.

Before I proceed, I wish to express my great personal sorrow that today our Hon'ble Prime Minister Dr Manmohan Singh and Shri Atal Bihari Vajpayee are unable to be present here due to their indisposition. On my behalf and on behalf of the House I wish to congratulate the hon'ble Prime Minister for his successful surgery and I am sure he will soon be able to resume his normal activities with perfect health and vigour.

I also convey on behalf of the House and on my own behalf our best wishes to Vajpayeeji for his speedy and complete recovery. We are happy that he is making good progress on his way to complete recovery. I also convey my very best wishes to my dear and young friend Shri Priya Ranjan Dasmunsi for a speedy and complete recovery.

The fourteenth Lok Sabha was constituted on 17 May 2004 and the House met for the first time on 2 June 2004. In all, the House had till today 332 sittings.

On 4 June 2004, the House bestowed great honour upon me by unanimously electing me to the august office of the Speaker. My colleague, Shri Charanjit Singh Atwal was also unanimously elected as the Deputy Speaker on 9 June 2004. It has been our sincere endeavour to conduct the proceedings and the deliberations of this House to the best of our abilities and in an impartial manner and uphold the dignity of the House. I also express my deep gratitude to the distinguished chairmen on the panel for the most conscientious and able manner in which they conducted the proceedings of the House.

As the Presiding Officer of this august House, it has always been my humble endeavour to promote quality debate on all issues by giving opportunities to all sections of the political spectrum in the House and to facilitate smooth and orderly transaction of the business in the House. To this end, I initiated several procedural reforms such as meeting with the leaders of parties and groups daily half-an-hour before the start of the day's proceedings to seek cooperation and support in obviating disruptions and disturbances in the House. As every minute and hour of the time of the House is precious, I started the practice of making a weekly statement every Tuesday on the business transacted by the House to make every member aware of the time well spent and the time wasted in the House.

As the hon'ble members are aware, much of the work of the House is done now by the committees. The parliamentary committees have, during the past five years, done excellent work. The departmentally related standing committees have been restructured and their number has been increased to twenty-four and their jurisdiction defined. This restructuring intended to bring about an improvement in the examination and scrutiny of the demands for grants of the ministries and departments has served its purpose towards ensuring effective parliamentary scrutiny of executive actions as envisaged in our constitutional scheme.

The parliamentary standing committees and the parliamentary committees functioned effectively and efficiently during the present Lok Sabha and made many important recommendations. The standing and other parliamentary committee presented as many as 626 reports. I am happy to record that the hon'ble members almost on all occasions considered the issues and problems which came before the committees in a non-partisan manner.

As the hon'ble members are aware, a new Direction 73A was incorporated in the directions by the Speaker which made it incumbent on all the ministers to make a statement in the House, on the status of implementation of the various recommendation/observations made by the standing committees in their reports within six months of their presentation in the House. In this context, the ministers made 388 statements regarding the status of implementation of the recommendations / observations contained in the reports of the standing committees.

Putting questions is an important instrument in the hands of the members to scrutinize the functioning of the executive. In the fourteenth Lok Sabha, 6218 starred questions were listed, out of which 929 questions were answered orally. I tried my best to give opportunity to members belonging to different parties, large or small. Written replies to the remaining starred questions along with 60,419 unstarred questions were laid on the table. Fourteen half-an-hour discussions were also taken up. Five short notice questions were also answered.

The fourteenth Lok Sabha enacted 258 legislations including Right to Information Act, 2005; the National Rural Employment Guarantee Act, 2005; the Protection for Women from Domestic Violence Act, 2005; the Disaster Management Act, 2005; the Commission for Protection of Child Rights Act, 2005; the Scheduled Tribes and Other Traditional Forest Dwellers (Recognition of Forest Rights) Act, 2006; the Unorganized Workers' Social Security Bill, 2008; and the National Investigation Agency Act, 2008 and the Rehabilitation Bill, 2009.

Personally it is a matter of great regret for me that we have not been able, during my tenure, to pass the Women's Reservation Bill which to my mind would have gone a long way towards genuine and effective empowerment of fifty per cent of our population. The Women's Reservation Bill has now been introduced in the Rajya Sabha during the 2008 budget session to ensure that the bill does not lapse with the dissolution of the fourteenth Lok Sabha. I am hopeful that all political parties will reach unanimity to evolve a clear consensus on the issue in the next Lok Sabha.

Coming to private members' business, 327 private members' bills were introduced during the fourteenth Lok Sabha. Nine private members' resolutions on important subjects were moved.

During this Lok Sabha, 3444 matters of urgent public importance were raised by the members after the Question Hour and at the end of the sitting for the day. Hon. members also raised 3485 matters under Rule 377. As the presiding officer, I had humbly tried to allow the members maximum opportunity to raise matters of importance. As a part of this approach, I allowed a larger number of matters under calling attention as compared to the number in the earlier Lok Sabha, which helped the members in getting response from the ministers to the matters raised by them. In fact, 115 calling attention matters were raised during this period. The ministers made 266 statements on various important subjects, which also include the statements made by the hon'ble Prime Minister.

In recognition of the right of the Opposition to move adjournment motions on urgent issues, I tried my best to allow a number of them consistent with the provisions of the rules, many more than allowed earlier.

In this context, I would like to recall some landmark decisions that were taken during the fourteenth Lok Sabha. As the custodian of the rights and privileges of the House and with a view to maintaining the dignity and authority of Parliament, I had to take painful decisions. Ten members had to be expelled from the membership of the House for their involvement in the cash-for-query scam. Another four members had to face suspension of their membership of the House for a certain period for irregularities in the implementation of the MPLAD scheme. I had also the painful duty to constitute several committees to inquire into alleged misconduct of members as in the alleged human trafficking case and the alleged bribery scam prompted by the unsightly display of wads of currency notes in the well of the House during the debate on the trust vote in July 2008. Some other members had to face expulsion from the membership of the House through disqualification under the Anti-Defection Act. In all such actions, this House has shown exemplary commitment to cleanse itself of the erring members and a firm resolve to adhere to the code of conduct expected from people's representatives, and this process of self-cleansing must continue whenever there arises any such occasion in the future also.

Outside the procedural plane, several other initiatives were taken during the life of the fourteenth Lok Sabha. The constitution of the parliamentary forums on different topical issues was one such significant development. We now have five parliamentary forums: one each on water conservation and management; youth; women and children; population and public health; and global warming and climate change. The underlying idea has been to provide members an important platform to interact with subject experts and key officials of the ministries concerned. These forums have been useful in equipping the hon'ble members with information and knowledge on specific issues and in helping them to adopt a result-oriented approach in dealing with particular issues. Member-conveners have been appointed for each forum and they have been very active in organizing several programmes of interest to the members during parliament sessions.

During the fourteenth Lok Sabha, a lecture series was instituted for Members of Parliament at the Bureau of Parliamentary Studies and Training to sensitize them on issues of topical concern and contemporary problems having a bearing on our socio-economic situation. So far, twenty-four lectures on various issues have been organized in which experts from India and abroad shared their perspectives with hon'ble members. The keen interest taken by hon'ble members and the meaningful interactions they had with the experts are indeed heart-warming.

I mooted the idea of an autonomous salaries commission for Members of Parliament which was accepted, in principle, by the government.

A prestigious annual parliamentary lecture has also been instituted in memory of one of India's most outstanding parliamentarians, Prof. Hiren Mukerjee. The inaugural lecture on the theme 'Demands of Social Justice' was delivered by the Nobel Laureate and Lamont Professor at the Harvard University, Prof. Amartya Sen, in the Central Hall on 11 August 2008. I believe all these initiatives have been received well and with good results and hope that members in the future also will continue to hold the same for which eminent persons will be invited to speak on important subjects.

Two round table discussions involving major stakeholders were also organized by the Lok Sabha on the theme 'Strengthening Parliamentary Democracy'. The first round table was held on 4 September 2008 and the second one on 1 November 2008. Both the round table discussions were interactive and addressed by very distinguished and eminent parliamentarians, jurists, journalists and civil society leaders. The deliberations were stimulating and thought provoking with the distinguished participants sharing their informed viewpoints on the state of our parliamentary democracy.

To take the institution of Parliament nearer to the people, I have the great satisfaction in being able to launch the Lok Sabha Television channel (LSTV). With the introduction of the 24-hour TV channel exclusively devoted to telecasting live all proceedings of the House, our people would be able to see the way their representatives discharge their responsibilities inside the chamber of the Lok Sabha, and find it as an effective interface among the people, Parliament and the government. Besides the coverage of parliamentary proceedings, several value-added programmes are telecast whereby parliamentarians participate in various programmes on contemporary topics and articulate the stand of their respective parties on important political, economic and international issues. The channel also telecasts plays, cultural programmes, films and documentaries on our heritage, beliefs, traditions, music and dance. We feel proud that this is the only TV channel in the world which is owned and operated by Parliament, without any executive control or even intervention. I conceived the idea of starting a TV channel for bringing the people close to Parliament and also to extend the space for the visitors' gallery to every home to let the country see what Parliament is doing. As the people are our real masters, they have the right to know how their representatives are serving them and the nation as a whole.

Recognizing the important role that the media plays, I had regular interactions with editors and senior journalists during the Parliament session and exhorted them to improve the coverage of the proceedings of the House. I do believe that as a result of these interactions the coverage has improved, though it is not yet in ample measure. A panel of experts was also constituted comprising among others media personalities to advise me on these aspects.

Another important initiative to bring Parliament closer to the people has been the setting up of the state-of-the-art Parliament Museum.

The museum, which was inaugurated by our the then Rashtrapatiji Dr A.P.J. Abdul Kalam on 14 August 2006 and is open to the public, has been designed to serve as a hi-tech, story-telling museum, depicting the continuum of democratic ethos and institutional development in India. The Lok Sabha Television and the Parliament Museum have been lauded by one and all, as important initiatives that would help to strengthen our parliamentary system.

I wish to sincerely thank all the leaders, especially the hon. leader of the Opposition for the kind help and guidance that he gave to me during the time when the museum was set up. I am happy to say that a large number of boys and girls, particularly students, are coming to see this museum. I hope members, who could not find time up till now, will pay a visit to the museum.

Yet another important initiative has been the widening access which we have facilitated to the Parliament library. I have endeavoured to ensure that the rich reservoir of knowledge we have in the Parliament library is also utilized by genuine research scholars from universities and institutions of repute, journalists, heads/members of educational institutions and others. We have also set up a children's corner in the Parliament library to cater to the information and knowledge needs of children. It provides opportunities to them to know of our parliamentary framework and about the country's progress and development, specially of matters relating to children and the youth.

With a view to promoting knowledge about parliamentary democracy among the younger generation, we have for the first time started the Lok Sabha Internship Programme. It is a year-long programme which provides an opportunity to five young postgraduates with outstanding academic records to acquaint themselves with the working of parliamentary democracy and democratic institutions, and especially about the Indian parliamentary system.

During the fourteenth Lok Sabha, we also had the satisfaction of observing two memorable occasions, namely, the 150th anniversary of our First War of Independence and the 60th year of our Independence, in the Central Hall, which programmes I believe were extremely successful.

I would also take this opportunity to mention that I have initiated a scholarship scheme for the wards of Group 'C' and 'D' employees of the Lok Sabha secretariat who have been admitted in professional courses in the disciplines of medicine including ayurvedic and homeopathic medicines, disciplines of engineering, chartered accountancy, MBA, LL.B. and architecture.

Under this scholarship scheme, six wards, one in each field mentioned above, shall be granted a sum total of the tuition fee of the course charged by the institution/college wherein the ward has been selected for pursuing his/her studies.

On this occasion, I would also recall the supreme sacrifice that an official of the Hindustan Petroleum Corporation, Shri Rajeev Saraswat, made while he was working as in-charge of the control room for the parliamentary committee on subordinate legislation at the Taj Mahal Hotel, one of the several places attacked during the dastardly terrorist assault on the city of Mumbai.

On behalf of the House, I had communicated our deepest condolences, to the chairman and managing director of Hindustan Petroleum Corporation and to the bereaved family. In this context, I would like to inform that the Lok Sabha secretariat has given ex-gratia amount to the family of the deceased and I have recommended to the government to allot a petrol pump to his family to secure their future.

These are some of the humble initiatives which the presiding officer took during this Lok Sabha with a view to strengthening the institution of Parliament. I must gratefully acknowledge the fact that I received unstinted cooperation and support from all sections of the House, the treasury as well as the opposition benches, in the discharge of my duties as the presiding officer of this House and for the new initiatives.

I will only be betraying my emotions if I do not refer to what I would painfully call certain aberrations and avoidable situations during the life of the fourteenth Lok Sabha which has somewhat lowered the esteem of this august institution in the eyes of the people. I am pained to say that politics of intense confrontation has gained the upper hand with the result that disruptions of the proceedings of the House through sloganeering, coming into the well of the House, walkouts, etc., have greatly eroded people's faith in the efficacy of this great institution. As we know now, this Lok Sabha spent a total of 1677 hrs 8 mins on actual sittings and wasted 421 hrs 5 mins at the end of the fourteenth session. The time wasted in disruptions and adjournments due to disorderly scenes amounted to a total of about 25 per cent of the time of the House which is very alarming.

The very edifice of parliamentary system of government is grounded in the clear delineation of powers and functions of the three different organs of the government – the legislature, the executive and the judiciary. As such, Parliament is the supreme law-making body which has exclusive powers to regulate its own proceedings and to discipline its members. As the custodian of parliamentary rights and privileges, it fell on me to defend and safeguard the rights and privileges of Parliament, and legislatures across the country. Members will recall that in March 2005, on a dispute that arose over the decision of the Jharkhand governor in appointing the chief minister, the Supreme Court passed an interim order which inter alia contained directions to the presiding officer on fixing of agenda of the House, maintenance of order and video recording of the proceedings in the House. Such matters fall under the exclusive jurisdiction of the presiding officer of every legislature under the Constitution, the rules of the House and even by convention. I had to assert the supremacy of the legislature in its exclusive domain, and in all this, I had ultimately the concurrence and support of all the leaders of parties in Parliament and the conference of presiding officers of legislative bodies in India, for which I am grateful to them.

Another such occasion arose when the expelled members in the cash-for-query scam filed writ petitions in the Supreme Court challenging their expulsion. As the presiding officer of the Lok Sabha, I had to defend the rights of this House to deal with all matters relating to discipline and misconduct of the members and to make it clear that the votes given by the members inside the chambers of Parliament cannot be questioned in a court of law. The Supreme Court subsequently dismissed the writ petitions and recognized the position that I took, that was endorsed by all sections of the House as well as the emergency conference of presiding officers of legislative bodies in India.

As we adjourn sine die today, it is a mixed feeling that I have – I have a feeling of quiet satisfaction, which I share with you in all humility, that I have honestly tried to uphold the dignity and prestige of the high constitutional office of the Speaker in regulating the proceedings of this House in the highest parliamentary traditions and in affording all opportunities to hon'ble members to participate in the proceedings and express their voices. In discharging my duty, it has been my endeavour to protect to the best of my ability the rights and privileges of the House and the hon'ble members irrespective of their political affiliations and to further enhance the functioning of our parliamentary system. If ever I did not come up to the expectations of the hon'ble members, I express my sincere sorrow for the same.

Once again I would like to express my gratitude to all sections of the House for their support and cooperation, notwithstanding the unkept assurances and frustration and disappointments at times, in discharging my duties and responsibilities as the presiding officer of this august House. I thank the hon'ble chairman of the Rajya Sabha, Shri Md. Hamid Ansari, for his active cooperation in coordinating the works of the two Houses of Parliament; the Hon'ble Prime Minister, Dr. Manmohan Singh; the Hon'ble leader of the House, Shri Pranab Mukherjee; and the Hon'ble leader of the Opposition, Shri L.K. Advani, for their support and cooperation in running this House; the Hon'ble Deputy Speaker, Shri Charanjit Singh Atwal, and the members of the panel of chairmen for sharing the onerous duty of the presiding officer of this House; the Hon'ble Deputy Chairman of the Rajya Sabha, Shri K. Rahman Khan, for his cooperation; the leaders of all parties and groups and each and every Member of Parliament for their contribution in making our parliamentary democracy work. I shall be failing in my duty if I do not express my sincere thanks and gratitude to the hon'ble chairpersons of the UPA and NDA for all the respect shown to the Chair and for their kind help and cooperation.

I also extend my gratitude to the secretary-general of the Lok Sabha, Shri P.D.T. Achary, for being a constant source of strength and support in running this august House, and his team of officers and to all the staff of the Lok Sabha secretariat as well as in the Speaker's office for their committed efficient and professional handling of all works related to the Lok Sabha. I also put on record my thanks to all the media persons accredited to covering the work of Parliament and the media in general for being a vigilant watchdog of democracy.

I also appreciate the services of the Watch & Ward Staff, CRPF, Delhi Police and other security agencies who are vigilantly protecting the Parliament House Complex. I also thank the CPWD and other allied agencies which have rendered their valuable support.

Hon'ble Members, along with fourteenth Lok Sabha which for all effective purposes is coming to an end today, I am also reaching my journey's end and in a short while I shall be leaving this chamber for the last time. I seek your kind indulgence for referring to my feelings on this occasion, when I shall be finally dissociating from this great institution. As a humble servant of the House of the people, I have had the great opportunity to serve the nation through this great institution for nearly thirty-nine years with a short break of eleven months.

I recall vividly that in the fifth Lok Sabha I was allotted seat No. 512 from where I had the privilege to listen with awe and admiration and as attentively as possible to some of the memorable speeches delivered by the outstanding parliamentarians. I had the great opportunity to serve the people of the country as a member of this august House from the fifth to fourteenth Lok Sabha. I was the leader of the party in the Lok Sabha for fifteen years till my election as Speaker. As the leader it was my duty to see that issues of the working class and vulnerable sections of the society were duly raised in the House. Lok Sabha provides the most important forum for articulating the urges and aspirations of the people and for raising matters of concern for the peasants and workers and for the common people of the country. I cannot but recall the great guidance and encouragement and affection that I received from my leaders, particularly Comrade Jyoti Basu. I am grateful to the Indian Parliamentary Group that selected me for the conferment of the Outstanding Parliamentarian Award in the year 1996.

I respectfully submit that as the presiding officer, I tried honestly and sincerely to uphold the highest traditions of the parliamentary institution and discharged my duties to the best of my ability.

I totally dissociated myself from any political activity whatsoever, in keeping with the essence of the Constitution of India, which demands discharge of duties with total impartiality and treat all the members as equal.

In consonance with the spirit of the Constitution, I took a considered decision to stand by the Constitution of India and not allow myself to take a course of action which my former party had taken. But I was completely overwhelmed by the tremendous outpouring of support and appreciation that I received from not only the citizens of this country but also from the Indian diaspora, on what they acknowledged as my principled stand on a very vital issue on the role of the Speaker, keeping the dignity of the institution and upholding the fundamental principles of the Constitution. I could not compromise on the role and expectations of the Speaker as enshrined in the Constitution.

Hon'ble Members, I wish to sincerely thank all of you once again for the great opportunity that you gave me and during the short time I am left with, I wish to closely follow the functioning of this great institution for all its glory and greater success.

I beg to convey my best wishes to each one of you for your success in the coming event.

Thank you.

APPENDIX II

Parliamentary Initiatives Taken during Somnath Chatterjee's Tenure as Speaker

Weekly Statements on Business Transacted

From 15 March 2005, I started the practice of presenting a weekly statement in the House, briefly recalling the business transacted by the House and the time, if any, lost due to unscheduled adjournments. My intention was to get the members to focus on what they had achieved and shame them about unfortunate disturbances. I must be honest that the objective was not wholly accomplished and the exercise became more of a routine ritual. But I hope it will be continued and its full potential realized sooner rather than later.

Departmentally Related Standing Committees (DRSCs)

I have always been an ardent advocate of parliamentary committees and cannot but acknowledge the extremely useful work taken up by them. The reports of such committees are preponderantly unanimous and the outcome of very serious deliberations and analysis. Sometimes I feel that the core functions of Parliament – of debating problems, issues, policies and legislations – have shifted to the committees. Having chaired many committees during my parliamentary career, I say this with some conviction.

On the basis of recommendations of the joint parliamentary committee to study DRSCs, I approved that their number be increased by seven and the membership streamlined. Rules of internal procedure were drawn up to improve their functioning.

What I consider my most significant intervention on this was the introduction of a new Direction 73A in September 2004, making it mandatory for the concerned minister to make a six-monthly statement in the House on the action taken on recommendations of a committee's report. Unfortunately, these valuable reports were seldom given proper attention in the ministries, and departmental secretaries were often not aware of their details. The situation definitely changed for the better because of Direction 73A. The DRSCs presented 626 reports and 388 statements were made in compliance with Direction 73A during the fourteenth Lok Sabha.

I had been very keen to empanel experts who could associate themselves with the parliamentary committees in specialized aspects of analysing legislations and policies. When I was chairman of the information technology committee in the thirteenth Lok Sabha, I had felt the knowledge gap rather acutely. My office prepared a note on the subject and I discussed it with leaders of parties and some chairmen of committees in March 2005. I was somewhat taken aback to encounter strong resistance to the idea. Sushma Swaraj, chairperson, committee of the home ministry, was particularly vociferous in her objection. Dr Karan Singh of the Rajya Sabha's ethics committee sounded quite alarmed at finding the word 'partnership' with experts and institutions in the note. I had to explain that this was not meant to be taken in the conventional sense but in a complementary, supportive sense. The committees would have gained greatly by allowing recognized expertise to enrich their work but I am sorry that I had to shelve this idea. I do hope that it will be taken up and institutionalized.

I prescribed time limits for presentation of reports, usually three months. Extensions were not encouraged, nor requests by ministers that bills not be referred to committees, unless there were very convincing grounds. I found the requests by some chairmen for extensions, after the last sitting in March 2009, particularly incomprehensible and expressed my annoyance in no uncertain terms.

Parliamentary committees undertake tours across the country to obtain a first-hand idea of different organizations and related issues within their remit. It came to my notice, and that of Bhairon Singh Shekhawat, chairman, Rajya Sabha, that many a time the tours did not serve their purpose and were more an all-costs-borne 'Bharat Darshan' for members and staff, with attractive gifts thrown in for good measure. There was much media and public criticism of this overindulgence. In May 2005, I discussed the matter with various leaders and amended the guidelines for the tours to make them more work oriented and less lavish. The numbers of tours and their duration were limited. I used to personally monitor the work taken up by committees, especially during tours, and ensure that bills were settled expeditiously. It was decided that Parliament, and not ministries, would pay for these tours. Initially, some objections were raised as my initiatives were wrongly perceived as an effort to curtail the existing rights of parliamentarians. It required quite a bit of effort on my part to clarify matters. Looking back, perhaps, the entire gamut of change envisaged was not effected. However, an important beginning was made, which will hopefully be built on in the years to come.

Members' Salaries and Allowances

A member is entitled to receive salary, allowances and other facilities under The Salary, Allowances and Pension of Members of Parliament Act, 1954. For the fixation and review of the amount of salary and allowances, a joint committee is constituted in every House.

During my earlier tenure as a Member of Parliament, whenever the question of re-fixation or increase of the salary and allowances of members had come up – any increase in the amount had to be brought about by amending the concerned Act of 1954 – I had expressed serious reservations about its propriety. I always felt that it was most embarrassing, if not demeaning, for members to fix their own salary. There was also a lot of criticism about this, especially as the majority of citizens did not find the role of parliamentarians exemplary, and as such worthy of being compensated. In no other Parliament in the world did members decide their own salary and emoluments. I believed strongly that there should be an independent body like a salaries commission to determine the matter and all its related aspects. I called a meeting of various political parties on 23 March 2005 to evolve a mechanism for periodical revision of salaries and allowances of MPs. There was unanimous agreement, in principle, to my proposal for setting up a salaries commission consisting of persons of eminence from different fields of finance, planning, constitutional law, etc.

During the debate in the House on 23 August 2006, Priya Ranjan Dasmunsi, minister for parliamentary affairs, stated that the government had agreed to set up a salaries commission but it would be taken up only in the next Lok Sabha. I have been kept in the dark about the reason for the postponement. I was rather intrigued, as the Prime Minister had written to me before the debate that the government agreed that the procedure should be institutionalized and that it would consider my proposal seriously. I was deeply hurt. I felt a great opportunity to improve the image of the Parliament had been lost. It seemed that the government did not want to give an impression to the MPs that the latter were going to lose their right to fix their own salary and emoluments. The fifteenth Lok Sabha, I hope, will address this unfinished business.

Parliamentary Diplomacy

Acknowledging the importance of people-to-people contacts, it was my endeavour to bring the parliaments of friendly countries closer to each other and foster more meaningful contact among them. I set great store on friendship, dialogue and understanding, as the accent should always be on what unites us and not what divides us.

Invitations to visit more than 150 countries were pending when I took office. I requested the foreign secretary to prepare, in order of priority, a list of the countries where a visit by a parliamentary delegation would be effective from the point of view of our country's foreign policy priorities, so that delegations would visit such countries. The involvement of the foreign secretary meant that selection was not based on the Speaker's personal choice of countries he wanted to visit. A list was submitted and the priority indicated was mostly followed, of course depending on the convenience of the host countries. I led all-party goodwill delegations of parliamentarians to several countries, including Japan, Trinidad and Tobago, Belarus, Bulgaria, Cuba, Turkey, Vietnam, China, Greece, Germany and Saudi Arabia. On each of these visits, I was struck by the great warmth of cordiality and hospitality we received and, above all, by the deep respect demonstrated for India. We felt honoured and humbled. Among the special moments of these visits, I must mention that my wife and I were given a rare audience – reserved for only a few heads of state – with Emperor Hirohito of Japan in November 2004. The sheer dignity and magnificent simplicity of the royal couple will remain etched in my memory forever. I found China's economic development – even in its semi-urban and rural areas – truly astounding. The remarkable progress Vietnam had made after decades of systematic destruction by imperialist powers was most impressive. I would have loved to call on the legendary Fidel Castro in Havana but because of his ill-health it was not feasible. My visit to Dhaka, on 21 and 22 February 2009, on the Bangladesh Speaker's invitation to address the newly elected members of the Jatiya Sansad, was memorable. The affection I received from parliamentarians and common people of Dhaka was amazing and went way beyond my expectations. Sheikh Hasina, the Prime Minister of Bangladesh, was exceedingly courteous and greatly interested in India and the functioning of our democratic institutions. In fact, she was disappointed that I cut short my address to the parliamentarians, in which she was completely engrossed. I was, of course, merely adhering to official advice not to exceed the time allotted to me!

In all these overseas visits, I found the Indian missions' support highly praiseworthy. The diplomats gave a very good account of themselves. I was happy to note that they represented our country's interests with commendable competence.

Twenty-five foreign delegations visited the Indian Parliament during the fourteenth Lok Sabha. These visits were organized with much care. I had given instructions that all details were to be looked into with great attention by the secretariat. Banquets were upgraded and training imparted to chefs and waiters so that they were on a par with Rashtrapati Bhavan and Hyderabad House. Protocol facilities were improved and programmes drawn up more innovatively. Gifts and mementos, which I consider very important, were redesigned to make them more appealing to represent India's best in arts and crafts and highlight our democratic ethos.

Forty-four parliamentary friendship groups with different countries – set up with the initiative of the Indian parliamentary group with members from the major parties of both Houses – were virtually moribund. I convened a meeting of the foreign secretary, Shyam Saran, with his senior colleagues, and discussed strategies to revitalize the friendship groups. It was agreed to build closer links with the respective high commissions and embassies in Delhi so that members would be able to obtain a more in-depth insight into the different aspects of the respective countries with which they were associated as part of the friendship group. Whenever foreign delegations visited India, interactions with the friendship groups were arranged. I was reasonably satisfied with the momentum built up with the initiative of the presidents of the friendship groups. I am hopeful that they will go a long way in building bridges among people of different friendly countries. There are proposals to constitute many more friendship groups on the basis of reciprocity, which I trust will be followed up.

I was, however, not happy with industry associations, like FICCI, which used the Parliament's logo without permission and tried to give the impression that their bilateral business groups – which had some MPs as members – were parliamentary friendship groups. I pulled them up and ensured that they did not convey misleading impressions to garner clout with foreign governments.

The Indian Parliament played a very significant role in the Commonwealth Parliamentary Association (CPA) under my guidance. Following the decision of the general assembly at its meeting in Toronto on 7 September 2004, India became a separate region of the CPA. Earlier, it was in the Asia region. The India region organized two Asia and India region conferences in 2004 and 2005 in Hyderabad and Delhi. I was elected vice-president, CPA, for 2005–06, during the 51st conference in Fiji in September 2005, and president, CPA, for 2006–07, during the 52nd conference in Nigeria in September 2006.

India hosted the 53rd CPA conference in New Delhi between 21 and 30 September 2007, on the theme of 'Delivering Democracy and Sustainable Development'. The conference was a resounding success and the best in the history of the CPA, as I was told by many of the participants. Over 800 parliamentarians, legislators, observers, clerks, secretaries general, officials and invitees attended. It set such high standards that other countries felt they would not be able to match it. For this, I give full credit to the team of dedicated officials and staff of the Lok Sabha secretariat. It reinforced my firm belief that India has so much going for it and a showcasing of its inherent capabilities on the world stage is a must. We have it in us to do it. It's just that we do not make the effort.

My long-standing admiration for Hashim Abdul Halim, Speaker of the West Bengal legislative assembly, who holds a world record for being Speaker for the longest tenure (twenty-eight years), prompted me to work in a well-planned and coordinated manner with the ministry of external affairs to secure his election as the chairman of the executive committee of the CPA at its conference in Fiji in September 2005. Hashim Abdul Halim has, during his tenure of over a quarter of a century, attended each and every CPA conference, in every corner of the globe. He secured 73 per cent of the votes and his victory was a signal one for India. Dr Balram Jakhar had held the position two decades back and won only by a single vote. Suresh Reddy, then Speaker of Andhra Pradesh assembly, Abdul Rashid Dar, then Chairman of J&K Legislative Council, G.C. Malhotra, former secretary general, as well as our diplomatic missions in Commonwealth countries worked hard and rendered great help for Halim's election. After completing an immensely successful, three-year tenure as chairman, Hashim Abdul Halim was elected to the post of treasurer at the 54th CPA conference in Kuala Lumpur in August 2008, a testimony to his leadership and popularity in the Commonwealth fraternity.

The importance of leaving our imprint for the world to applaud is what I have always impressed on MPs and officials. I do not accept that participation in international conferences and seminars would be primarily about planning logistics and most attractive itineraries and have very little to do with substantive issues. The orientation had to change and it did under my watch. The conference branch of the Lok Sabha secretariat was rejuvenated and cells set up for planning and following through important events. Some important conferences like the CPA and Inter-Parliamentarians' Union (IPU) received my focused attention. I decided that, unlike the previous practice of leaving nomination of participants for these conferences and seminars to the parties, I would do so myself only after going through the qualifications and performance of members. This was initially resisted by the BJP. However, as I endeavoured to give all parties, big and small, an opportunity to participate in these events, according to a fair formula, there were no complaints. Of course, I would always receive requests from members for inclusion in delegations if the conferences were held in the more coveted destinations. Members attended eighty overseas conferences and seminars. I admit to having been a hard taskmaster during the overseas trips and at the conferences and seminars that I led. Every day's schedule, hour-to-hour, had to be planned in advance and all delegates fully briefed by officials. At the end of the day I would make it a point to sit down with them, however late it was, for debriefing and reviewing. Not that it was all work. After all, these tours were meant to broaden one's horizons and get to know the best of different cultures. And if there was a football World Cup final, which came as a bonus, as it did in June 2006 in Germany, what more could we ask for! I wish to mention in this connection the help and guidance I received from K. Rahman Khan, deputy chairman of the Rajya Sabha, who was a delegate to CPA and IPU conferences, and from the Lok Sabha secretariat, the Lok Sabha secretary general as also the principal secretary with the Speaker's office, who facilitated our participation in these conferences.

I was not prepared to compromise on the dignity of the Chair during these overseas trips. In April 2005, I cancelled a trip to Australia to attend the executive committee meeting of the CPA, as I was told that I would be frisked at the airport. I could not accept that the Speaker of the world's largest democracy might be a security threat! I was not obliged to visit any country where the Speaker was treated as a potential terrorist. Surprisingly, passengers (any passenger) who arrive by chartered flights are not subject to such checks at airports by the Australian authorities! While we in India extend courtesies to visiting dignitaries, Australia chooses not to reciprocate, quoting rules which have the provision for exemptions. It just prefers not to invoke them in the case of India. I was surprised to find that the UK also adopted a similar discriminatory stance against me in October 2008. I requested the Prime Minister to give these countries an appropriate reciprocal treatment, but I doubt if my suggestion was heeded. We need to be much more mindful of our national pride and dignity. I received a number of congratulatory messages for my stand. As expected, there were a few critical and caustic comments from the media which misunderstood me and passed off my principled position as 'tantrums' and an obsession with receiving special treatment. So much for the objectivity of the media and support for upholding the dignity of a constitutional authority!

I made it a point to never go back to a country where I had taken exception to any security requirements on my first visit there. It was my decision to keep away personally, as Speaker, from those countries. In that sense, I never understood why anybody could take exception to the Speaker of the largest parliamentary democracy in the world not allowing himself to be treated as a possible terrorist, while India laid red down red carpets for ministers or Speakers of such countries.

Parliamentary Forums

I believe that Parliament should not lose sight of the need to upgrade and retrofit the skill-sets of its members. Between 2005 and 2008 I constituted parliamentary forums on water conservation and management, children, youth, population and public health, global warming and climate change.

I would like to narrate how the idea struck me in the first place. I was very moved by a news report of a young boy in Delhi who was killed in a stampede while collecting drinking water from a tanker. I wanted to involve Parliament in ensuring that such unfortunate tragedies did not recur. I observed in the House on 12 May 2005 that parliamentarians need to do much more to build up awareness and sensitize policy makers on burning issues like shortage of water. To begin with, there were doubts among members on how exactly these forums would work and whether they would, inadvertently or otherwise, encroach on the domain of the departmentally related standing committees and the consultative committees. They were also apprehensive that the ministries would be confused about the jurisdiction and authority of these committees. I was clear that these were groundless apprehensions and had the guidelines spelt out meticulously. The sole purpose of these parliamentary forums was to hone the knowledge base of the members so that they would find a proper reflection in the conduct of parliamentary proceedings. I must say that this was met to a large extent and members of the forums participated in the deliberations and programmes enthusiastically. Many parliamentarians specially requested membership of forums in which they were interested. The member convenors – Naveen Jindal, Vallabhai Kathiria, Prema Cariappa, N.K. Singh and Tarlochan Singh – deserve my special praise for their wholehearted efforts in energizing these forums.

Lecture Series for Members

As part of my endeavour to empower members with information and expertise, I introduced a lecture series in 2005. The Bureau of Parliamentary Studies and Training organized the lectures, mostly during Parliament sessions. Between 2005 and 2008, twenty-four lectures were delivered by experts, eminent persons and parliamentarians which included Anne Veneman, executive director, UNICEF; Jeffrey D. Sachs, director, Earth Institute, Columbia University; Meghnad Desai, member, House of Lords, UK; Sam Pitroda, chairman, Knowledge Commission; Prof. Sugata Bose, Harvard University; Al Gore, ex-vice-president of USA, and Dr R.K. Pachauri, chairman, TERI, both Nobel laureates;

Thich Nhat Hanh, acclaimed Vietnamese Buddhist monk; B.G. Verghese, veteran journalist; Prof. Irfan Habib, eminent historian from Aligarh Muslim University; Prof. M. Swaminathan and Prof. K. Kasturirangan, both renowned scientists and members of the Rajya Sabha; Sunita Narain and Rajendra Singh. Even though the lectures were not always well attended, I believe that some interested members gained from them and over a period of time the appreciation index will improve.

In 2008, I instituted an annual lecture in honour of the erudite parliamentarian, Prof. Hiren Mukherjee. Nobel laureate and Lamont Professor at Harvard University, Prof. Amartya Sen, delivered the inaugural lecture on 'Demands of Social Justice' to a spellbound audience in the packed Central Hall on 11 August 2008. This was the one lecture in Parliament which members probably did not miss! I sincerely hope that this prestigious annual lecture is held regularly and is addressed by persons as distinguished as Prof. Amartya Sen.

Citizen's Right to Information

The Right to Information Act, 2005, was one of the landmark legislations of the UPA government. It was enacted to empower citizens, promote transparency and accountability in the working of the government, curb corruption and make democracy work in a more effective and meaningful manner.

The Lok Sabha Secretariat Right to Information (Regulation of Fee and Cost) Rules, 2005, were framed under this Act. A central public information officer was appointed along with the appellate tier. Information sought by the public on various activities of the Lok Sabha and its secretariat were provided, under my explicit instructions, without taking recourse to confidentiality clauses. In 2005, only twenty petitions were received, which increased in

2006 to 318. By April 2008, the number had touched 805. This was evidence of the great interest evinced in parliamentary activities, which is vital in a democracy. From the number of days the Parliament sat in a year, to the nature and number of disruptions in the House, the expenditure incurred on parliamentary business, various subjects taken up for discussion, participation of members in debates, in raising questions, their tours within the country and overseas, their salaries, allowances, medical reimbursement, facilities, legislation passed, privilege matters, petitions, implementation of MPLADS, etc., the information sought covered a range of issues.

With regard to the assets and liabilities of MPs, the Members of Lok Sabha (Declaration of Assets and Liabilities) Rules, 2004, tabled in the House on 10 June 2004, provided that the register of declaration of assets and liabilities of elected members would be kept confidential, unless authorized otherwise by the Speaker. I made this information, too, available, even when sought under the RTI Act, unlike the PMO and the judiciary, without making any distinction between a member and a minister. No applicant under the RTI complained about accessibility to records pertaining to assets and liabilities of members of the Lok Sabha during my tenure.

However, I do have strong views on the likelihood of misuse of the RTI Act by those with vested interests. In my address at the valedictory session of the third convention of the Central Information Commission on 'RTI and Its Ramifications for Good Governance' on 4 November 2008, I asserted that an efficacious right to information regime implemented for bona fide purposes would promote a culture of probity in the functioning of all governmental organs but if we were not alert, the true spirit of the Act may be undermined by design or default or by recklessly taking recourse to its provisions without the right intentions. As in

Public Interest Litigations (PILs), it could be used as an instrument to unsettle well-established norms of governmental functioning, to pursue personal agendas in the garb of public interest, or as a short cut to easy fame, even cheap publicity, or as a means to earn a livelihood in the guise of social activism or to discredit people's institutions.

Parliament Museum

To enable more people, especially the young, to get a better idea of our democratic heritage – which is not a mere inheritance from British colonialists – I fast-tracked the proposal to set up a museum in the Parliament House complex. The museum was to be focused on events rather than objects, ultra-modern and hi-tech and of an international standard. Dr Saroj Ghose, an eminent museuologist and former president of the International Council of Museums in UNESCO, Paris, and retired director-general of the National Council of Science Museums, developed its concept and blueprint at my request. The continuum of democratic India's heritage was depicted by walk-through period settings, sound-light-video synchronization, interactive computer multimedia and impressive visualization, along with multi-screen panoramic projection, virtual reality and animatronics. The design was cleared by leaders of various parties in Parliament on 21 April 2005. I also took care that the script was made available to the leaders for their comments and approval. Only Rupchand Pal, MP belonging to the CPI(M), made some suggestions to the script, which were accepted and incorporated.

The museum was completed in a record time of eleven months and inaugurated by the then President, Dr A.P.J. Abdul Kalam, on 14 August 2006. He greatly appreciated it and mentioned it in his address to both the Houses as well. It was opened to the general public on 5 September 2006. Over 65,000 visitors had visited the museum till April 2009, including the Prime Minister and many other dignitaries like the Chief Justice and other judges of the Supreme Court. The current President, Pratibha Devisingh Patil, was kind enough to visit the museum on 1 May 2009 and was very impressed.

I made it a point to go through the visitors' book of the museum regularly – which people thought rather unusual for someone in my position – and tried in my own way to popularize its use. It gave me immense satisfaction to know about the views of visitors, most of whom were schoolchildren. Entry was free for children and indeed for all students. They found the visits most educative as it made their textbooks come alive. What most of them unfailingly highlighted were the sections on the Dandi March, the multimedia presentation on the transfer of power and the animated 'Tryst with Destiny' speech of Pandit Nehru, patterned on the Gettysburg speech of Abraham Lincoln. Visiting foreign delegations to Parliament were, almost always, given a conducted tour and they all lavished praise on it. Many wanted to set up similar museums in their parliaments and sought our technical advice. The museum has by now found pride of place in Delhi's prestigious tourist guides. But I regret that many MPs either did not know of the museum or had not visited it. The loss, I believe, is entirely theirs!

To further extend the reach of the museum to the people, an interactive website on it was launched on 19 December 2007.

Parliament Library

Because of my love for children, I had a children's corner set up in the Parliament library. Inaugurated on 21 August 2007, it is the only one of its kind in the world. Care was taken to ensure that children of marginalized sections of society, who did not have access to a good and resourceful library, could avail themselves of these facilities. Children's books, encyclopaedias, magazines, CDs and DVDs were put together in an interesting layout. A special child-friendly ambience was created to make it attractive for children to delve into the treasure trove of books and nurture the habit of reading. I was hopeful that this initiative would make the concept of parliamentary democracy more relevant to children and they would learn the value of its institutions. The corner became very popular. Regular activities were organized on children's day and other important occasions by the secretariat, in association with reputed NGOs, drawing children to Parliament in large numbers, which had not happened before.

Another important initiative that I was happy about was to make the library accessible to scholars and professionals so that they could tap into its vast reservoir of invaluable collections. This was greatly welcomed and over 800 persons had availed themselves of this facility till 2009. I used to remark that if members did not have time to use the library, other interested citizens should certainly be enabled to make proper use of it!

Internship Programme

B.G. Verghese, a senior journalist and a member of the board of experts I had constituted, suggested the introduction of an internship programme in Parliament to serve as a bridge with the youth. It would motivate them to come forward to do their bit instead of sitting back and joining in the sterile chorus of general condemnation of murky politics in the country. Such programmes are successful in many democracies, like the United States. I found the concept interesting and exciting and accepted the suggestion straightaway. Through the year-long internship programme, inaugurated in January 2008, a group of five young professionals with outstanding academic and extracurricular achievements, from different parts of the country, were selected after a rigorous screening process and given a close-up view of the working of parliamentary institutions. I was immensely satisfied to know of the tremendous response the programme evoked and its positive impact.

Round Tables on Strengthening Democracy

In order to encourage public debate in civil society on the apparent deficiencies of the parliamentary system of governance, I organized two round table discussions with highly respected and eminent persons from diverse backgrounds across the country on 4 September and 1 November 2008. These were very well received and seen as setting a new trend, with Parliament playing a lead role in safeguarding and revitalizing democratic institutions. I was assured that the dialogue would be carried forward in a meaningful manner. Among the participants were Jaswant Singh, Era Sezhiyan, Dr M.S. Swaminathan, Soli Sorabjee, Shashi Tharoor, Vasant Sathe, Girija Vyas, Jaya Prakash Narayan, E.A.S. Sarma, Justice Rajinder Sachar, Fali Nariman, T.R. Andhyarujina, Dr Harish Khare, Kuldip Nayar, Vinod Sharma and Prabhas Joshi.

Administrative Reorganization

I realized that the support structures in the secretariat called for a thorough revamp to enable them to do greater justice to their duty of servicing the highest institution of democracy. I had been deeply disappointed to find that when it came to administrative matters, there were no systems in place. The Speaker exercised almost all administrative powers, except what he chose to delegate. I delegated many powers to the secretary general and his officers, often against the advice of those who believed in preserving and concentrating power. There was great scope for streamlining and rationalizing procedures, rules, conventions and practices and for introduction of hi-tech mechanisms to bring in greater efficiency, transparency and accountability in the functioning of the secretariat. For the first time in the history of the Lok Sabha, a comprehensive cadre review was conducted by an outside agency, the reputed Indian Institute of Management, Kolkata, and major restructuring of the organizational structure effected. As a result, the career prospects of a majority of employees improved dramatically. Around 1800 promotions were made during my term. Direct recruitment was introduced at different levels to bring in fresh blood. Training programmes, which had been long neglected, were resumed on a regular basis. A grievance redressal mechanism was set up for employees to resolve their problems expeditiously. Service-related court cases and vigilance cases were monitored closely. The difference all these initiatives made to the morale of the staff was palpable. Many of the recommendations of the Sixth Pay Commission were adopted. A pay committee was constituted after a gap of ten years. Its generous package was accepted with some modifications, in April 2009. Although there was some opposition from the government I resolved the sticky issues with the cooperation of the chairman, Rajya Sabha.

Recognizing that there was a crying need for additional office space, I took up the matter which had been pending with the ministry of urban development. After persistent efforts by the secretariat, all the approvals were finally obtained in April 2009. I had made it clear that the staff should get priority and precious space should not be wasted on lavish committee rooms or office rooms for chairmen, which would be used only occasionally. That meant changing the design – which took time – but I did not settle for a compromise with staff welfare. The foundation stone for an annexe to the existing Parliament annexe building was laid on 5 May 2009, at a cost of Rs 268 crore, which I consider a worthwhile investment in our human resources, which are among the best in the world.

Residential accommodation was also augmented. A special ladies' pool was carved out, meeting a long-felt need. Welfare measures for the staff were upgraded and full scholarships provided for their meritorious children to allow them to pursue professional courses in recognized universities for the first time ever. I always encouraged the staff to develop their cultural and sporting talents and build multifaceted personalities. Many scintillating performances were held by the staff and their families in the Balayogi Auditorium. Such an opportunity had not come their way earlier and they greatly cherished it.

Functions to commemorate the 150th anniversary of the first war of Indian independence and the sixtieth anniversary of Independence were held in the Central Hall in 2007, with star performers including Pandit Jasraj, Amjad Ali Khan, Shabana Azmi, Javed Akhtar, Shubha Mudgal, Gulzar and Jagjit Singh. There was a special sound and light programme based on the uprising of 1857 at the National Stadium, Delhi, which had the audience enthralled. Members recalled these unforgettable functions for a long time.

At my instance, Parliament commissioned distinctive statues of Nobel laureate Rabindranath Tagore and the much revered and loved Shaheed Bhagat Singh. These are the only two statues, along with Mahatma Gandhi's, which have been funded by Parliament. All the other statues in the complex are donated by state governments, institutions/organizations or members. Tagore's statue in the Parliament library, unveiled on 7 December 2005, is my favourite, not only because I represented the constituency where he set up his world-famous university, Visva-Bharati, but also because it was an exquisitely crafted work of art by Gautam Pal.

I had a number of anxious moments prior to the installation of Shaheed Bhagat Singh's eighteen-foot statue in the central courtyard of Parliament on 15 August 2008. The statue was sculpted by award-winning sculptor Ram V. Sutar. There were conflicting views on the appearance and dress of the martyr. Thankfully, these were resolved to everyone's satisfaction by the joint committee of statues and portraits. The media attempted to raise some controversies and there was a demand that the statue be replaced. That was, however, not pursued. In this connection, I must record my deep sense of gratitude to Dr Karan Singh, a member of the Rajya Sabha and a distinguished member of the joint committee on statutes and portraits, for his most valuable help to me and the committee in respect of the emotive issues that came before the committee. He dealt with them with wonderful felicity.

APPENDIX III

A. Occasions when the Prime Minister was not allowed to speak and was interrupted during his speech in the Fourteenth Lok Sabha:

S. No.	Date	Subject	Remarks
1.	13.08.2007	Prime Minister's statement on Indo-US nuclear deal	Not allowed to speak
2.	05.03.2008	Motion of thanks to the President's address	Prime Minister spoke amidst continued interruptions by Opposition members. Later, Opposition staged a walkout.
3.	22.07.2008	Reply to the debate on the motion of confidence	Not allowed to speak because of interruptions and disruptions by the members of the opposition parties and his speech had to be laid on the table of the House.

B. Instances when Budget was passed without discussion during the Fourteenth Lok Sabha because of interruptions in the House

S. No.	Session	Particulars	Date Of Passing	Time Taken Hrs. Mins.
1.	Second	(i) Demands for Grants (Railways) for 2004–05 (ii) Demands for Grants (General) for 2004–05	23.08.2004 25.08.2004	00 02 00 07
2.	Seventh	Demands for Grants (Railways) for 2006–07	11.03.2006	00 02
3.	Tenth	Demands for Grants (Railways) for 2007–08	26.04.2007	00 03
4.	Fourteenth	Supplementary Demands for Grants (Railways) for 2008-2009	22.12.2008	00 01
5.	Fifteenth	* (i) Interim Budget (Jharkhand) for 2009–10 * (ii) Supplementary Demands for Grants (Jharkhand) for 2008–09	19.02.2009	00 05

* Taken up together

C. Instances when government bills had to be passed without discussions during the fourteenth Lok Sabha because of the continued interruptions and non-cooperative attitude of some members

S. No.	Session	Title of the Bill	Date of Passing
1.	Second	The Finance (No. 2) Bill, 2004	26.08.2004
2.	Third	The Delegated Legislation Provisions (Amendment) Bill, 2004	23.12.2004

S. No.	Session	Title of the Bill	Date of Passing
3.	Sixth	i) The Chartered Accountants (Amendment) Bill, 2005, *as passed by Rajya Sabha*	23.12.2005
		ii) The Cost and Works Accountants (Amendment) Bill, 2005, *as passed by Rajya Sabha*	23.12.2005
		iii) The Company Secretaries (Amendment) Bill, 2005, *as passed by Rajya Sabha*	23.12.2005
4.	Seventh	The Delhi Special Police Establishment (Amendment) Bill, 2006	22.03.2006
5.	Ninth	The Indian Rifles (Repeal) Bill, 2006, *as passed by Rajya Sabha*	08.12.2006
6.	Tenth	i) The Banking Regulation (Amendment) Bill, 2007	16.03.2007
		ii) The National Institute of Pharmaceutical Education and Research (Amendment) Bill, 2007	16.03.2007
		iii) The Taxation Laws (Amendment) Bill, 2007	19.03.2007
		iv) The National Tax Tribunal (Amendment) Bill, 2007	19.03.2007
		v) The National Rural Guarantee (Extension to Jammu & Kashmir) Bill, 2007	19.03.2007
		vi) The Constitution (Scheduled Castes) Order Amendment Bill, 2007	14.05.2007
		vii) The Securities Contracts (Regulation) Amendment Bill, 2007	14.05.2007
		viii) The National Institutes of Technology Bill, 2007	14.05.2007
		ix) The Central Road Fund (Amendment) Bill, 2007	16.05.2007

S. No.	Session	Title of the Bill	Date of Passing
7.	Eleventh	i) The Competition (Amendment) Bill, 2007	06.09.2007
		ii) The Apprentices (Amendment) Bill, 2007, *as passed by Rajya Sabha*	07.09.2007
		iii) The Aircraft (Amendment) Bill, 2006	10.09.2007
		iv) The Carriage by Road Bill, 2007, *as passed by Rajya Sabha*	10.09.2007
8.	Twelfth	The Armed Forces Tribunal Bill, 2007, *as passed by Rajya Sabha*	06.12.2007
9.	Fourteenth	i) The Drugs and Cosmetics (Amendment) Bill, 2008, *as passed by Rajya Sabha*	23.10.2008
		ii) The Gram Nyayalayas Bill, 2008, *as passed by Rajya Sabha*	22.12.2008
		iii) The Information Technology (Amendment) Bill, 2006	22.12.2008
		iv) The Supreme Court (Number of Judges) Amendment Bill, 2008	22.12.2008
		v) The Prevention of Corruption (Amendment) Bill, 2008	23.12.2008
		vi) The Code of Criminal Procedure (Amendment) Bill, 2008, *as passed by Rajya Sabha*	23.12.2008
		vii) The Post-Graduate Institute of Medical Education and Research Chandigarh (Amendment) Bill, 2008, *as passed by Rajya Sabha*	23.12.2008
		viii) The Collection of Statistics Bill, 2008, *as passed by Rajya Sabha*	23.12.2008
		ix) The Agricultural and Processed Food Products Export Development Authority (Amendment) Bill, 2008	23.12.2008
		x) The South Asian University Bill, 2008, *as passed by Rajya Sabha*	23.12.2008
		xi) The Constitution (Scheduled Tribes) (Union Territories) Order (Amendment) Bill, 2008, *as passed by Rajya Sabha*	23.12.2008
		xii) The Compensatory Afforestation Fund Bill, 2008	23.12.2008

APPENDIX IV

Messages Received by Somnath Chatterjee after His Decision Not to Resign as Speaker in the Wake of the Trust Motion in July 2008

In July 2008, when the erstwhile supporters of the UPA, the Left parties led by the CPI(M), decided to withdraw support to the Manmohan Singh-led government on the issue of the Indo-US nuclear deal, the CPI(M) asked me to resign as Speaker, arguing that I was a member of the party and as such the party's decision to withdraw support from the government was binding on me. I thought over the matter at great length and came to a decision that it would amount to a betrayal of my mandate as Speaker of the Lok Sabha if I resigned as dictated by my party. I argued that as Speaker I was expected to be non-partisan and nothing would induce me to toe a party line. I paid a heavy price for my decision, to the extent of being removed from the CPI(M), the party I had counted as my own for over forty years.

What made the despair of those days bearable was the literal avalanche of messages of support from all over the world, from people from all walks of life. I cannot resist the temptation to reproduce extracts from some of the messages which convinced me that I had done the right thing. I would like to take this opportunity to thank everyone who supported me during those bleak days.

Please allow me to express my sincere admiration for your leadership, guidance and dignified conduct during the special session on the confidence motion. This has endeared you to the people of India, and also to all freedom-loving and democratic nations of the world. ... Your cool and composed disposition was commendable and worthy of emulation ...

– General J.J. Singh, PVSM, AVSM, VSM (Retd)
Governor, Arunachal Pradesh, 24 July 2008

I salute you for upholding and maintaining the dignity of the high office of Speaker of the Lok Sabha above party politics ... the whole country is proud of you for enhancing the prestige of this high office in the most dignified manner ...

– Tarun Gogoi, Chief Minister, Assam, 24 July 2008

... You, as Speaker of the largest democracy of the world, have set a fine example of maintaining impartiality, prestige of the Chair ... It would be my endeavour to carry forward this tradition in the most democratic, transparent and impartial manner to further enhance the prestige of this august constitutional position.

Mohammad Akbar Lone, Speaker
Jammu and Kashmir Legislative Assembly,
Srinagar, 17 March 2009

~

You have throughout your tenure as Speaker exhibited total independence and impartiality, for which the country is proud. You will be remembered for long as one of the outstanding Speakers that this country has had.

– K.K. Venugopal, Senior Advocate, New Delhi, 25 July 2008

~

I was in the Rajya Sabha box watching the two-day debate on the motion relating to the Vote of Confidence moved by the Hon'ble Prime Minister. ... Sir, your honesty, integrity and indomitable courage of conviction have always been on display under different situations ... I have always looked upon you with great admiration and as a symbol of a value system which this country needs to emulate at all levels of society. ... Coming from a very distinguished family, enjoying a decent level of prosperity, and with an enviable professional career, it needs a great sense of sacrifice to choose to work in an environment which places very high demands both mentally and physically. Sir, I take this opportunity to wish you many years of further public service for the benefit of the country ...

– Dr K. Kasturirangan, Member, Rajya Sabha, 25 July 2008

~

Heartiest congratulations. You have raised the level of the whole parliamentary democracy in India.

– Lord Swraj Paul, London, 23 July 2008

I am studying in the ninth standard and I write this letter to appreciate your proud and courageous stand of not withdrawing from your position. ... The coming generations of India need leaders like you. The stars are twinkling in the sky. There are so many bright stars in the sky. But you are the golden star which is twinkling in the Parliament. ... You will not be forgotten by the people who love the country and who are ready to dedicate their life for the country.

– Jitty Mol Thomas, Kavalam, Kuttunadu, Kerala, 24 July 2008

I teach Indian history at the City University of New York ... I greatly admire the stand you have taken in Parliament in recent days. You will be remembered as having done the right thing.

– Satadru Sen, New York City, 23 July 2008

You have certainly changed my perception of politicians. Mahatma Gandhi died before my birth, but I see his values and ethics in you ...

– Durgesh Mathur, Noida, Uttar Pradesh, 23 July 2008

I am a proud citizen of India. This letter is to express my great admiration for the way you stood your ground and continued to be the Speaker in spite of intense pressure on you to resign from the post. ... Sir, we admire your courage and steadfastness in continuing in the post. I wish we have several people like you who want to serve our nation without craving personal gain or profit. May you continue to be a beacon of light to all of us.

– K.V. Mathew, 25 July 2008

~

… History honours the student who stood in front of the tank, not the tank driver. You did the right thing, the honourable thing. You saw this coming. You knew that you might lose the party you have given everything to for the last forty years and you still did it. Because it was the right thing to do. And that is why history will remember you.

– Shashwata Chatterjee, 23 July 2008

~

We have been following the developments both inside the Lok Sabha and outside. … we are very proud of the way in which you have conducted yourself since you took office and also during the last few weeks. We hope you will always have the inner strength to speak objectively and take decisions that reflect both wisdom and the rule of law.

– Winston and Viju James, Oman, 2 August 2008

~

Some people get glorified with the post. Some people bring glory to the post. We are proud of you for having brought Himalayan glory to the post you have been adorning. Hats off to Comrade Somnath Chatterjee.

– apdght@aait.aero, 24 July 2008

~

I am a common man who happened to witness the proceedings of Parliament on 22 July 2008. I was totally impressed by your personality and charm in handling such a sensitive happening. I was proud to have experienced it. Whatever you did is possible only by total commitment and dedication in what you are doing. I am inspired, and you would have similarly inspired many others …

– Dr Suresh Akella, Hyderabad, Andhra Pradesh, 22 July 2008

The whole of India and many millions the world over are proud of you. It takes tremendous courage of conviction to dare and be different. Rabindranath Tagore so convincingly exhorted us, '*Ekla Chalo*.' Sir, you are well and truly doing that, and the whole world is watching in admiration with great respect and pride …

– A.E. Jacob, Thiruvananthapuram, Kerala, 16 July 2008

It will be nothing new to you when I tell you that all my Indian friends whom I met do hold you in very high esteem and speak most respectfully of you. I think you have added by your personality enormously to the prestige of the position of Speaker and have made this position not only known but also important to the ordinary citizen of your country. … I am sure you will always be remembered as a great Speaker of the House. Your father would be very proud of you.

– Klaus Benz, Germany, 24 July 2008

I feel very proud that Parliament has a Speaker of your standing and calibre. You have not only enhanced the prestige of this important office but have also provided a remarkable example to be emulated by those in public life in this country. May I express my deep admiration for your statesmanship and your role as parliamentarian …

– Dr R.K. Pachauri, Director General,
The Energy and Resources Institute
New Delhi, 27 July 2008

I congratulate you for conducting the session of the Lok Sabha to discuss the confidence motion with authority and dignity. You also deserve our sincere felicitations for standing firm against communalism and in support of secularism ...

– (Maulana) Arshad Madani, President, Jamiat Ulama-i-Hind
New Delhi, 26 July 2008

We wholeheartedly congratulate you for conducting the proceedings of the special Lok Sabha session on 21 and 22 July 2008 under trying circumstances ... Parliamentary democracy stood upheld under your stewardship when it mattered the most. You have stuck to your duty when Parliament and the people of this great nation needed you most. ... Our country's constitutional apparatus and parliamentary obligations would have been thrown out of gear had you not applied your mind and wisdom and risen to the occasion. You have saved the day for the nation. We are proud of you. India needs farsighted leaders like you. Please carry on your good work.

– H.N. Arengh, Secretary General, All India Garo Union
Shillong, Meghalaya, 5 August 2008

Most discerning people, scholars and reputed intellectuals have commended your impartiality and dignity in maintaining the position of the Chair ... Whatever you have done befits the honour and dignity of the office and the rare personal credibility as politician and parliamentarian. No one else could have done better ...

– Era Sezhiyan, Former Member, Lok Sabha, 11 August 2008

Congrats! Today the whole world is looking towards the Indian Parliament. Democracy has been strengthened by you. Thanks a lot for improving the quality of Indian democracy.

– L. Venkatasubramanian, Malaysia, 22 July 2008

~

We Indians in the United Arab Emirates are proud of you, for the decision and stand you took as the Speaker of the Lok Sabha. ... We appreciate your action in being neutral and in saving democracy. History will remember your for your right decision ...

– Saravanan, Dubai, UAE, 24 July 2008

~

We salute you, Sir, from the depths of our hearts ... Our countrymen are proud of having a parliamentarian and leader of your stature as Speaker of our Parliament. ... You have become and idol and a role model for the presiding officers of parliaments and legislatures of the world.

– Abdul Rashid Dar, Former Chairman
J&K Legislative Council, 23 July 2008

~

... you have upheld the principles of the Constitution and also gave dignity to the office you are holding. Please accept my most patriotic respects and salute that I have to offer. I am proud to be an Indian because of you.

– Biju Jose, Riyadh, Saudi Arabia, 2 August 2008

~

I was a judge of the Supreme Court of India from 1978 to 1987. I am writing this letter to congratulate you for the very dignified manner in which you conducted the entire proceedings of the Parliament when the Prime Minister moved his motion of confidence. No one could have done better. I too believe in Marxism as you do but I am wholly unable to understand the criticism of some leaders of the party. I am glad you stood your ground.

–Justice O. Chinnappa Reddy,
former judge of the Supreme Court

Hearty congratulations for exhibiting constitutional morality and statesmanship while not only conducting the proceedings in the Parliament but also after the result … you have enhanced your stature by rising above self-interest … As Speaker of the Lok Sabha, you minced no words to pull up the members, irrespective of parties, whose conduct was inconsistent with parliamentary norms; you did that with distinction and tact … I congratulate you for your extraordinary patience in conducting the proceedings and upholding the dignity of the office, rising above self, by which you brought laurels to the office of the Speaker of the Lok Sabha.

Dr Justice K. Ramaswamy,
former judge of the Supreme Court

APPENDIX V

Farewell Letter from the Speaker's Team

Respected Sir,

You have heard it before and you will, no doubt, hear it for a long time to come. Today it is our turn to tell you how proud we, in your team, are of you for having successfully etched a place in the annals of the country's history as a distinguished parliamentarian and Speaker. You truly epitomized the expectations and aspirations of the people as well as their fervent hope that parliamentary institutions would deliver on their constitutional mandate. You set your sights high, always strove for perfection and never compromised with your principles and values. We have often heard it said of you and with full justification that you were the first 'People's Speaker' who went the proverbial extra mile beyond the strict confines of rules, procedures and conventions, to uphold the image and dignity of the world's largest democracy. There are not too many like you on the political firmament today!

As we gather to bid a farewell, we have only one request to ask of you. Please don't refer to your Speakership as the 'worst period' in your career, as it was, in our perception, certainly not so and you have many enduring achievements to your lasting credit.

As officers and staff who had the privilege to be associated with you from 2004 to 2009, we take this opportunity to convey our deepest appreciation for what you have stood for, the courage of your conviction and all that you have accomplished. The recounting of details is not called for on this occasion as they are already well known and greatly acclaimed.

For all of us, this will certainly count as amongst the most memorable phase of our careers, as we deemed it a rare honour to be able to contribute in some measure, to the translation of your grand vision of an effective, transparent and accountable parliamentary institution, into an enduring reality. We will always cherish this rich experience, more so, as you treated each one of us exceptionally well. There were no doubt, few moments of stress and frustration, which are only to be expected in as important an office as the Hon'ble Speaker's, but with your statesmanship, resoluteness of purpose and magnanimity, you handled them admirably. For any inadvertent failures or shortcomings on our part, we crave your indulgence and are sure you will not deny it to us.

In fact, we believe, this is not a farewell in the literal sense, as there can be none in as unique a relationship as this. But we would certainly like to let you know that our heartfelt and very best wishes will always be with you for most fulfilling and meaningful days ahead. Someone of your stature cannot simply 'fade away' as you, at times, 'threaten' to! We know you will continue to be active in public life and provide noteworthy leadership to the people. We also wish you good health, peace and contentment. May you have plenty of time to all your own, for all the interesting things your heart has long yearned for, but which had to be put aside because of the call of duty.

We are there for you, wherever you may be and wherever we may be.

And, above all,
Thank you for being you!

Shri Somnath Chatterjee,
Hon'ble Speaker, Lok Sabha

Dr. T. Kumar
Principal Secretary
HSO
20 May 2009

APPENDIX VI

Statement issued by Somnath Chatterjee on 12 September 2009 responding to charges made in *People's Democracy*, the weekly organ of the CPI(M)

My attention has been drawn to a publication described as 'A Rejoinder to Somnath Chatterjee's Charge' in the weekly *People's Democracy* of 31 August–6 September 2009, a copy of which has been obtained by me after I saw the news item based on the same published in *Ananda Bazar Patrika* of 6 September 2009. I could not get a copy of even the Kolkata edition of the weekly earlier, because it is not readily available. Hence the delay in my response.

The so-called rejoinder, to my mind, displays the current political culture of the present leadership of the CPI(M), which has made the party and Left politics in our country almost irrelevant. In its anxiety to indulge in its laboured accusation against me, it has discovered some meanings allegedly hidden in my statement, which I had made to a Delhi daily a few days earlier.

I had made it specifically clear in my statement to the daily that I had heard only a rumour (and I also said that I had no proof of my own) that the Left parties were probably aware that the trust vote debate in Lok Sabha would be disturbed. I never stated that 'the Left had some foreknowledge that the cash-for-trust-vote scam would come up in Parliament' nor I had 'insinuated that there was some coordination between the BJP and the Left in this matter'. It is further alleged in the so-called rejoinder that it has become my practice 'to level baseless charges against the CPI(M) and the Left ever since he decided to cross over to the government side after the Left withdrew support to the UPA government'. I am amazed at the deliberate distortion of facts in the mouthpiece of the CPI(M), which during my long association with the party, I have never seen it to have ever indulged in. I had never mentioned the name of the CPI(M). Then why this virulent reaction? I get the impression that in its anxiety to justify its unfathomable decision which has brought the party to its present sorry state, the CPI(M) through *People's Democracy* has made a desperate effort to indulge in character assassination, which seems to be a new tactic adopted by the party. I would ask the party leadership to point out what are the 'baseless charges against the CPI(M) and Left' I had made. Although I could have, and indeed many well-meaning citizens of the country had urged me to give my views on the party's decision to expel me, I did not make any allegation against the party and on the other hand I admitted in my public statement that the party had the right to expel me and there was no occasion for me at all to ask for a review of the same or to file an appeal. It is a canard and a calumny to allege as deliberate falsehood that 'I had decided to cross over to the government side'. It is a blatant untruth and an atrocious lie. It makes one fully convinced that the alienation of vast sections of its supporters from the party has been due to the leadership's tantrums not only in relation to the political developments in the country but also for its deviation from the path of truth and exactitude. I cannot but reject totally the most baseless charge made against me. It seems that the present CPI(M) leadership has a guilty conscience because of its abysmal failure in conducting the affairs of the party and is now trying to find excuses for its total rejection even by the common people.

On the very day itself, immediately after the despicable incident that took place in the Lok Sabha chamber, I had described it as the most heinous act which had greatly tarnished the image of Parliament and it had reached its nadir. I had immediately convened a meeting of the leaders of the parties where I announced my decision that I was going to constitute a committee, consisting of the representatives of all the parties, to inquire into the matter. The committee, in which the CPI(M) was represented by its deputy leader, could not come to a unanimous conclusion and recommended further investigation in the matter by an appropriate authority. On the basis of the recommendation, I referred the matter immediately to the ministry of home affairs, Government of India, which has different investigative agencies under its authority. It was not for me as the presiding officer to select a particular agency for the purpose.

If CPI(M) leaders had proof that 'hundreds of crores of rupees were spent on purchase of MPs belonging to the opposition', it was the duty of the party to disclose the facts before the nation. I had not condoned any act of impropriety. In the defection cases brought before me, I disqualified a number of MPs for violating their party whips as they had voted in favour of the motion. It is amazing to note the weekly's unsolicited advice that I should have been worried about 'this brazen suborning of MPs and the farce it made of democratic norms'. It is obvious that no sensible person could come to a conclusion without the facts being fully known or proved and that is why I had forthwith appointed an enquiry committee consisting of hon'ble members of different political parties. If the sordid wrongdoings were known to the CPI(M) before or during the debate, why did they not expose the same before the people? I am thankful for the reference to my role in the debate held in the Lok Sabha when there were allegations and charges against the Narasimha Rao government of indulging in illegal acts and purchasing MPs' support. Interestingly, I was found suitable by the then party leadership (of course then not dominated by the present one) to be the leader of the party in the Lok Sabha, which position I held for nearly fifteen years until my election as Speaker. Certainly, I was proud to have enjoyed the confidence of the party leadership as well as of my colleagues in Parliament. The order of my expulsion exposed not only the intolerance shown by the present leadership of the party but also its wrong understanding of the role of the Speaker in a parliamentary democracy. It seems that the party's present leadership has not found time to go through my strongest criticism of the sordid event that took place in Parliament, which I made in many of my speeches and also interviews given to the media and has chosen to make deliberately incorrect and calumnious accusation against me.

It is a travesty of truth to allege that I had, as it were, condoned criminal activities committed within the precincts of the chamber. I can humbly claim that no other presiding officer in the past had tried to get rid of the corrupt and criminal elements from Lok Sabha as much I did and that too successfully.

The rejoinder is a clear attempt to indulge in deliberate falsehood, calumny and character assassination to justify the party's untenable action against a member of the party, who had humbly and to the best of his ability and without any self-interest the great distinction of being not only an ordinary member of the party but also a member of the West Bengal state committee and a member of the central committee of the party. It is now well known that large sections of the party have not supported the arbitrary action of the party. That is why many members and active supporters of the party on their own still keep close touch with me and I have had the honour to have been asked to take part in many important programmes, in which leading party members are present or associated with.

I had hoped that the party leadership at the highest level would do some introspection and would try to find out why it is now in splendid isolation and why the party even in West Bengal and Kerala, the two major states where only it has its existence, is today facing such serious erosion of popular support. No sensible supporter of the party nor any right-thinking citizen has approved of the queer attempts of the present leadership of the CPI(M) to bolster up a so-called Third Front with disparate elements, with ridiculous assurance to its members and supporters that the so-called Third Front would come to power and would provide opportunity to the party's general secretary even to head such a government. Large sections of the supporters and members of party had extreme reservations about the efforts of the central leadership. They were bewildered at the almost desperate and comic attempts of the leadership to come closer to certain political outfits, many of which are embodiments of crime and corruption in politics. Even the die-hard supporters of the party could not countenance such deviation in its policies and basic philosophy.

I repudiate each and all the allegations and insinuation made against me in the so-called rejoinder. It contains clearly a laboured attempt on the part of the leadership to foster untruth and divert peoples' attention from its abject failure on all fronts. I can only sympathize with the editor of *People's Democracy*, as he had to provide space in the weekly for such tendentious rigmaroles.

INDEX

ACKNOWLEDGEMENTS

The idea of writing my memoirs had never occurred to me, though from time to time Dr T. Kumar, IAS, who made exemplary contribution towards the proper functioning of the office of Speaker, in her capacity as the principal secretary to the Speaker, had been prodding me to record my experiences of all those years in Parliament, as she said that I owed a duty to my country. However, I never gave a serious thought to her suggestion. A few important editors and publishers, of whom the first was Amit Agarwal of HarperCollins, had been requesting me to write about my experiences. There was also mounting pressure on me from many of my friends and colleagues. However, if anyone can claim the credit of finally persuading me to write the memoirs (I am no writer by any means), I must unhesitatingly concede it to Dr Kumar. She has not only been a tower of strength to me in the discharge of my duties and functions as Speaker, but has also organized and helped to gather material for the book and to decide about its format. Without her encouragement, her constant help and her excellent leadership in trying to build the supporting staff, this book would never have seen the light of the day.

As the Speaker, I hardly had much spare time to devote to the writing of my memoirs, covering a period of nearly four decades. Thus it has taken me quite a long time, during which I have been given polite reminders by the publishers, though I had the full-fledged support of my staff and guidance and goodwill of a number of friends.

I have received considerable help from Indranil Banerjie, Paranjoy Guha Thakurta, Professor Bidyut Chakraborty, Rajinder Pandey, Tarun Bose, Dilip Banerjee and Amitabha Bhattacharya from time to time in the preparation of the book and I convey my thanks to all of them.

I am thankful to Dr Jaydev Sahu and G. Rangarao and to Vijaykrishnan and D.R. Kalra of the Lok Sabha Secretariat for all their help in obtaining copies of my speeches and some important parliamentary information, but for which it would not have been possible to make much headway.

Of course, I could not have made any progress without the most competent assistance and help of Subrata Majumder and Sunil Minocha, my additional private secretaries in the office of the Speaker, who are extremely competent. The services rendered by Sutanu Chatterjee at my Kolkata office were indispensable to me in all matter and at all times. I have always received most efficient and most sincere help from them. All my best wishes will always be with them. I also received considerable help from Vivek Kumar, IAS, former secretary to the Speaker, K.J.S. Cheema, IAS, and J.R. Gulati, former secretaries to the Speaker, H.K. Kapoor, Rupasree Roy, Prasanna Kumar, P.J. Antony, Swapan Roy,

Prodyot Chatterjee, Jagdish Kashyap, D.K. Sharma, Lalit Kumar, Manoj Chowhan, Manoj Bundela and Lokesh Kumar, who were part of the Speaker's office. P.D.T. Achary, secretary general, Lok Sabha, and Indevar Pandey, IAS, secretary in the office of the Speaker also constantly, along with other friends and well-wishers, provided me encouragement and urged me to complete the book, which at one time I felt I would not be able to do because of the many disturbing and frustrating events that had been unfolding. I express my thanks to all. But for their help, I could not have gone much further with the writing of the book.

Thanks are also no doubt due to Amit Agarwal and Shantanu Ray Chaudhuri of HarperCollins for their help and patience.

Of course, without the constant encouragement from my wife and other members of my family, I could never have embarked upon the difficult job of writing my memoirs and they have been a constant source of inspiration to me.

While writing this book, I have often consulted Ramachandra Guha's *India after Gandhi* for reference material and I wish to acknowledge the great help I received from the treatise.

It will more than satisfy me if the book is treated as a sincere and responsible attempt to project our highest representative institution and is found informative by my readers.

If there is any error or shortcoming, the responsibility is entirely mine.

ABOUT THE AUTHOR

Born in Tezpur, Assam, in 1929, Somnath Chatterjee was educated at the Presidency College in Calcutta, at Jesus College in Cambridge, and at the Middle Temple. Chatterjee began his career as a lawyer and joined active politics in 1971, when he was elected to the Lok Sabha. He continued to remain an MP till he stepped down from active politics in 2009.

In his long and illustrious career as an MP, Somnath Chatterjee adorned several parliamentary committees as chairman and as member. He served with distinction as Chairman, Committee on Subordinate Legislation and Standing Committee on Information Technology, Committee of Privileges, Committee on Railways, and Committee on Communications. He has been a member of the Rules Committee, General Purposes Committee, Business Advisory Committee and the Ethics Committee, to name a few. As a barrister and as a senior lawyer, he brought his legal acumen to the sphere of legislation, both in the House and its committees. In 1996, he was conferred the most Outstanding Parliamentarian Award by the Indian Parliamentary Group.

In 2004, he was unanimously elected Speaker of the Lok Sabha. His conduct of the proceedings of the House evoked widespread appreciation from a cross section of citizens from India and overseas.

He now lives near Santiniketan.